DOCUMENTARY
DIARY

BOOKS BY PAUL ROTHA

CELLULOID: THE FILM TODAY (1931)

DOCUMENTARY FILM
(1936, 1939, and with Richard Griffith and Sinclair Road, 1952, 1966)

MOVIE PARADE
(1936, and with Roger Manvell, 1950)

ROTHA ON THE FILM (1958)

WORLD OF PLENTY
(book of the film, 1945)

PORTRAIT OF A FLYING YORKSHIREMAN
(the letters of Eric Knight to Paul Rotha, 1952)

Editor of TELEVISION IN THE MAKING (1956)

SOME FILMS BY PAUL ROTHA

Feature
THE SILENT RAID (De Overval) (1963)
CAT AND MOUSE (1957)
NO RESTING PLACE (1950)

Documentary
THE LIFE OF ADOLF HITLER (1960–61)
CRADLE OF GENIUS (1958)
WORLD WITHOUT END (with Basil Wright) (1952–53)
THE WORLD IS RICH (1947–48)
A CITY SPEAKS (1946)
LAND OF PROMISE (1944–45)
WORLD OF PLENTY (1942–43)
THE FOURTH ESTATE (1939–40)
NEW WORLDS FOR OLD (1938)
THE FACE OF BRITAIN (1935)
SHIPYARD (1934)
CONTACT (1932–33) etc., etc.

DOCUMENTARY DIARY

An Informal History of the British
Documentary Film, 1928–1939

by

PAUL ROTHA

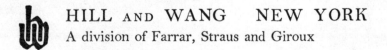 HILL AND WANG NEW YORK
A division of Farrar, Straus and Giroux

To the Memories of Five Men
Who Knew about and Believed in the

DOCUMENTARY FILM

Robert J. Flaherty
John Grierson
Richard Griffith
Eric Knight
Richard Winnington

I am the richer for having known them.

BUT

Because this book should not be only of past experience, I address it with modesty also to the young documentary film-makers who are growing up today in so many parts of the world. May they have the same fire within them to win battles without which films cannot be made for the betterment of human well-being.

Acknowledgements

The following authors and their publishers are thanked for giving permission to print extracts from their books:

Benjamin Britten, by Eric Walter White, Boosey & Hawkes, 1954, reprinted, Faber, 1970; *The Changing Scene*, by Arthur Calder-Marshall, Chapman & Hall, 1937; *Cinema*, by C. A. Lejeune, Maclehose, 1931; *Garbo and the Night Watchmen*, edited by Alistair Cooke, Jonathan Cape, 1937, new edition, Secker & Warburg, 1972; *Grierson on Documentary*, edited by H. Forsyth Hardy, Collins, 1946; reprinted, Faber, 1966; *The Mind in Chains*, edited by C. Day Lewis, Muller, 1937; *On Native Grounds*, by Alfred Kazin, Harcourt Brace Jovanovich, 1943; and *Rain on Godshill*, by J. B. Priestley, Heinemann, 1939.

The Canton Film Appreciation Group kindly supplied me with a transcript of Richard Griffith's tape-recording made as an introduction to *The Fourth Estate*; some photographs came from the National Film Archive by courtesy of Sheila Whittaker, and the same body screened many films for me from the 1930s and 1940s for which I was obliged; other still-photographs came from the Edinburgh Film Guild and the Museum of Modern Art, New York; the photograph of Robert Flaherty on page 2 was supplied by Mr John Monck; while the photographs of 21 Soho Square, 37 Oxford Street, and Dansey Yard were specially taken by Mr Wolfgang Suschitzky, that admirable cinematographer and friend. My thanks also to Mr Russell Madden for the photograph for the jacket.

If some acknowledgements have not been made, it is because their source has been untraceable.

P.R.

Contents

Plates
between pages 164 and 165

xi

Preface

Every critic, historian and student knows the mythology, the anecdotes, the reminiscences and no less the gossip that surround and follow a movement in the arts. A typical example is the mass of memorabilia that has grown up around the French post-Impressionists or the German Expressionists. As the years pass, inevitable distortions bud and bloom and are likely to become alcoholic coloured; only the works themselves remain aloof. A fringe element thrives on all this and I despair to think of the money made by the parasites out of Van Gogh and Modigliani and the others who died destitute. When as in recent years an art becomes integrated with modern methods of communication, the danger is even greater because of the ephemeral character of the electric media.

Up till 1940, there was only one real coherent movement in the young art of the cinema which was destined to have an influence on Western film-making and to attract world attention among critics and audiences; that was the movement of documentary film-making in Britain in the 1930s. The great works of Flaherty, of a few Europeans and some of the Soviet film-makers were earlier milestones, but they were the films of individuals and not those of a unified movement, except perhaps in the Soviet Union. It has been thought worth while, therefore, to set on record now, while memories are reasonably clear, facts available and most of the protagonists alive and alert, something of that period of film production. The record will tell of the main aims, influences and achievements, as well as of the mistakes and failures, in those formative years. Some opinions and deductions may well be debatable, but the facts, I hope, cannot be refuted.

One day it could be instructive for some critical assessor to compare the documentary film people and their work in the 1930s with a similar generation growing up at the same time in

xiii

Preface

Britain in the field of literature. Auden, Isherwood, Day Lewis, Warner, Spender, Graham Greene, Calder-Marshall and others were all exploring poetry and the novel at the same time as we were exploring the cinema medium. Without wishing in any way to denigrate their work, it is worth considering if anything written by this group of authors could compare in social influence to the work of the documentary film group. Undoubtedly the size of the audience reached by the films was far greater than that reached by the writers. *Night Mail*, for example, must have made a far greater impact on a far bigger audience than *The Ascent of F.6*. Which made the larger creative contribution to its time is a matter for debate. I would suggest, too, that in the US around the same years, writers like Mac-Leish, Agee, Odets and Dos Passos were having a much deeper social meaning than anything written by their English confreres. That again must be a matter of controversy. It is interesting that for a time Auden worked at the GPO Film Unit and wrote verse for Strand Films, but he cannot be said to have entered the medium in the same way that William Coldstream, the artist, did, although the latter, having renounced painting in the 1930s, returned to it again after the war.[1] It is strange that whereas in France, writers and the film *avant-garde* worked closely together, in England there was no similar rapport, until much later Rex Warner and Calder-Marshall wrote some scripts and commentaries and wrote them very well.

Research for this book and the writing of the first chapters were begun with the aim of producing an objective historical survey. It became clear, however, that because, like others, I was closely concerned with the documentary development, personal involvement could not be avoided. It was agreed that the book should have a dual approach. First, it would tell factually and critically the origins and growth of the documentary film movement in Britain from 1928 on; second, alternative chapters would tell some of my own experiences while making films at that time. I also privately hoped that this would make the book less dull. Anyway, that is how it evolved. Whether this dual approach works or not is impossible for me

[1] Vide: *Rotha on the Film*, A Painter Looks at Films, pp. 50–2, Faber, 1958.

to judge. It has one obvious drawback, an overlap in the march of events, but these have been dovetailed in what is believed to be a practicable and continuous way.

Since the term was first coined by John Grierson in 1927, and then publicised by those of us who wrote books and articles and gave lectures, documentary has been gradually and loosely used to cover a multitude of kinds of film-making, especially since the spread of mass-television. (I can well remember when I joined BBC-TV in 1953, Huw Wheldon asked, 'Tell me, Rotha, what *is* a documentary film?'). It is hard to say if this has been due to sheer ignorance on the part of new protagonists of the original principles and definition of the documentary idea as set out by us, or to the fact of our own obsessive zeal to get the term widely known. No one can claim any title to the use of the word; but it was first thought up by Grierson in the *New York Sun* and was propagated by us from 1929 onward.[1] In the 1930s it was considered in some areas as a dirty word, anathema in Wardour Street where it spelt bad box-office. (The Associated Realist Film Producers in fact substituted the word 'realist' for 'documentary'. Not all of us agreed, but a majority vote won.) Now hardly a day or evening passes without its use in talk, newspapers, theatre, radio, fiction, and of course television could not live without it. To some extent, I suppose we should be gratified for this attention. In spite of the attempted use of 'realist', 'documentary' obstinately stuck. To some people, the term means a film which is a document, which is far from the case. *Louisiana Story* was no document; but it was a documentary film and a very fine one at that. But for myself, understandably I hate to see the word abused and applied to almost any performance or publication that comes under the general heading of actuality. Another popular word, reportage, is often used to mean documentary, which it is not.

For some 25 years or more documentary had a clear definition. What exactly that definition is has most often been evaded; and I have been one of the worst evaders. I do not intend to over-clarify it here. It will, I hope, emerge from my

[1] 8 February 1926. Grierson's exact sentence in his piece ran: 'Of course *Moana* being a visual account of events in the daily life of a Polynesian youth, has documentary value.'

book as a whole. You can take your choice between Grierson's phrase, 'The creative treatment of actuality' and my own expansion, 'The use of the film medium to interpret creatively and in *social* terms the life of the people as it exists in reality.'[1] But I must stress that it is not the subject matter of a film which is in dispute. Much of *Nanook of the North* and *Louisiana Story* by Flaherty was faked, while the material in *Transfer of Power* by Shell was factual and accurate. What matters basically is the *creative* approach of the film-maker himself, especially in its human connotations. The fact that the boy in *Louisiana Story* had never paddled a *piroque* in his life until Flaherty had him taught, or that Nanook never caught a seal as Flaherty showed us, that the men of Aran had never harpooned a shark until they did it for Flaherty, or that the herrings in *Drifters* were actually shot in a marine tank at Plymouth, does not matter. What does matter is Flaherty and Grierson's approach to and use of their material. Several sequences in John Taylor's *The Londoners* and my *The Fourth Estate* were studio-shot, but no one will dispute that these were documentary films. In the 100 minutes or so of *The Life of Adolf Hitler*, there was only one fictional shot – the first in the film, and this is declared to be so by the commentator; the rest is all newsreel or actual film record, but it would have been a dull and dusty collection of shots if a creative approach had not been adopted in their selection and constructive arrangement as a creative concept of history. There is a vast difference between, say, a boring FitzPatrick travelogue of Ceylon and Basil Wright's poetically evocative film of that island's people and places. Therein lies the definition of documentary, if one is needed. But now I must stress something else. I have always seen documentary as a part of *all* creative cinema art, not as something specialized and out on a limb. Over the last thirty years I would include Pabst's *Kameradschaft* under the documentary label, and Pontecorvo's *Battle for Algiers*. That is why I have always avoided until now any kind of hard definition.

In subsequent years, especially since television, the term documentary has been thrown around without discrimination. Critics, especially television ones, are particularly at fault here;

[1] On title-page of *Documentary Film*, second edition, Faber, 1939.

xvi

film critics even more so because they have time to do their homework and read some of the literature that has grown up round film-making.

It has been tempting to restate certain conclusions about the documentary idea, its birth and growth, its aesthetic and technical developments, already set out at some length in my book in 1936, written the previous year.[1] I have tried to avoid this; the book is still readily available. Re-reading it before starting on this present work, I saw fit, perhaps in vanity, to think that my theoretical conclusions formed then, some 35 years ago, have changed little. Policies may have shifted a bit, events have inevitably replaced events, and people people, but the basic principles have remained true to their conception.[2] In post-war years, these principles may have become blurred and sometimes wholly discarded but that is no challenge to their original validity.

The wide popular success of television documentaries, moreover, has proved how right we were in the 1930s in believing that public audiences wanted to see our films and how dismally wrong were cinema exhibitors and distributors who were reluctant to market and show them. The wholesale and retail sides of the film industry, even today, have too often been inadequate in their assessment of public taste. The faceless men who book films for whole circuits of theatres have little real contact with public taste.

Sometimes I wonder if the many young makers of television documentaries in recent years appreciate how much they owe to our film labours in the 1930s. Would there have been a *Cathy Come Home* or an *Edna* without the spadework of people like Ruby Grierson and John Taylor? It is a debatable point, but I feel often that not enough courteous acknowledgement is made to the overall documentary tradition in Britain which was plotted and toiled over, long before television became a reality in almost everybody's home.

.   .   .

[1] *Documentary Film*, Faber, 1936, 1939, 1952 and 1968.
[2] I remember well Grierson reading the MS in 1935. 'Why the hell do you have to include Marx in the thing, it'll only make it more difficult for me with the Treasury.'

Preface

Recognition of the historical importance of the documentary film to our present age of living, and in particular the British contribution, has been the main reason why several bodies and individuals have made practicable this survey. In June 1967, the University of Manchester generously awarded me a Senior Simon Research Fellowship for twelve months to undertake the necessary research for the projected book. That is to say, to explore and discover material that might exist over and beyond that which was in my own extensive collection of memoranda, correspondence, files, programme notes, press-cuttings etc. (My father was after all a museums curator all his life.) This grant was made to cover 18 months. In the summer of 1969, a publisher's agreement, with adequate advance royalties, helped to make possible the start of the writing. Later, the Arts Council of Great Britain made a grant for the work to be continued. From 1970 on, various bodies such as the Royal Literary Fund, the Society of Authors and the Cinema and Television Benefit Fund helped to keep the writing going. My thanks are due to all these bodies. At the same time, learning of my task, and also deeming it of some importance in the history of the cinema, various colleagues in the production side of the British Film Industry contributed to make practicable the completion of the book. My gratitude, and that I am sure of all those concerned with the documentary film record in this country and overseas, is made to them for their belief in what, I trust, will be a worthwhile and lasting undertaking. Without such aid from different sources as listed above, this book would certainly not have been produced.

Here, too, I should like to set down my appreciation to those who encouraged and indeed urged me to undertake this work because, they told me, a young generation of would-be documentary makers is around in many parts of the world who want to know more than legend and pub talk about the people and their films, as well as the struggles and successes, of the early documentary days in Britain. Among the most insistent urgers were some of those who once worked with me on production – Stanley Hawes, Donald Alexander, Francis Gysin and Robert Kruger. And there were my older friends who were a constant stimulus, John Trevelyan, Carl Foreman, John Schlesinger,

Joseph Losey and David Lean; they maintained their enthusiasm when my own may have flagged. I thank them also.

It goes without saying that my old friend and colleague, the late John Grierson, continually spurred me on when we met from time to time at Devizes, conveniently placed near to where we both lived at that time. It was most fortunate for all concerned with this survey and those who may read it, that Grierson devoted his Christmas in 1970, when he was briefly back from Canada, to going through a large part of the MS, in particular the chapters dealing with the EMB and GPO Film Units. He found no errors of fact but sent me several pages of valuable notes, from some of which I have quoted. My great thanks also go to another old friend and co-worker, Basil Wright, who read the final complete MS, corrected a few factual errors and made several good points in general argument which have been adopted. He in particular early on made available a great deal of correspondence and memoranda, much of which will be of value in the future.

The MS has also been read in part or in whole by four other friends who know the period well: Mrs Jere Knight, Mrs Ann Griffith, Donald Alexander and John Taylor. I am indebted for their comments. My especial thanks are due to Elizabeth Sussex, who was asked by my publisher to be editor of the book, Her care, patience and skill have been of great value in the final stage of the MS, on which so many years have been spent.

In the course of research, it was my pleasure as well as duty to have talks with as many relevant people as possible. Like most documentary film-makers, I have a good and, I hope, reliable memory, but I was taught early on in life to check dates and facts wherever possible. (This is another valid reason why this work has taken so long to surface.) So I listened to rather more than 70 persons who worked in some capacity or other, production or office, in British documentary in the 1930s (and of course in later years). Many others courteously replied to my enquiries by letter and where I have quoted, acknowledgement has been made.

Since it was published in 1947, the Arts Enquiry Report called *The Factual Film* has been a mine of information for students and research workers. Set up in 1943 at the instigation of the Dartington Hall Trustees, it was one of several enquiries into the arts. The group which met so frequently and produced the Report has for many reasons remained anonymous. I see no good reason why it should remain so and have secured permission to identify them. Under the Chairmanship of Prof. H. L. Beales of the London School of Economics, there were: Miss Dilys Powell (film critic of the *Sunday Times*), Mr G. T. Cummins (Producer of British Paramount Newsreel), Mr Basil Wright (of Film Centre), Mr Edgar Anstey (Producer at the Shell Film Unit at that time) and the present writer. Miss Calley Calvert did most of the research at our bidding, while the drafting and final Report were the work of Mr Sinclair Road. We met many times in those blacked-out nights at PEP's offices in Westminster. If nothing else, the group could claim a big share in the complete reorganization and restaffing of the British Film Institute, as well as a revision in the make-up of the British Council Film Committee. In our aim to see a National Film Board established in this country, we were unsuccessful for reasons which will emerge in these pages.

Of the films themselves (which after all many people will say are what matters most), of the period, those about which I write critically were of course seen at their time of making (they were touched on in my earlier book), but in many cases I have reseen them, thanks to the cooperation of our National Film Archive. What to me was exhilarating in this screening was that so many of the films, though more than 30 years old, have so much vitality today. That is in part due obviously to their factual subject matter. Techniques of camera, sound and editing, however, suffer considerable changes in the film medium but far less, I suggest, in the documentary *genre* than in the story-film. Whereas feature films like *The Way Ahead* or *San Demetrio, London,* are fairly dated in technique when seen now, documentary films like *North Sea* and *Night Mail* are not. Except for some technical advances, in more mobile cameras and better quality sound-recording, one cannot conceive a more up-to-date technique than that of *Song of Ceylon.* That should be a gratifying thought to their makers today, living maybe in some cases off their old-age pensions. Television has certainly not invalidated such films. If anything, old in cinema years though they may be,

Preface

these early documentaries show up much contemporary television technique for its amateurishness, shoddiness and lack of expertise, unless that is, television relies on using films, and then it becomes only a medium for transmission of another medium, and not an act of creation in itself.[1]

Criticism of documentary films in this survey is of two kinds; my own judgement, for what it is worth, and reviews by responsible critics at the time, for example, Mr Graham Greene and Mr Forsyth Hardy. There are also some reviews made in hindsight, such as Mr Richard Griffith on *The Fourth Estate*. I have tried to keep a balance on such critical assessment. Over the years, the work of the EMB and GPO Film Units, as well as that of Strand and Realist, has sometimes been both decried and eulogized. Often the precepts have been misunderstood, as frequent pieces in American books and journals and our own *Sight and Sound* have shown, mainly because of superficial research and plain ignorance. One aim here has been to set the British documentary movement of the 1930s in some perspective while we can remember. At the time, as will be seen, we ourselves set it around with a kind of lustre (of which Grierson and I were the main burnishers), because first we passionately believed in the concept of documentary and, second, not unreasonably, we sought some kind of a modest and worthwhile living for ourselves and our dependants.

This survey is also intended to reveal that it was not only the artistry, technical skill and social conscience behind some of the films that characterized British documentary in the 1930s as a factor significant in cinema history, but the strategy and political manoeuvering that made the production of such films practicable at all. This continued to be equally true during the war years, 1940–47, which will be the subject of further survey. The fact that what was called the 'national interest' required Government sponsorship of many documentary and other kinds of factual films in wartime, thus giving producers a kind of modest but hard-fought-for stability, did not in any way lessen the need to see that basic documentary principles were both

---

[1] Cf. My views about television in the Introduction to *Television in the Making* (Focal Press, 1956), formed after two years as Head of BBC Television Documentary.

maintained and developed. This fact, I regret, as will be seen in time, was not to be remembered by all involved.

There is room, obviously, for more than one observer's point of view on our subject. Rachel Low will, I know, be giving documentary her special attention in the next and fifth volume of her invaluable *History of the British Film*. Elizabeth Sussex has spent much time tape-recording some of us oldsters who had a part in the documentary story, and will edit these interviews into a book. These two ladies charmed me into giving what help I could; they are serious authors and, short of making my own research available, I told them all I could. I wish their books well. The facts in each of these books will be the same, but the two ladies will have the advantage of objectivity which I cannot claim. They will most likely provoke dispute and argument among the old bulls of British documentary but that will be no bad thing. Professor Jack C. Ellis, of the School of Speech at North-western University, Illinois, is believed to be undertaking a biography of John Grierson, but it is some little time since I had news of this work.

Another very good reason for writing this book at this time is to prevent any kind of future myth being dreamed up about British documentary and its makers. Happily its story is within easy living memory. What I mean is that in the last two decades a young generation of film addicts for all kinds of cinema, not just documentary, has sprouted to adulate a hung-over era in cinema that they did not experience at first hand. I refer to the glorification of the Hollywood years of the 1920s–40s. I find it almost as nauseating as when I see partly-educated teen-agers flashing Swastika badges and cloth Iron Crosses when I see this salivating over the Hollywood years of whoredom. The men who really knew and suffered its reality told the truth but the young disregard this. 'Hollywood,' said Stroheim on BBC-TV in 1954, 'Hollywood is just a whore'. And said Flaherty after *Moana*, 'Hollywood is like floating over an open sewer in a flat-bottomed glass boat.' There was nothing romantic or glamorous or fabulous about most of the characters who held the power of hire or fire in those ugly days – the Fox's, the Laemmles, the Zukors, the Schencks, the Mayers, the

Preface

Cohns, the Warners, the Selznicks and all their countless hangers-on. They were as parasitic to society as their counterparts in banking, insurance, accountancy, real estate, property development, alcohol trading and of course, corrupt local politics. They dealt in entertainment in terms of flesh as others dealt in drugs, drink and property. I find it slightly revolting that servile adulation should be given to such gangsters at our national film theatre but assume that it is due to youthful ignorance and a lack of historical perspective on the part of those who are supposed to have a 'policy' for their cinema. There have been, be it noted, several accurately observed books about Hollywood, exposing it for what it really was, such as Ezra Goodman's *The Fifty-Year Decline and Fall of Hollywood* and Lillian Ross's *Picture*, but they have not prevented a cult being developed and fostered.

This kind of eulogizing of the Hollywood myth reflects the fact that the British Film Institute, for all its changing chairmen and governors, has never had a genuine *creative* policy towards the cinema. It has organized, collected, compiled, catalogued, indexed, administered and even disseminated information about the cinema, but its approach has never been *creative* towards the medium it is supposed to represent and appreciate. If a similar approach were applied to documentary I could imagine some future cult season at the NFT, with the late Sir Arthur Elton being portrayed as a bearded aristocratic gentleman bemusing himself with a Cornish beam-engine financed by the Shell Company; Mr Edgar Anstey, OBE, as a maker of home-movies about toy trains financed by Messrs Bassett Lowke and the National Union of Railwaymen; Mr Basil Wright eulogizing the Ceylonese and Greek Colonels sponsored by Lloyds and the CIA; Mr Grierson himself, having made a legendary film of the sardine fleet called *Heads Without Tails*, perpetuated as a lay preacher advocating Empire Trade and 6p postage with finance from the Fish Marketing Board and Marie Elizabeth. It sounds a good trip, but with a new generation of film addicts unwilling or too lazy to research into their facts, let alone discover back perspectives, it could happen as logically as the recent idolizing of Hollywood at its most garish. Perhaps this book could prevent it.

Preface

In October, 1958, the Museum of Modern Art Film Library
paid me the honour of presenting a four-week Retrospective
season of films produced and/or directed by me since 1933. On
my way back from Australia, where I had been the guest of the
Government's film department (headed by Stanley Hawes) and
of Unesco, I broke my journey for a few days in New York. I
dropped into the Museum's auditorium towards the end of *Land
of Promise*. On the way out, I mingled with the audience. In
front of me was a matron and her son (or nephew). 'Now if you
want to grow up and make films,' she said, 'that's the way how
not to make them.' It was salutary, but you could hardly expect
a Manhattan matron to be interested in Britain's housing problems. They say in the film world, 'Once you've had a Retrospective, you've had it.'

Three further small points I should like to make. If the US
chapter is more anecdotal than others, it is because I was in a
new place meeting new people, and undertaking a kind of
informal public relations job. I was not making a film, which is
my normal work. Second, to the young reader, it should be
made clear that the description of the making of *The Fourth
Estate* in 1939–40 refers, of course, to *The Times* newspaper and
its staff at that time, and not to the paper since it was acquired
by Lord Thomson's Organization in 1966. At the end of the
1930s, *The Times* film was the most technically complicated
British documentary to be attempted to that date, and therefore
its method of production is given its adequate space in this
survey. So many persons involved in its making, both on the
staff of the paper and of the film crew, are now not among us
that in a way the chapter is a small tribute to their patience and
work.

Photographs of the main exponents of British documentary
films at the time under review have been hard to find. Several
exist said to be of Grierson when making *Drifters* but I suspect
they were made later when he made *Granton Trawler*. That
used here was given me by himself. The one of Edgar Anstey is
an enlargement from a frame of film required by Customs on
the end of each reel of negative exposed overseas; it was taken
when he was making *Uncharted Waters*. The only photograph
of Mary Watt was as a 'glamour' boy in his Ealing Studios

days; I am sure he will be glad I do not use it, but his absence is missed. A few stills have been used before; this was inevitable. Documentary stills of that period are scarce.

To find and keep a perspective when you yourself were so much involved is almost impossible. I only hope that the passage of years has given an objective backward look. Quotes from letters of the time are relevant; they spark events. I was not at all inhibited when I wrote at such length to Eric Knight and Richard Griffith in America. I shamefully used them as catalysts. On my side at least, the vast correspondence was a safety-valve. For most of the time, my correspondents were not themselves involved in documentary's day-to-day working, but they became closely concerned with its ideological purposes. I have also had occasion to read through the detailed diaries I kept during the war years because they contain a number of entries relating to the 1930s seen in hindsight. These passages have been used with care; others have not been used at all because they refer to persons who are alive and active today, or the relations of those who are dead. It should be remembered, as will come clear later, that although British documentary in the 1930s, and to a lesser extent in the war years, was presented as a unified movement to the outside world, its inner workings were inevitably the stage for personal conflicts, perhaps even jealousies and one or two cases of disloyalty. Today I prefer to forget these happenings; they are locked away in my diaries for safe-keeping for some very future date, even if then.

Although it is all of ten years since I made a picture and even more since I was in close touch with the documentary film-makers of recent years, it does not mean that I dissociate myself in any way from the documentary purpose as I have known it over the past 43 years. But of my actual leaving of documentary production after Basil Wright and I made *World Without End* together in 1952–53, I shall write another day.

As I write this now, a book has just come in from America called *The Documentary Tradition*, edited by the indefatigable Lewis Jacobs.[1] It is an anthology by many critics and film-makers in this field, mostly American. It seems a useful addition

[1] Hopkinson and Blake, New York, 1972.

to documentary literature, but already I have spotted numerous factual errors about British documentary films and some misconceptions about their origins and purpose. This fact oddly cheers me; it means that my own survey herewith is needed to set the record straight.

P.R.

1967–72
Didsbury, Manchester; Wendover, Bucks; Market Lavington, Devizes; and Upton, Aylesbury.

Life is a gift from the few to the many, from those who know and who have, to those who do not know, and have not.

AMADEO MODIGLIANI

Prestige never bought anybody a ham sandwich

ROBERT J. FLAHERTY

The cinema is man dreaming as well as man in conflict and action with man and nature. By which I mean, the cinema is the first method of art to catch up with the speed and range of man's instantaneous comprehensive vision in that condition between sleeping and waking – the cinematograph daydream.

RICHARD WINNINGTON

1. *Background Picture*

The drop of bombs from airships, round about and over London. Thousands of shattered windows in Queen's Square, Bloomsbury. Gothas and Fokkers shadowed against a moonlit sky. A gun mounted in a truck blazing away at nothing but making an awful lot of noise. This is in my memory, but I shall not be writing a sequence of childhood memories. Instead, here are a few facts.

My father and mother were tolerant, liberal, wholly apolitical and far from well-off people. One came from Yorkshire, the other from Lancashire. One had a medical training, the other was a nurse. They must have been tolerant and also patient, because I went to and left thirteen schools in less than that number of years. I learned little but was encouraged by a bearded man called Brown to draw and paint whatever came into my mind. At all my thirteen schools, as soon as I became aware of feelings, I loathed not sport itself but the fetish made of it by boys and staff alike. I feared the quick use of physical violence, sensing its evil power over adolescents. I have retained both those feelings.

At my last school, where I somehow remained longer than usual, my form-master wisely said, 'You'll learn nothing in this classroom. But this school has a fine library, which nobody ever uses. Go and use it. Get to hell out of here to the library! I'll cover up for you at the end of term.' I never regretted his advice and wish I knew his name so that I might commemorate it. All those years at those thirteen schools were a waste of time and my father's ill-to-spare money. Maybe they were the wrong kind of school? At the last one I won the annual Art Prize two years running much to the abuse of my mates. The end of term in summer, 1923, saw all five hundred odd boys and many of their bourgeois parents assembled in the fake Great Hall. After

1

speeches, boys due to leave filed one by one past the Head Master to be given his blessing. It was the first and only time I came face to face with him, with his fiery complexion and bloated eyes. He stank of whisky. 'And you, my boy, what are you going to do?' he asked the youth two ahead of me in the line. 'Accountant, sir.' said the boy. 'Good, you'll do well! Next!'. The youth in front of me shuffled forward. 'And you, young fellow?' 'I'm going to join my father, sir. He's a stockbroker.' 'Excellent! Make lots of money! Next!' I stepped up. His red eyes glared at me. I glared back. 'And you?', he asked. 'An artist', I replied. He paused a moment, looked past me to the boy behind, and said, 'Next!'

It was a never-to-be-forgotten moment in my life. Many years later, I had a letter from the Honorary Secretary of the Old Boys' Society of the school, of which I was not a member. It said that a fund had been started to build an extension, or a laboratory, or a fives court, or something, at the school and it was to be named after the Head Master who was now dead. As an old boy of 'wide repute' (it was not stated for what), it was felt sure that I would send a donation to the fund. In fact, I sent a description of the above incident, and thought no more of it. But back came a reply, 'You're not the only one!'

At sixteen it was mutually agreed between my father and myself that schools were no use to me or I to them. So I left. But I must remember that broken limbs at sport gave me the freedom twice a week to go to all the local picture-houses in the area. Anything that was billed, I saw. From early years, I took notes of them. In World War I, my father, in addition to his normal work as a museum curator, was a Commandant of a voluntary Military Hospital. He opened it only a few weeks after the declaration of war in August 1914. Wounded soldiers from the French, or maybe Belgian, front, in red, white and blue cotton uniforms were given free seats at the local fleapit. Naturally I went too. The red plush curtain, the fetid tobacco smoke, the whirring projector, the endlessly throbbing piano, and above all the flickering shadows on the screen of blue, orange, or just black-and-white are strong images. The manager, or maybe he was the owner, was a Mr Tipping. He had a nicotine-stained moustache and a permanent cigarette-end. There were such

2

romanticisms as *Beau Brocade* and *Prisoner of Zenda,* and some
very early Douglas Fairbanks pictures like *He Comes Up
Smiling* and *The Man from Painted Post.*

Before that, my father had taken me to the Scala Theatre in
Charlotte Street to see the *Delhi Durbar* film in Kinemacolour,
with a John Bunny comedy. After the 1918 Armistice, but not in
London, I saw many serials, such as a favourite, *The Mystery of
the Double Cross.* Of features I recall Elsie Ferguson in *Barbary
Sheep,* especially the scene when she put eau-de-cologne on a
lump of sugar, and Fairbanks again in *Mr Fix It* and *The
Americano.* There were the action pictures of Wallace Reid, like
Watch My Smoke and the original African-made *King Solomon's
Mines.* Occasional visits to London produced more Fairbanks in
The Three Musketeers and *Robin Hood.* When eventually I met
him in some London hotel, I was disappointed that his sole con-
cern in life seemed to be golf.

It is pointless to record the hundreds of films I saw in this
habitual way. My only wish is to stress how I grew up, like
many others of my generation, with the movies. Their continuous flow over me must have made deep subconscious impact.
Years later, somewhere around 1952, David Low, that admirable cartoonist, told me that every day except Sunday he went
to his local cinema after lunch to let films just 'float' over him;
he had no idea what he saw, the movement hypnotized him, as it
possibly does those who perpetually watch television today. The
fact that I can still remember in great detail the rescue over the
ice-floes in *Way Down East* and Fairbanks swinging from the
draperies across the baronial hall in *Robin Hood* is of significance
to me. It was the movement itself that has remained in my mind,
not the episode involved. In the same way later, it is the movement in *Song of Ceylon* that remains so significant but now I
remember the reason for this movement and not just the movement itself. The Fairbanks films were fulfilling a desire for
pleasurable emotion; Basil Wright's film was conveying a
sociological meaning through its movement.

In those early years the most outstanding film event for me
was in 1922, when I was taken to see *The Cabinet of Dr Caligari*
at the old Marble Arch Pavilion. The originals of E. McKnight
Kauffer's posters hung in the vestibule. (What happened to

them?) So much has been written about this unique film that I need not say here more than what a deep impression it made. I was fortunate in later years to have as a friend Carl Mayer who, with Janowitz, wrote the script. Many, many evenings in some pub in Fleet Street during the air-raids Carl told me about how *Caligari* came to be made; but he talked even more about how the veil of expressionism and theatricalism fell from his eyes on the day he saw *Potemkin*. And how standing outside the Palast am Zoo, staring into the swirling traffic, he conceived the idea of what became *Berlin: Symphony of a City*. Carl Mayer, like Griffith, Pabst, Eisenstein, Pudovkin and Dovjenko, was one of the very great men of cinema. So were Flaherty and John Grierson.

When I went to the Slade School of Art in 1924, the greater part of my time was still spent in seeing films. For that reason, my work was not especially distinguished, although I got a top students' prize for theatre costume design at the International Theatre Exhibition in Paris in 1925. It brought me a most welcome £50, with which I began a bank account. The Slade, however, gave me a basic training in design and especially, visual composition within the frame, which was to be both a hindrance and a guide. The rigid edges of a canvas or a sheet of paper induce a static concept as opposed to the dynamic of the cinema screen. Most of my first film was observed in static terms, except for the editing. But as will be seen, my searching for movement was frustrated because I had no access to equipment which was helpful for camera movement.[1] It was at the Slade that there arose my first and everlasting interest in typography. I find as much aesthetic as well as functional delight in Gill's Perpetua as I do in a John drawing. I suppose it is called graphics. It has a lot to do with the cinema.

Among co-workers at the Slade were Oliver Messel, Rex Whistler, Bill (now Sir William) Coldstream, Humphrey Slater (who wore tartan trousers), a Strachey of some variety (who wore no socks), and Robert Medley. There was also a nicely crazy American named Skelton, who one afternoon returned to the life-room and with great care and patience stuck up on the wall a complete set of fifty cigarette-cards of British

[1] Vide: p. 73

4

insects. 'That', he declaimed, 'is Real Art'. Among our skilled and respected teachers headed by Professor Henry Tonks, whose fine work is perhaps overlooked today (go and see his pastels of paraplegics in the Royal College of Surgeons which my father commissioned), were Franklin White, who drew divinely, Wilson Steer whose painting left me cold, and the anatomy-fiend George Charlton. It was Charlton's teaching that you should observe the outer contours of a human body from its inner bone and muscle structure that greatly helped me in film work, especially when I related it to Freudian analysis. About this I was to write in *The Film Till Now* in the section dealing with film psychology about which I also had long talks with the great Pabst. Of all things about the Slade, however, that stay in my mind were the superb nude drawings by Augustus John which hung in the passage that led to the men's life-room. There was a man who saw from the inside to the outer surface.

Of the various painters whom I tried to understand, Van Gogh was the first. I found him in the Tate Gallery and in many books. His letters to his brother, Theo, made a deep impression on me, especially those in which he wrote of a guild of artists, an ideal in which Gauguin evilly betrayed him in that visit to Arles. It was Van Gogh's socialist notion that possibly first stirred in me a social conscience. His letters and drawings from the Borinage have always stayed with me. In later years, I spent much time, after a visit to Holland, trying to find a source of money to make a film about him. Korda said, 'Who in the public will be interested in a man who is only remembered because he cut off his ear.?' I deplored the Minnelli film perhaps less than the shocking novel from which it was adapted.[1] But Resnais did him well.

Many of us ate day and evening at the Bertorelli's restaurant in Charlotte Street and went afterwards to the Fitzroy Tavern opposite. The popular meal was *spaghetti al sugo* and a *demi-tasse* which cost in all 5d. Paper table-cloths but an inimitable atmosphere. Other haunts at night were *The Cave of Harmony* in Gower Street, run by Elsa Lanchester, Charles Laughton and Harold Scott, and the *Ham Bone Club* in Ham Yard just off

[1] Vide- *Rotha on the Film*, Faber, 1958, pp. 192–4.

Piccadilly. I began to hear my first jazz, this in *The Nest* in Kingley Street.

I came to know London streets, parks, squares, courts and alleys better than some taxi-drivers of later use. I found this out in the only way, by walking, mostly at night. The West End, the East End, the City, the Docks, the Embankment, King's Road and all Hampstead I knew like the veins in a leaf, but I never went much into Kensington and that part of the West. Notting Hill, Praed Street, around Euston and King's Cross and up Pentonville Rise to Islington, these were all familiar. They had individual character, most of which has vanished since the war. Property developers, living in penthouses or on a yacht or some tax-free West Indian haven, have wholly torn London's character to shreds. Uncontrolled exploitation for private profit has strangled what was one of the humanly most warm cities in Europe – not the most beautiful, for that you must go to Prague or Amsterdam or Copenhagen or Athens or Rome or what is left of Paris. Property developers are as great an assassin in our living these past 25 years as the industrial polluter of water, air and open country. No one in places where controls can be used, cares, or uses their controls with real purpose. They are corrupted by their personal needs. The great vision of a city, sprawling as it may sometimes be, has vanished from London. For many years I lived just off Fleet Street and was there all through the Blitz. It has all changed and not just the buildings but the atmosphere. I do everything in my power now to avoid going to London, where once I loved and lived and worked. Its ruination has all been due to exploitation for private profit, the greed of a few people who do not even live there.

Money for my fees at the Slade ran dry. I had paid them by doing some enlargements of mediaeval woodcuts to hang in a museum. For a time commercial work, such as book illustrations and book-jackets, posters and even menu designs, brought in a kind of living. The theatre design world was a closed shop, prised open by social influence which I did not possess. One or two established designers, such as George Sheringham, were kind and even enthusiastic but led nowhere. Theatre design was rarely commissioned and when it was it went to a chosen few. Endless letters to film studios seeking work usually brought no replies. A friendly talk with Anthony Asquith (who was then making *Underground*) gave a warning not to try any further. Balcon took on a few recruits but they all had a respectable university background. For some months *The Connoisseur*, an expensive monthly magazine devoted to antiques and old masters, found me a place doing make-up for the paper. The Editor, the most charming C. Reginald Grundy, thought, however, that his journal should keep up with the times if in a cautious way. Thus I found myself with great impertinence reviewing exhibitions of so-called modern painters which included Van Gogh, Modigliani, Toulouse-Lautrec and Marie Laurencin. I had no qualifications to write about their work but as they were already dead I suppose no harm was done. Mr Grundy had on his desk a small framed notice facing a visitor which read: Ten Minutes Means a *Long* Interview.

Evenings and weekends were spent as usual in seeing films. At this time the energetic but not very knowledgeable Stuart Davis (whose brothers owned the Pavilions at Marble Arch and Croydon) was in charge of the small Shaftesbury Avenue Pavilion, an awkward house for film-booking in competition with the big theatres in the West End. He hit on the idea of running what he billed as Unusual Films, which he picked up on the Continent very cheaply. In this way, many enthusiasts for films other than the routine American and British showings were able to see French, German and Russian films which otherwise would have been restricted to the Film Society's members. Stuart Davis's minute office on the first floor of his theatre became a rendezvous for those who were discovering the cinema. I recall his showing of *Moana* made its first impact on me here, and also Pabst's *The Love of Jeanne Ney*, retitled as *Lusts of the Flesh* by Wardour Films who imported it. Stuart little realized what effect the films he booked in Paris and Berlin at small cost would have on future film-makers.[1] Among other films he played were: *En Rade, Rien que les heures, Finis Terrae, The Italian Straw Hat, Les Deux Timides, The Fall of the House of Usher* and *Turksib*.

By now I realized that my future, if I was to have one, could

[1] A full story of this enterprise was printed in *Documentary News Letter*, June 1940, and reprinted in *Rotha on the Film*, Faber, 1958.

only be in the medium that excited me so deeply. One rainy day I strapped a portfolio of drawings and designs on the back of a bicycle and rode from my small room in Hampstead out to the British International Film studios at Boreham Wood. When the commissionaire heard that I had no appointment with the Art Department, he refused admission in that way which only commissionaires at film studios can. I had asked to see the Supervising Art Director, not knowing if there was such a person. It so happened at that moment he was passing through on his way from the canteen. His name was Norman Arnold and he was a water-colorist *manqué*. He overheard my enquiries and took me up to his department. My work was liked but there was no vacancy. He would get in touch with me but meantime advised a study of architecture and interior design and furniture. During the next month or two, I undertook this study in spite of the fact that my commercial hackwork brought in less than £1 per week. My instruction was mainly gained in the Victoria and Albert Museum.

Unlike most people in the film business, Norman Arnold fulfilled his promise. Three months after my visit to the studios, a telephone message told me that a job was available. It was what was called an 'outside man'. Each evening I was supplied with a list of furniture, ornaments, properties of all kinds (including animals), required by the art-director for a set to be built the next day and 'dressed' the day after. With a Ford van and a driver, armed with the list, it was my duty to go to London, visit the suppliers of the articles needed, drive a bargain for the hire of same, and then return with my load to the studio usually around 8 pm. Often it was found that, in my absence, the director had changed his shooting-schedule and left orders that the set which had been built that day should be ready 'dressed' by 8 am the next morning. As in most cases the set-dressers had gone home at 6 pm, the 'outside man' (who had clocked in at 8 am that morning), had to turn 'set-dresser' overnight. When the set was ready for shooting the next morning, on many occasions the director (with a hangover) did not appear until after lunch. All this was for 25 shillings a week and, of course, no overtime. But I had begun in the Film Industry.

Memories of that year, 1928, are not important. The first

8

picture to which I was assigned was *After the Verdict*, directed
by a German (it was fashionable to bring over European
directors at that time), Henrik Galeen, who had made the
beautiful *Student of Prague* in 1926, a film that had much impressed me. One day during the lunch-break (it was a day off
from London), I found Galeen sitting alone on the set. Daring
to approach him, I said how much I admired his films, especially
Student of Prague. His reaction was instant. It seemed that I was
the only English person in the whole studio who knew his work.
He was delighted. We became very good friends and he told me
much about the German cinema, of what I later called The
Golden Period when I wrote *The Film Till Now*. He gave me
his own album of stills from the film I admired so much.

When *After the Verdict* (a bad film but no fault of Galeen)
was finished Norman Arnold found a minor place for me as a
draftsman in BIP's regular art department. The work was unin-
spiring; drawing plans for interminable boudoirs and night-
clubs that made up most of the current needs in British pictures.
During the year, however, I was able to meet that gifted
Austrian art-director, Alfred Jünge, who had been brought over
to do the sets for E. A. Dupont's *Piccadilly*. It began a long
friendship and I learned much from him. Another German
director with whom I made good contact was Arthur Robison,
who had made the memorable *Warning Shadows* in 1922. He
was currently directing the first version of Liam O'Flaherty's
The Informer, with Lars Hansen (from Sweden), Lya de Putti
(from Germany) and Carl Harbord (from England), with sets
designed by Walter Reimann, who worked on *Dr Caligari*. (For
some reason, an English art-director was given the credit on
the screen instead of Reimann.) Little shown because it came
during the transition from silent to sound films, it was a far
better film than John Ford's much over-praised version of the
same book. Robison's *The Informer* was mutilated in the editing
by a crude attempt to add some post-synchronized dialogue.
Like Galeen, Robison was working in a studio alien to his ideas.
At the same time, Hitchcock was making a best-forgotten
picture called *Champagne*; he is remembered then as a practical
joker, usually at the expense of the crowd players.

These meetings with gifted European film-makers, whose

talent was little appreciated in English studios, were my main pleasure and reward in working at Elstree. Someone else with whom a good friendship was made was the charming and gifted actress, Anna May Wong, who had been brought from Hollywood, where she had made an impact in Fairbanks's *Thief of Bagdad*, to play in *Piccadilly*. She kept herself aloof from most of the studio with whom she found small sympathy. Theodor Sparkhul and Werner Brandes were two German cameramen with whom I also made friends; the former had shot several of the big-scale historical films so popular in Germany in the early 1920s.

At the same time, there were the usually rewarding Sunday afternoon performances of the Film Society, which had been founded in 1925 by Ivor Montagu, Iris Barry, Ted McKnight Kauffer, Edmund Dulac, Frank Dobson, Sidney Bernstein and W. C. Mycroft. It was the first such society in the world. There we saw between October 1925 and December 1930 such classics as (in order of their presentation): *Nju, Menilmontant, The Hands of Orlac, Dr Mabuse, Greed, The Joyless Street, New Year's Eve, Nana, Berlin: The Symphony of a City* (with Edmund Meisel's superb music), *Tartuffe, Mother, Dracula (Nosferatu), Rien que les heures, The End of St Petersburg, En Rade, Bed and Sofa, Drifters, Battleship Potemkin* (again with Meisel's powerful music, forbidden to be played in some countries), *New Babylon, Storm Over Asia, Voyage au Congo, The General Line, Earth, La Passion de Jeanne d'Arc* and many others. In addition, there were dozens of short experimental and *avant-garde* films which would not have been seen in Britain without the Film Society. Although it had a distinguished council, there is no doubt that the inspiration behind the choice and importation of films was due to Ivor Montagu. Film-makers, critics and historians of my generation owe a great debt to his energy and judgement, not least to his programme notes compiled for each programme. The Society's last performance was at the New Gallery Kinema, 23 April, 1939. It had presented 108 programmes over fourteen years. There are today more than seven hundred film societies in the United Kingdom.

Late in 1928 my creative urge, if such it was called, rebelled against the imbecilities and vulgarities of the Elstree studios.

Background Picture

Under my name an article appeared in *Film Weekly* with the heading 'The Technique of the Art-Director'.[1] The morning on which it was published, Norman Arnold said that the General Manager of the studio wished to see me at once in his office. I thought I was going to get a rise. It was my first and last meeting with John Appelby Thorpe, an unimpressive small fat man. He waved a copy of *Film Weekly* at me. 'Did you write this?' he demanded. Proudly I said, 'Yes.' 'Then you're fired!' he shouted, 'I will not have employees of this studio knocking the pictures we make here.' My piece did deplore the crudities of set design in British studios, comparing it unfavourably with the creative work in German and French films. When I told Herbert Thompson, editor of the paper, he said he'd call Thorpe but I restrained him. He also said he'd like to have any further articles I cared to submit. Which I did.

In any case, there would have been no work at the studio within a few months. With Hollywood going over to sound films, British production was mainly suspended so that studios could be equipped with sound-recording systems. A skeleton staff was kept on by a studio but the rest went on the unemployment roster for a year or so.

In spite of the frustrations, my year at Elstree was not wasted. What I learned was twofold. First, almost everyone making British films was fully occupied in a rat race. Second, it was important, if not essential, to acquire the knack of personal showmanship. Here is an example. Walking through the studio one evening after shooting had stopped I found a set for a typical, middle-class, living-room. The only thing which drew my attention was that the three-ply floor was painted in big blue and yellow squares. Sets were always done in monochrome. I saw the art director who I knew had designed the set standing looking at it. I asked him, 'Why the blue and yellow, instead of black and grey?' He replied, 'For the same damn-fool reason you ask. All day everybody has asked the same question, That twit,' and he named the executive producer of the studio, 'even came to look at it. He was so puzzled that he's given me a rise and a contract for three more pictures.'

One final thing that I learned was that the great majority of

[1] 12 November 1928; reprinted in *Rotha on the Film*, Faber, 1958.

English persons (but not all) making pictures at that time were far more interested in football and racing results than they were in film production. As a result, technical standards were not exactly high.

While at the studio, the Anglo-Frenchman, Edmond Greville, had become a friend. He had been second assistant to Dupont on *Piccadilly*, and like me had recently been fired. He had gone back to Paris, where he lived, and wrote that he had raised some money to make a film to be called *Midnight* and would I go over and do the sets? Two weeks were spent in a sordid little Montparnasse hotel, after which the money did not appear. I returned to London, but I had at least met René Clair, Jean Epstein, Georges Lacombe and Cavalcanti of the *avant-garde*, if only over a drink. There was one big difference; they had all made a film, I had not.

For some time I had made up my mind that if I couldn't make films, I could write about them. This I did for *Film Weekly* but it was not enough to live on. Then I met again the novelist, Norah C. James, who was in charge of book design at Jonathan Cape, the publishers. She had from time to time given me book-jackets and illustrations for children's books to do. Her first novel, *Sleeveless Errand*, had just been a matter of a court action, which resulted in it being banned and all copies confiscated. It was her idea one evening at Bertorelli's that I should write a book about the cinema. If I drew up a synopsis, she undertook that Jonathan Cape himself would consider it. I had an interview with Mr Cape. He liked the project, he said, but it would have to be largely a labour of love. There was little precedent for books on the subject and for his firm it was a gamble. He offered me a contract with modest advance royalties payable in thirds, the first of which would allow visits to Berlin and Paris to see films.

Early in 1929, Erich Pommer, the head of the big Ufa company in Berlin, told his publicity man, Paul Davidsohn, to give me all I asked for. Cooperation could not have been better. Many German films, old and new, were projected for me and the Ufa files of stills made available. More than 30 years later in Hollywood, I reminded Pommer, now a crippled old man, of his great kindness in 1929, and again thanked him. He just said,

Background Picture

'I heard that in later times in London you too were kind to many film people who had to leave Germany – Fritz Kortner, Carl Mayer, Berthold Viertel, Alfred Jünge, George Pabst, Ernö Metzner and many others, I now thank you.'

Then to Paris again, where equally good help was forthcoming. In particular the Soviet Trade Agency was all too willing to show me many Soviet films whose titles were in many cases unknown to me. They also supplied an interpreter. I spent 10 days seeing nearly 100 films, short and long, which I could never have seen in England. My advance from Cape had almost run out but I returned to London enthused.

At that time I rented a small, furnished room in Hampstead. I reported to Jonathan Cape on the success of my journey and he generously advanced more money, not much but enough just to live on while writing the book. The following months often saw a daily diet of four stale doughnuts (1d.), ten cheap cigarettes, half a pint of mild and something left over for rent and shillings for the gas meter. Someone who was very helpful at that time was Hugh Perceval, who worked in films. He gave me a big file of Press cuttings he had collected, mostly from the better Trade journals and I also had my own Press cutting books which I had started in 1924.

While working on the book, Sergei Eisenstein, the great Soviet film director and theorist, came to London. His visit has been described in detail by Ivor Montagu in his intriguing book *With Eisenstein in Hollywood*[1] and by Marie Seton in her vast biography, *Eisenstein.*[2] From memory I gave Miss Seton the following anecdote. Miss C. A. Lejeune, film critic, of *The Observer*, Norah James and I took Eisenstein to lunch in Soho, after which he much wanted to visit the Black Museum at Scotland Yard. This was impossible for an alien but instead I took him to the collection at the Royal College of Surgeons of which my father was then Curator. Miss Lejeune had to go see a film, but Norah James accompanied us. All Eisenstein was interested in were pickled penises but he declared himself very satisfied. He asked for some English tea. Norah James excused herself. So I took Eisenstein to a Lyons Tea Shop next to Holborn Underground station. We sat and he talked for some

[1] Seven Seas Books (Berlin, 1968).   [2] The Bodley Head (1952).

13

two hours and he drew a great deal on the marble-top table. I regretted that I could not take the table top away. It was during his visit that Ivor Montagu arranged for Eisenstein together with Hans Richter, the German *avant-garde* film-maker, to give some film classes, held I think in an upstairs room at Foyle's Bookshop, but I could not afford the fee. Basil Wright attended.

The MS of *The Film Till Now* was finished early in 1930 but it was far too long, more than 200,000 words. After reflection, G. Wren Howard, who was looking after the book at Cape's, suggested that two people experienced in sub-editing go through the MS with me to see what could be shortened or deleted. He also proposed that the theoretical part of the book be put last and the historical survey first, an idea which was adopted. With the help of an old journalist friend, Osbert Lumley, then assistant editor on *Public Opinion*, and F. Gordon Roe, assistant editor on *The Connoisseur*, the work was done in the evenings. The revised MS was delivered to the publisher in the Spring and was published in the following September. With what pleasure I made the design for the book-jacket from film-strips obtained from Grierson's *Drifters*, Asquith's *A Cottage on Dartmoor* and Blakeston's abstract film *Light Rhythms*. It was around then that I coined the phrase, 'A film is a microcosm of a microcosm'. To this day it has made no sense, but it has been admired and used by various psychiatrist friends later.

In general the book had a good reception both here and in America, but the Trade Press slated it. If it had been in my mind that the top men in the studios would be impressed by a display of cinema knowledge and experience, this notion was soon shattered. In the film industry the book made me many enemies. Over the years it has been steadily reprinted, updated in 1949 with the help of my friend Richard Griffith, and updated again in 1960 and 1963. At the time of writing today, it is still in demand among the ever-growing number of film students attending film schools, motion picture departments at universities and film societies. Its sales in developing countries, in Africa and Asia, are especially encouraging.

Above all, the book brought me friendships that were to last over many years. First, there was Eric Knight, Motion Picture Critic of the *Philadelphia Public Ledger* at the time of the book's publication in the US, with whom my long correspondence began in 1932 and lasted until his death in 1943. Second, there was Richard Griffith, a student in 1932 and also with whom I was to exchange hundreds of letters until he was tragically killed in an automobile accident in the Fall of 1969. Third was Richard Winnington, one of the best of all film critics, a close friend until he died in 1953. The book also destined me to be asked to open many film societies which sprang up in the 1930s in the UK, and to give innumerable lectures in many countries.

When the Shaftesbury Avenue Pavilion closed in 1929, not through lack of audience support but because the lease ran out, Stuart Davis had given me his mailing list of some 12,500 names and addresses in the London area. With several enthusiasts, including J. B. Holmes and F. Gordon Roe, we formed what we called the Film Group with the aim of starting a cinema for the showing of specialized films. A prospectus was issued, and a postcard questionnaire asking the recipient if he or she would support regularly a cinema created along such lines as we suggested, was sent to everyone on the mailing list. The response was impressive. Over 70 per cent were favourable. We then approached several small theatres in the West End but none was available for rental. In the meantime, Miss Elsie Cohen, who was running the Windmill Cinema (later to become famous as the Windmill Theatre under Vivian Van Damm), latched on to Stuart Davis's policy and began playing Continental films, mostly running pictures that had already been shown at the Shaftesbury Avenue Pavilion. She joined with our Film Group in intention and through her we met Eric Hakim, who had a white elephant on his hands at the Academy Cinema in Oxford Street. The rental he asked was far too high for our estimated budget. A week later Elsie Cohen informed us that she had made a private deal with Hakim and that she was shortly opening the Academy Cinema for showing specialized films. That ended the Film Group project.

Again there was no employment. Maybe a few drawings sold here and there. But let us go on to events of which a small part involved myself.

2. The Beginnings of British Documentary

Sometimes it is said that the roots of the British documentary film lay in the work of professional or amateur cameramen who accompanied expeditions of exploration and adventure, or maybe went solo. Notable as records and often well photographed within the technical qualities available at the time, such a film as Herbert G. Ponting's *The Great White Silence*[1] or the wild-life films of Cherry Kearton as far back as 1908, were not documentary films in the sense that the term is meant all through this survey. Nor were many other examples of scaling mountains and crossing deserts, several examples of which are given by Rachel Low.[2] The film camera was simply being used in its basic capacity as a moving photographic recording instrument. Harry Bruce Woolfe and Percy Smith in their long series of films, *Secrets of Nature* (1919–33), also fully explored the camera's technical resources, including many examples of the beauty of slow motion. They demand credit for their perseverance in the use of the film medium for popular instructional and educational purposes. After World War I, Bruce Woolfe, with the collaboration of such directors as Geoffrey Barkas and Walter Summers, was also responsible for a number of films about major war events, such as *Armageddon* (1923), *Zeebrugge* (1924), *The Battle of the Falkland and Coronel Islands* (1927) and *Q Ships* (1928). These films linked authentic combat footage shot by official cameramen and newsreel-men with sequences reconstructed on shore or at sea. Jingoistic in purpose, they were

[1] Re-edited in the early 1930s with a sound track and issued under the title of *Ninety Degrees South*.
[2] *History of the British Film, 1918–1929*, Vol. IV, Allen & Unwin, 1971.

commercially very successful and provided a good revenue for their distributor, New Era Films.[1] A skilful early maker of travel films with some imagination was Geoffrey Barkas whose series *Tall Timber Tales* (1923–24), made in Canada, was of note. The British were not the first to explore this non-fictional exploratory use of the cinema but they were among the pioneers and struggled hard against general Trade apathy.

The authentic origins of the international documentary approach lay of course in Robert J. Flaherty's film *Nanook of the North*, made in the Hudson Bay Territory in 1920–21, financed by Revillon Frères, the New York furriers. It not only recorded Eskimo life, admittedly with some reconstruction, but unconsciously perhaps brought a creative art into its observation. The actual term 'documentary' was not used until 1926, when Grierson found it to describe Flaherty's second film, *Moana*.[2] So much has been written about Flaherty's work that it is pointless to analyze and describe it again here.

In the early 1920s, on the other side of the world, the Soviet film-makers under the stimulation of Lenin's recognition of the cinema and the direction of Lunacharsky, Education Commissar, were becoming aware of the powerful social and political value of the actuality cinema. The work of Dziga-Vertov and Esther Schub made use of newsreel and other authentically shot footage in many early films.[3]

The next milestones in the documentary story were in France and Germany. They were Alberto Cavalcanti's *Rien que les heures* (1926), being Paris seen through a cross-section of 24 hours, and Walther Ruttmann's *Berlin: Symphony of a City* (1927). Both these films made a deep impact on the young British documentary people. Both have been written about a

---

[1] Bruce Woolfe, who began as an exhibitor, was a fervent Empire loyalist. Grierson wrote of his film *England Awake!* 'Toot, toot! Here Comes the British Empire'.

[2] Cf. p. xiii. For the full story of Flaherty's life and work, see *The Innocent Eye* by Arthur Calder-Marshall, based on research material by Paul Rotha and Basil Wright, W. H. Allen, 1963, and *The World of Robert Flaherty* by Richard Griffith Gollancz, 1953.

[3] See *Kino* by Jay Leyda, Allen & Unwin, 1960. Many of these films were revived in connection with the Fiftieth Anniversary Celebrations of the October Revolution of 1918.

great deal but a very good analysis, not before published, was by Richard Griffith. He wrote:

Chiefly preoccupied with abstract aestheticism, the French *avant-garde* films of the silent era sometimes forsook Freud and Dada to touch upon the contemporary scene. Panoramas of Paris during the period 1920–27 occasionally contrasted the rich and the poor, filth with splendour, taking elementary symbolism where they found it but leaving social implication out altogether. Deriving in part from their example, Cavalcanti's *Rien que les heures* was one of the first films to attempt to deal intimately with industrial civilisation, as Flaherty had dealt intimately with the remnants of a world passed away. Cavalcanti's film revealed in spreading images the passage of a day in the life of Paris, touching lightly upon the occupations, surroundings and events of a series of more or less typical Parisians. Its clumsiness and preening preciosity are not the worst faults of the film seen later. There is a social meaning in the film but Cavalcanti leaves it locked inside the material; the spectator must dig it out for himself. He seldom comments; always he presents, and from an aesthetic point of view. Sliding along his slender thread of temporal continuity, he selects each shot for its compositional value. And yet the film, concerned as it is with presenting an aspect of Paris rather than its total actuality, cannot escape wholly into aestheticism. It is, after all, a modern city we are shown and, seeing it, we are forced to apprehend the human implications that even an aspect suggests. Jerkily but inevitably, the carefully rehearsed aesthetic rapture of the visual pattern is broken by sympathy and indignation.

If Cavalcanti's film is in purpose a glorified travelogue, Walther Ruttmann's *Berlin* was surely intended as an *étude* in rhythmic abstraction. Carl Mayer, formerly scriptwriter of many famous German silent films, and Karl Freund, skilful and experienced camerman, are credited with assistance in making it as a *Kontingent* picture for Fox-Europa during the 18 months of 1926–27.[1] Like Cavalcanti, Ruttmann was not so much concerned with the meaning of city life as with creating from it a self-sufficient pattern. This time the pattern was achieved through rhythm as well as from the individual composition of the shot, as with Cavalcanti. Ruttmann gained richly from studying the editing methods of the Soviets. It was upon editing and tempo that *Berlin* relied chiefly for its 'symphonic' effect. Rhythm gave it the excitement and liveliness which *Rien que les heures* lacked. It suggested how the film medium might dramatize fact with striking emotional effect . . . Like Cavalcanti

---

[1] Mayer only supplied the idea and later dissociated himself from the film.

18

in his different style, Ruttmann was concerned with the creation of filmic rhythms for their own sake rather than for what they might reveal.[1]

A significant observation may be made on the above brief background to documentary development outside Britain. Neither Flaherty's *Nanook* nor the Soviet films were financed in the normal way of commercial film production. The first was intended as prestige publicity; the second served the needs of the State. This idea for finding finance with which to make films other than from commercial sources was to influence the whole of documentary's future, especially in Britain.

In 1924 a young Scotsman named John Grierson was awarded a Rockefeller Research Fellowship in Social Science. He was to spend the next three years in the US – in New York, Chicago and Hollywood – looking into the effect on the general public of what today are called mass-communications, at that time the Press, the Film and Radio. He was also to interest himself deeply in public education, an interest which was to concern him greatly in future years. He was to have a good deal to do with the preparation of the famous Soviet film, *Battleship Potemkin*, for its New York presentation, and was thus enabled to analyze its revolutionary technique with which he was deeply impressed. Grierson was to become the founder and developer of the British documentary film and to carry the ideology behind it to many countries during the next four decades. He died on 19 February 1972.

He was born at Deanston on the Sterlingshire–Perthshire border in Scotland in 1898. His forefathers were men of the sea. His father was a schoolmaster. He made, it is said, a 'brilliant entry' to Glasgow University, where thirty-three years later he was to receive a Doctorate of Law. The war years were spent in minesweepers. He returned to the University after the war, graduated in English and Philosophy, and for a short time lectured at Durham University, from where he went to the US. He has said that the concept of the use of the cinema for public

---

[1] Extracted from some Programme Notes written at the Film Library, New York, Winter, 1937–38, but unpublished.

influence was partly inspired by his interest in Political Science at the University of Chicago. He was certainly impressed by the theories and writings of Professor Charles Edward Merriam, whose book *American Political Ideas: 1865–1917*, contained this pertinent passage:

To Whitman it appeared that democracy was not merely a form of government. 'If ever accomplished,' he said, 'it will be at least as much (I think double as much) the result of democratic literature and arts (if we get them) as of democratic parties.' It seemed to him that democracy must have its own art, its own poetry, its own schools, and even its own sociology.

Grierson also acknowledged another influence: 'We noted,' he wrote, 'the conclusion of such men as Walter Lippmann, that because the citizen, under modern conditions, could not know everything about everything all the time, democratic citizenship was therefore impossible. We set to thinking how a dramatic apprehension of the modern scene might solve the problem, and we turned to the new wide-reaching instruments of the radio and cinema as necessary instruments in both the practice of government and the enjoyment of citizenship.[1]

He continued at a later date:

The idea of documentary in its present form came originally not from the film people at all but from the Political Science School in Chicago round about the early 1920s. It came because some of us noted Mr Lippmann's argument closely and set ourselves to study what, constructively, we could do to fill the gap in educational practice which he demonstrated. At first, I must confess we did not think so much about the film or about the radio. We were concerned with the influence of modern newspapers . . . It was Mr Lippmann himself who turned this educational research in the direction of the film. I talked to him one day of the labour involved in following developments of the Yellow Press through the evanescent drama of local politics. He mentioned that we would do better to follow the dramatic patterns of the film through the changing character of our time, and the box-office records of success and failure which were on the file.

I took his advice and a young man called Walter Wanger[2] opened the necessary files. A theory purely educational became thereby a theory involving the directive use of films. That directive use was

[1] Vide: *Grierson on Documentary*, edited by H. Forsyth Hardy, revised edition, Faber, 1966, p. 207.
[2] Later, a well-known Hollywood producer.

based on two essential factors: the observation of the ordinary or the actual, and the discovery within the actual of the patterns which gave it significance for civic education.[1]

Such reasoning influenced all Grierson's work and through him more than one of those who either worked with him, or have been closely associated with him. It was to be the main-spring of documentary thinking and development.

The first opportunity for Grierson to introduce his ideas in film came not in the US but when he returned to Britain and met a remarkable civil servant, Sir Stephen Tallents, at that time the Secretary of the Empire Marketing Board in London. The EMB, as it became known, had been set up by a Conservative Government at the recommendation of the Imperial Economic Committee for 'furthering the marketing in this country of Empire products'.[2] Its Chairman was Mr L. S. Amery, then Secretary of State for Dominion Affairs. In its first year it had a grant of £500,000 and for future years an annual grant of £1 million. Its work provided for the making of grants for scientific research into problems of production and marketing, the initi-ation and development of economic investigation and intelli-gence, and a publicity and educational campaign. Its activities were widely varied and included Tropical and Sub-Tropical Agricultural Research stations, Low Temperature Research, Entomological Research, Animal Husbandry, Economic Botany, Fruit Growing, Dairy Research, Poultry Research etc. As part of its Publicity and Educational activity it arranged nation-wide Press advertising, Poster Displays, Exhibitions and Fairs, and Empire Shopping Weeks. Last on its list was Cinema, of which it said: 'By arrangement with the Department of Overseas Trade a cinema-hall for the Board has been constructed at the Imperial Institute, South Kensington.' No mention was made of the actual making of any films; in fact, no indication was given as to what films would be screened at the cinema-hall or from where they were to come.

Tallents's own conception of the EMB's aims were set out in his imaginative and, still today, highly relevant pamphlet, *The Projection of England* which, although not published until 1932,

---

[1] Ibid: pp. 290–1.   [2] Cmd. 2898. June 1927.

contained his thinking since the inception of the Board.[1] For an account of the first meeting between Tallents and Grierson, access has been had to the former's recollections supplemented by Grierson himself. Both are obviously made in hindsight.[2] Tallents had become interested to add the film medium to the other media of publicity being used by the EMB as a result of a visit to Rudyard Kipling. He wrote the following:

One summer afternoon in 1926 – the first summer of our work at the EMB – I had driven to lunch with Mr Rudyard Kipling at his house at Burwash. Mr Kipling, who had so far fought shy of films, confirmed our belief in the possibilities of the cinema and held out hopes that he himself would guide the making of a film for us. This seemed to me to be a magnificent opening. I had little difficulty in persuading my Board to pursue it. I had much more difficulty in selling the idea to an extremely sceptical Treasury. In the end, however, I got leave to employ a man named by Mr Kipling as particularly suited to work with him; and we embarked on a film of fancy to be called *One Family*, which was to begin with scenes of society ladies impersonating the different Dominions in the Throne Room at Buckingham Palace.[3]

The man was called Walter Creighton.

It is cinema history that *One Family* played for one week only to almost empty houses at the Palace Theatre, London, in 1929, and thereafter sunk into oblivion. Robert Herring wrote of it:

We have waited for a march-past of the British Empire on the screen and now we get it we find it allied to a Christmas shopping tour conducted by a little boy with ungracious manners and a squeaky voice.[4]

This was kinder than most critics who were vitriolic in their disdain and mimicry. To be fair to Walter Creighton, he did

---

[1] Faber, 1932. Reprinted by Film Centre Ltd, 1955.
[2] From a MS of a part of Volume II of Tallents's autobiography, dated October 1945, unfinished and unpublished. He died in 1958. The MS was made available to the author while research was being done for the writing of the biography of Robert J. Flaherty in 1958. It is used now by kind permission of Mr Timothy Tallents. A somewhat similar account was given by Tallents in his Cobb Lecture delivered to the Royal Society of Arts, November 1946, and printed in the Society's journal, December 1946. It was also reprinted in *Documentary News Letter*, Vol. VI, No. 55, January 1947.
[3] Ibid:
[4] *Manchester Guardian.* Reprinted in *Garbo and the Night Watchmen*, compiled by Alistair Cooke, Cape, 1937; new edition, Secker & Warburg, 1971.

take some nice footage during his tour of the Dominions but unhappily the little boy was in most of the scenes. However, a nice small film was made of what was left, *Southern April*. Creighton's previous film experience had been as a producer of pageants and tattoos.[1]

Preparation for *One Family* was under way when Grierson met Tallents and it was too late to interrupt its production. To return to Tallents' recollections:

In February 1927, a young man called to see me one day with a letter of introduction from Robert Nichols, the poet. It was for a certain John Grierson who, Nichols said, had ideas which marched closely with his own. He begged me to give Grierson a chance of putting into practice the theories about the cinema which he had formed as a Rockefeller Research student of psychology [*sic*] in Hollywood and elsewhere in the USA.

I took to Grierson at first sight. He put his ideas, as he has always done, with persuasive conviction. I did not fully grasp their purport at the moment, but, looking back, I can give a clearer account now than I could have done at the end of that first meeting. Grierson had been steeped but never dyed in the colours of orthodox education, which he had seen as never rising above the information level to that at which apprehension enlists with the imaginative faculties. The meagreness which he found in modern community life seemed to him due to a lack of essential understanding of the stuff of which that life is made up. If life itself was to yield its riches, then the raw materials of life must be worked up by processes which would elicit not merely its bare facts but its essentially dramatic qualities.

Grierson had been led to this conviction by his own personal experience; but he would have certainly subscribed to the pregnant saying which Walt Whitman included in his *Backward Glance O'er Travelled Roads*. 'Whatever may have been the case in years gone by the true use for the imaginative faculty of modern times is to give ultimate vivification to facts, to science, and to common lives, endowing them with the glows and glories and final illustriousness which belong to every real thing, and to real things only.'

Grierson also would have been at home, I am sure, with a sentence which I came across in a letter written shortly before his death by J. B. Yeats in America to his son in Ireland. 'It is easier to write poetry that

---

[1] He subsequently made a film to celebrate the Centenary of the Great Western Railway, but this did not achieve a showing at all except to the Directors in their boardroom.

is far away from life, but it is infinitely more exciting to write the poetry of life – and it is what the whole world is crying out for, as pants the hart for the water brook.'[1]

Grierson himself was quick to pick up a sentence by John Stuart Mill quoted by Tallents in *The Projection of England*, which 'said a good deal of what some of us were thinking round about 1928. It is the artist alone in whose hands truth becomes impressive and a living principle of action'.[2]

Continued Tallents:

But in those days a purely aesthetic approach to the screen was apt to be regarded by young aspirants for cinema distinction as the only alternative to commercial cinema. A sense of this danger, combined with his native Scottish puritanism [*sic*] upbringing, made Grierson shy of much talk about art films. He demanded that only 'the affairs of our time should be brought to the screen in any fashion which strikes the imagination and makes observation a little richer than it was'. The approach, as he saw it, should sometimes be frankly journalistic; sometimes it might rely upon the beauty of stark lucidity; sometimes again it might rise to poetry and drama. It was really an accident that led him to choose film as his medium. The motives, as he has so often later insisted, both of himself and of those who came to be associated with him, were social rather than aesthetic; and those motives might equally well have led them to the writer's pen, the painter's brush, or the broadcaster's chair.[3]

'His line of approach fitted in with ours. The EMB, before he joined, had determined to bring the Empire alive to the minds of its citizens and in doing so to substitute for talk and theories about it a vivid and exciting representation of its infinitely various lives and occupations.

Grierson wrote of his outlook around that time:

Yes, there was the runaway from the synthetic world of the contemporary cinema, but so also, as I remember it, did documentary represent a reaction from the art world of the early and middle 1920s – Bloomsbury, Left Bank, T. S. Eliot, Clive Bell and all – by people with every reason to know it well. Likewise, if it was a return to 'reality', it was a return not unconnected with Clydeside Movements, ILP's, the

---

[1] *Letters to His Son*, J. B. Yeats, Faber, 1944.
[2] 'Story of the Documentary Film', *Fortnightly Review*, August 1938.
[3] Grierson greeted with enthusiasm the coming of the television medium although as an exponent he still relied on film for his material.

The Beginnings of British Documentary

Great Depression, not to mention our Lord Keynes, the London School of Economics, Political and Economic Planning and such. Documentary was born and nurtured on the bandwagon of uprising social democracy everywhere; in Western Europe and the United States, as well as in Britain. That is to say, it had an uprising majority social movement, which is to say a logical sponsorship of public money behind it.[1]

Much as Grierson impressed him, Tallents could not add to his permanent staff in 1927. Instead, he arranged that for a fee Grierson should prepare a number of reports on how various European countries were using films for purposes other than casual entertainment. The French, for example, were making instructional films for agriculture. While thus busy, Grierson implemented the EMB's powers to have projection equipment installed in the Imperial Institute. From then on, the EMB Film Committee and their guests were shown at regular intervals programmes of films chosen by Grierson which he thought had bearing on their outlook. Among pictures shown were: *The Covered Wagon*, *The Iron Horse*, *Grass*, *Berlin*, *Nanook* and *Moana*. The controversial Soviet films *Battleship Potemkin* and *Storm Over Asia* were also seen and discussed. Grierson, the all-time persuader and inspirer, must have been eloquent at such performances.

Tallents continued:

Meantime Grierson began to discuss with me the possibility of his making a film of his own for the EMB . . . I was anxious to gain him the opportunity and we framed a proposal that he should make a modest film about herrings. There were four good reasons for this choice of subject. It seemed wise to start this wing of our programme un-ostentatiously. ('If the Civil Service or any other public service must have its illegitimate infants, it is best to see that they are small ones,' said Grierson later.) Then we needed to do something for the home fishing industry. Grierson had served in mine-sweepers. Mr Arthur Samuel, Financial Secretary to the Treasury, from whose department we anticipated the liveliest opposition to our scheme, had made a study of the history of the English herring industry and had committed his learning to a book, *The Herring: Its Effect on the History of Britain*.

Tallents recorded that the decision for Grierson to make his own film took place at a meeting in Mr L. S. Amery's office at

[1] Preface to *Documentary Film*, third edition, Faber, 1952.

the Dominions Office on 27 April 1928. Six persons were present – Mr Amery, Mr Walter Elliot (Chairman of the Film Committee), Sir John Craig (later Deputy Master and Comptroller of the Royal Mint), Mr Arthur Samuel, Tallents and Grierson. The Treasury, be it noted, had previously sought to overrule a recommendation by the Board for a possible new film in addition to *One Family* at a meeting at which they had not even taken the trouble to be present. This had angered Mr Amery.

Tallents recalled:

Our plans had not been laid without guile. Mr Samuel opened the meeting with a salvo. As a director of the soft-drink manufacturers, Apollinaris, he knew much about advertising; and he could assure us that it was sheer waste of time to think of increasing the sale of Empire products by means of films. Mr Elliot and Mr Amery, in that order, explained that this was to be a background film, not advertising, designed to create an atmosphere by presenting British life and character. Then we dangled our herring bait in front of the Financial Secretary. The meeting ended with Mr Samuel genially offering to help us with his deep knowledge of the herring industry and ourselves warmly welcoming his offer. The official Treasury voice insisted, as a postcript, that one 'semi-expert' and one office-man should be sufficient for our needs.

In this way, Grierson's *Drifters* came to be born.

It had already been agreed that Walter Creighton's debutante's pageant should cost some £18,000, which left Grierson £2,000 for his film. He was officially appointed Assistant Films Officer. To produce the film, however, the Board itself could not undertake production and a contract had to be entered into with a commercial company, New Era Films, who eventually also distributed the film. The exact relationship between the EMB and New Era was complicated. The one was an official body operating with public funds; the other a Trade company operating on a profit-making basis. This arrangement will not be discussed here, but a detailed investigation was made in the Report by the Select Committee on Estimates, ordered to be printed by the House of Commons, 2 July 1934, and will come up for quotation when the story of the GPO Film Unit is reached.

The Beginnings of British Documentary

Tallents's record of the making of *Drifters* continued:

The decision to embark on this second EMB film involved two top-ranking Cabinet Ministers; and the making of the film itself created, I am sure, agonies as sharp as ever attended the making of, say, Eisenstein's Mexican film, *Que Viva Mexico*, or Rank's *Caesar and Cleopatra*. A drifter, *The Maid of Thule*, was hired at Stornoway, chiefly on the strength of the crew's supposed photogenic quality. John Skeaping, the sculptor, designed a cabin set which was erected near the harbour. A fisheries protection cruiser obliged with power for the interior lighting. The underwater shots were supplied by dogfish chivying small roach about a tank at the Plymouth Marine Biological Station. Then *The Maid of Thule* couldn't find any herrings and operations had to be transferred to another drifter at Lowestoft on the East Coast. Next the Chairman of New Era films (Sir Gordon Craig) with whom the contract had been made to provide services, turned up in my office one evening with a long face to declare that the film was a predestined flop and had better be abandoned. I left Grierson to deal with him.[1]

Grierson's own description of the making of *Drifters* ran:

It is about the sea and fishermen, and there is not a Piccadilly actor in the piece. The men do their own acting and the sea does its – if the result does not bear out the 107th Psalm, it is my fault. Men at their labour are the salt of the earth; the sea is a bigger actor than Jannings or Nikitin; and if you can tell me a story more plainly dramatic than the gathering of the ships for the herring season, the going out, the shooting at evening, the long drift in the night, the hauling of nets by infinite agony of shoulder muscles in the teeth of a storm, the drive home against a head sea, and (for finale) the frenzy of a market in which the said agonies are sold at ten shillings a thousand, and iced, salted and barrelled for an unwitting world – if you can tell me a story with better crescendo in energies, images, atmospherics and all that make up the sum and substance of cinema, I promise you I shall make a film of it when I can.[2]

Many years later, in 1954, Grierson added to his earlier comments:

It is the hauling of the herring nets in heavy weather off Smith's Knole

[1] Sir Gordon's qualifications to pass comment on the film were given as: Liveryman Gold and Silver Tyre Drawers Company, Vice-President Old Contemptibles, Assoc. President Hackney Branch British Legion. Clubs: Royal Thames Yacht, Sunningdale Gold. (*Kine Yearbook*, 1933).
[2] *Close-Up*, Vol. V, No. 5, November 1929.

in the North Sea and it is, of course, very spectacular. We're in a drifter called *The Mirabel* off Lowestoft. The camera is moving around a very slippery deck indeed, noting detail after detail, and part of the time it is poised perilously up on top of the wheelhouse trying to get the swing of the ship. What seemed new to people 25 years ago was this use of the camera, the detail, the piling of one shot on another and this business of filling the screen as full up as a modern painting. The big close-up, it was a sort of demonstration of, a reminder of the camera's power of natural observation, taking all the little bits and pieces and binding them together. Another thing in it seemed a revolution in its time – it was about working people. We said then that it was the first picture of the working classes. That, of course, was an exaggeration. For some all this seemed to express a new sort of pride – a pride in the beginning of the Century of the Common Man, and it was expressed as far as we were concerned in this first experiment with describing the smoke and the funnels and the engines and the winches of the modern industrial world around us.[1]

Drifters was finished in the late Summer of 1929. It cost less than £2,000. It had its first showing in the same programme as the British premiere of *Battleship Potemkin* (which had long been held up by Censor problems) at the London Film Society's 33rd performance, 10 November. This was an astute move, typical of Grierson's flair for showmanship; half of London's intellectuals and most of the national Press would come to see the much-heralded *Potemkin*. Grierson chose his own music from discs in which Mendelssohn's *Fingal's Cave* played a prominent part. The film was an immediate success both with the audience that afternoon and in the Press.

The *New York Times* (no date) was less warm. Under the title *Drifting*, it wrote:

This film was made by John Grierson, the Scotch film critic, whose knowledge of the mechanics of picture construction is evidently less than his critical ability. . . . There is no element of suspense, none of the feverish activity implied in the sub-titles, that better cutting might have achieved and only a feeling of comfortless menotony that one sees frequently in short features called nature studies. Its efforts at human interest in showing the men either cooking, eating or idling are far from exciting.

[1] In a transcript of a BBC-TV programme, *The Projection of Britain*, 23 November 1954.

The Beginnings of British Documentary

The review refers to the film as a day in the life of the Gloucester fishermen (*sic*).

Drifters was double-booked for cinema release by New Era with an amateur pierrot musical, *The Cooptimists*. It should have made a very good return but that would have depended on what kind of a shared distribution deal the EMB had made with New Era. No figures are on the record. It is known, however, that the Board was delighted by the revenue returns but even more delighted by the assurance this implied that a wide public in the United Kingdom and overseas would see the film. This, after all, was the intention, not a financial return.

Tallents wrote:

That fact alone more than justified this film venture of ours against those who had counted on its failure . . . If *Drifters* had done no more than that, its making would have been amply justified. But *Drifters* was a real pioneer and more. It rejected the escapism of the ordinary box-office film. It did not seek to spirit its audience away from real every-day life to dream. It had no snob appeal, making falsely glamorous and desirable to humble people the fundamentally commonplace and vulgar luxuries of the rich. It took as its raw material the day-to-day life of ordinary men and from that neglected vein won interest, dignity and beauty . . . It differed from Robert Flaherty's work in that it did not go to the far North or the South Seas in search of the remote or the exotic. It differed from the work of the Soviets in that it was harnessed to no political theme. Owing much to those two sources, it yet enjoyed a greater liberty and struck a more universal note than *Nanook* or *Turk-sib*.[1]

So this modest and cheaply produced film, in spite of its weaknesses which any documentary film-maker of today would avoid, caught at the time both the attention of qualified critics and the interest of unrelenting audiences and, by virtue of its original and pioneering quality has since become something of a legend.[2]

But there has been the occasional voice of dissent. In an article attacking Flaherty's film *Man of Aran*, David Schrire criticized the romanticism of British documentary.[3] Grierson

---

[1] A Soviet film by Victor Turin of the building of the Turkestan-Siberian railway, on which Grierson helped Turin prepare the English version. This film, more than any other except *Potemkin*, made a profound impression on British documentary film-makers.

[2] Cobb Lecture, 27 November 1946.

[3] 'Evasive Documentary', *Cinema Quarterly*, Vol. III, No. 1, 1934.

replied. The two articles became the basis of an argument carried on by correspondence between Mr Schrire and the author.

Is it true that powers of production alone were responsible for *Drifters* lacking a full expression of social purpose? Isn't it a little romanticised and in an oblique way under the influence of Flaherty? Remember the contempt Grierson had for the actual marketing of the fish, the regret he appeared to express that the fish, the fruits of the glorious adventurous fishermen, was bought and sold for money. Shouldn't his protest have been that the fish was often thrown back into the sea, or used as manure, because of the economic system which did not allow people to afford to buy it? Isn't Grierson's approach here just the other side of the Flaherty romantic, escapist medal? Flaherty ran away into the anthropological present; Grierson dealt with actual industry or occupation but ran away from its social meaning. He said, as it were, I like the adventure, the joy of the catch, but when I see that it is sold just like a pair of trousers in Petticoat Lane, my soul revolts and I would rather no fish were caught.[1]

A different criticism arose in reaction to an article by an intelligent critic of the *Newcastle Chronicle*, Ernest Dyer (who died all too young), in which he greatly praised both Grierson and his film. It had been written for *Education: Elementary, Secondary and Technical*, the official journal of the Association of Education Committees. The Editor accepted the piece but returned a proof to Mr Dyer commenting, 'I showed your article to one of the people who has been foremost in advocating the use of the cinema in schools.' This anonymous film educator is then quoted as follows:

More serious is the question of Grierson and the EMB. What Grierson has done, badly needed doing. The trouble is that in my view he has done it thoroughly badly. I saw *Drifters* at the London Film Society and everybody I spoke to there afterwards, judging it purely from the point of view of technique, thought that it was a very childish imitation of the Russian manner that contrived to be obscure without being original or vivid. I had looked forward to showing the film but thanks to this pseudo-Russian manner, I cannot now do so; and may add that I am a very profound admirer of the *real* Russian film. Grierson calls his film, a film for schools. Whom did he consult in making it with a knowledge of schools?

[1] 25 November 1935

He has behind him the money of the EMB and the publicity of the Imperial Institute showings. It seems to me to be shameful that he should be allowed to produce at his own sweet will without, so far as I am aware, consulting anybody who is interested in the subject from the school end. For these reasons, I personally deplore any praise given to his work at the present time, however imaginative and enterprising it may be, as I think that both administratively and artistically, it is along entirely wrong lines and is likely to remain there until he and the EMB come down to real life and consult people with knowledge about schools.[1]

Ernest Dyer refused to amend his article and it was published. The criticism typified the kind of hostility to which Grierson, and later the whole documentary movement, were to be subjected.

What is perhaps forgotten about *Drifters* today is that it revealed the poetry of movement. Like most of the EMB films that came after, it had no words, no story and no chance for depth of human characterization. Instead it discovered the dynamic and aesthetic of movement to express poetic images on the screen. It was not just movement of action within the screen frame or movement of the camera itself, but the all-important movement created by editing shot after shot.

If a good share of space has been given here to John Grierson and his film *Drifters*, it is because I have at times in subsequent years heard it called a flash-in-the-pan film, and its maker decried as a one-man film-maker. Revolutionary as it was both in its use of the camera and the cutting-bench, and in the poetry and drama of its approach to its subject matter, it is not just as an isolated film that *Drifters* must be judged, but by what it stood for. It brought a unique new character into British film production. It brought a completely fresh way of thinking into the use of the film medium and it was, as will be seen, the beginning of a wholly new movement in film-making in Britain. Lastly, but not least significantly, it suggested and proved a new way of finding finance for film-making which, not without its restrictions, was at any rate independent of commercial profit-

---

[1] Quoted from a letter to John Grierson from Basil Wright, 20 February 1931. The former was in Canada at the time. It was found that the letter had been written by a commercial film producer interested to explore the educational film market.

making. The importance of *Drifters* cannot be overestimated in the history of the cinema, let alone in the story of the documentary film.

After this success both in policy and artistry, Tallents and Grierson were faced with a vital problem for decision. Should the EMB proceed to capitalize on the prestige of its first film? Provided money was forthcoming from the Treasury, should Grierson now direct a second film? He did in fact talk about one to be called *Smoke and Steel*, but it came to nothing.[1] He did make two marionette films at the Wembley Studios but no one, least of all Grierson, remembers anything about them. He also began to shoot considerable footage, with Sydney Blythe as cameraman, over many weekends in the London docks for a projected film about the Port of London but it was never completed. (Much of the footage found its way into later EMB films, notably *Industrial Britain*.) But in Grierson's mind a much more important policy took shape. He proposed to Tallents that the most sensible and far-sighted purpose for the EMB would be to create a small unit of film-makers who, under Grierson's supervision and tuition, could develop the course pioneered by *Drifters*, as well as try out other film experiments to meet the needs of the Board.

Tallents wrote,

We should aim at a school of young directors, selecting carefully for the purpose young men (and women) of first-class ability and intelligence but requiring of them not necessarily previous film experience. We should, however, require hard and concentrated work from them and put them through a severe apprenticeship in the basic craftsmanship of film-making. Then we should employ those of them who showed promise, according to their aptitudes, on the production of a considerable number of films of different types. In so doing, we should keep strictly within our EMB commission; but we must provide room for experiment. We must expect, too, a percentage of failures. ('You can no more contract for the quality of a film than you can contract for the character of a baby,' Grierson was once to write to me.)[2]

[1] Associated Sound Film Industries, of Wembley Studios, announced in its 1930 programme that John Grierson would direct a subject with this title. (*Close-up*, Vol. VI, No. 3, March 1930).
[2] Cobb Lecture, 27 November 1946.

The Beginnings of British Documentary

In the mid- and late 1920s in Britain many young men were attracted to the cinema as a new and vitally exciting art medium. The poetic films from Scandinavia and France, the decorative and craftsmanlike work of the German Golden Period, the *avant-garde* experimentalists in Paris, Berlin and Holland (Cavalcanti, Clair, Richter, Ruttmann, Ivens *et al.*) and above all the explosive and technically stimulating films from the Soviet Union, each in turn made their impact on would-be young British film-makers who could find no entry or encouragement in the sterile and corrupt commercial film world. The cultish little magazine *Close-Up*, mainly written and published from Switzerland from 1927 on, attracted its share of readers who were derided in Wardour Street. For the most part, these young discoverers of the powers of the film medium were actuated by its aesthetic qualities.

Tallents went on:

There was no difficulty about finding would-be recruits for such a venture. Youth, fired by the success of *Drifters*, and thwarted in its search for a self-respecting way of access to the screen, at first in its tens and later in its hundreds [*sic*] wrote to Grierson and asked to join him.[1]

Thus, in January 1930, there was set up the EMB Film Unit. Outside the Soviet Union, it was the only experimental workshop for film-making in the world. Grierson had made a brave and unselfish decision; he would henceforth give up the intense pleasures of actual film-making himself and instead become a teacher, a producer, an inspirer and a catalyst for the basic documentary idea and purpose. It was a most courageous decision and one for which many people should be grateful.

Yet much criticism of Grierson was made when he gave up making films himself to become producer. One example was the change in attitude by the film critic, C. A. Lejeune, of *The Observer*, whom Grierson had befriended and who was a frequent visitor to the pub at that time used by the documentary people. At first, be it noted, she was one of the most fervent admirers of the EMB Film Unit, sometimes to the point of embarrassment. 'At the moment there is practically no other

[1] Op. cit.

33

workshop than the EMB in which a film apprentice can learn his job with a mixture of imagination and hard commonsense.'[1]

In her book published later the same year, however, a note of criticism crept in.

Miss Lejeune wrote,

John Grierson, whether we regard him as a director, as organiser, as cutter, as teacher, as critic, is the most considerable intelligence attached to the cinema in England today . . . I can believe almost anything of Grierson, even major achievement; his short film *Drifters* has in it all the qualities of fine movie-making; but belief has no place in my perspective; it is the finished work alone that can stand up to a general survey, and Grierson's finished work is too scant and too specialised to bring him yet into the focus of an observation at long range.[2]

A year later, under the heading 'This Documentary Fetish', she was to write,

If anyone were to ask me to name the keenest critical intelligence without hesitation I should plump for John Grierson. If anyone were to ask me the most dangerous influence directed towards the development of new production, I should give the same answer. Grierson has done perhaps more than any man in this country to create an appreciation for real movie in England, perhaps more than any other man in England he now stands blocking the way between theory and its practical end.

'Five years ago [*sic*] Grierson made *Drifters* . . . From that moment – and all against the grain of his Scots nature – he became the sign and figurehead of the cinematic *avant-garde*. Without any other film to his credit than the classroom experiment, *Conquest*, and a couple of marionette shorts, he came to be accepted as a documentary dictator. As chief of the EMB film unit he has achieved a kind of legendary omnipotence. A hundred applicants a week [*sic*] thirst to be numbered among Grierson's Bright Young Men.

That's all to the good. Grierson's sympathies are catholic, his judgements acute, and he has a fine capacity for promoting enthusiasms . . . But – and it is a very big but – his peculiar combination of qualities makes him essentially dangerous as a tutor of talent in the making.

Grierson's recruits are apt to miss the essential lesson of first things first. They acquire something of the Grierson touch without mastering

[1] *The Observer*, 14 June 1931.   [2] *Cinema*, Maclehose, 1931.

the reasons for it . . . All over the country today [*sic*] there are pro-
fessionals and amateurs shooting, cutting and editing [*sic*] in what
they believe to be the Grierson manner, inverting sequences here,
fashioning hortatory captions there; working with immense enthusiasm
and a considerable capacity for a cinema whose first principles they
don't in the least understand. . . .

But sometimes I wonder whether the same efficiency could not be
achieved in half the time by an apprenticeship among the hard facts of
the newsreel – in some practical body like *Movietone News* or the *Ideal
Cinemagazine* . . .

(Here followed an attack on Arthur Elton's film *The Voice of
the World*, produced by Grierson.)

Miss Lejeune concluded:

For in the end it comes down to this, in spite of his promises, in spite of
his precepts, in spite of his position Grierson is still a one-film man, he
is still known as the director of *Drifters*. The material he has collected
for the Port of London film may be audacious and magnificent, but still
there is no Port of London film. He is gradually developing into a
paper-director, and the EMB would be wise to cut him loose from the
cares of an executive position, and send him off with a camera and a
definite order to deliver. Outside, and on a job, I believe Grierson
might prove himself our best native director. Inside, on somebody
else's job, he is becoming a rather tiresome tradition . . . The British
avant-garde have been trailing along too long after the man who made
Drifters. He must make another *Drifters*, or they must go their own
way.[1]

Seldom in all its story have the principles and purposes of the
British documentary idea been more misunderstood. Fortu-
nately, Tallents and Grierson were far too occupied injecting
their policy for the future into the Treasury, the Civil Service
and the EMB to pay heed to such gratuitous advice, which was
also ill-informed. How wide off the mark was Miss Lejeune's
prophecy became clear in the subsequent work of the EMB
Film Unit and of others working near by. Her most important
error of all, beyond any recognition of documentary policy as
being formulated by Grierson, was her complete failure to see
the documentary group as a whole, to grasp that it was a
growing movement by a number of film-makers who gave it

[1] *The Observer*, 21 August 1932.

impetus. The significance of *Drifters* as expounded earlier was wholly ignored by this critic. She saw it as an isolated work.

Grierson wrote later,

The business of running a creative concern within the Civil Service is, of course, relatively new. Round about 1905, Mr A. J. Balfour set out for the British Civil Service a policy which was to guide it in such matters. This policy was, 'The Civil Service is geared to the administration of the Act, not to the creative services. If such are needed, have them done outside on contract.' This policy was still operative in the late 1920s when two or three of us came into Whitehall with very different ideas. The factors governing our theory were as follows:

1. The inevitable trend is away from *laissez-faire* towards Government planning, Government coordination and Government leadership in all matters affecting the economic and social life of the nation.

2. With initiative imposed upon it by Parliament must come of necessity the duty of explaining plans, securing coordination and giving the information, etc., which are the essence of leadership.

3. Modern governments, therefore, cannot forgo their duty on the educational plane, which is the common basis of national thought.

4. Nor can they forgo their duty on the imaginative plane where sentiments are crystallized and patterns of interest and loyalty created; whence their especial and direct interest in the imaginative media – radio, films, posters, etc.

The Civil Service – in particular the British Treasury – resisted this theory as they resisted the attempt to put it into practice. Ironically, Mr Balfour was one of the first to give support. The fight went on roughly between 1927 and 1933 with the Treasury gradually breaking down. The point was won with the establishment of strong creative services at the EMB (films and posters), the Department of Overseas Trade (exhibitions) and, later, the Post Office (films, posters and exhibitions), with the Departments of Labour and Agriculture moving in. But we should note, with the limitations that ordinary Civil Service practices in the matter of Treasury accounting and Treasury appointment were insisted on.

It was slow, hard going but we were greatly helped by the spectacular and publicly acknowledged success of certain of the Government services developed; in particular, the creation of the documentary film, first at the EMB, and later, at the GPO Film Units. There was also the raising in standards of the nation's poster and typographical styles by the EMB and the great strides made in exhibition work by the Department of Overseas Trade; also by the realisation that the Government's interest in the creative arts was *of a kind* in which outside agencies were not tutored and could not as *outside* agencies be expected readily to appreciate.

There came then the conception of the public servant trained in creative work, or alternatively the creative worker trained in the public service. There came also the conception of the creative unit working directly within a Government department.[1]

If the above passages of Grierson's letter have been quoted at some length, it is because they reveal an informative and searching analysis of the relations between the Government's Civil Service, the Treasury and the arts and mass media in Great Britain which is of the utmost importance. It does much to explain how, for example, the reactionary attitude of the Treasury and the Civil Service to the arts and mass media castrates any attempt since the war to explore imaginative information services. It explains, too, the reasons, other than personal political ones referred to later, for opposition to any proposal for a National Flm Board in Britain and provides one of the explanations for the abrupt abolition of the Crown Film Unit in 1952 (successor to the EMB and GPO Film Units), although commercial Trade interests also had a hand in this assassination of creative work. It, more than anywhere else, explores the underlying motivations of British documentary that were little understood by some film-makers themselves at the time, or even in later years. It explains how Grierson's remarkable grasp of all this subtle machinery-within-machinery was missing from post-war documentary development.[2]

[1] In a letter, 12 November 1945, to the Hon. Brooke Claxton, Defence Minister in the Canadian Government.

[2] Cf. Chapter 12.

3. The Empire Marketing Board Film Unit (1930–33)

Grierson and I first met in January 1931. He and Basil Wright used to have coffee in the mornings at Legrain's Coffee Room in Gerrard Street, right around the corner from the minute cutting-room rented by the EMB Film Unit in a slum back mews off Wardour Street called Dansey Yard. *The Film Till Now* had been published the previous September and I used it as a pretext to introduce myself. I told him how much *Drifters* had impressed me. He made no comment on my book. He had a wide-brimmed black Borsalino hat and a dark raincoat that was to do service for a good many years. So far as I recall, Wright said little. There was nothing for me at the Unit for the moment, Grierson said, but asked me to call and see him in April.

Actually, I had already been to the cutting-room round the corner in the previous summer in search of work. There I had found a young man, John Taylor, Grierson's brother-in-law, who kindly gave me some negative slips from *Drifters* which I wanted to form a part of the dust-jacket design of my book. John Taylor was a kind of dogsbody to the tiny Unit and remained so for some years until he blossomed out into a very good cameraman and later a producer/director. That afternoon, there being nobody else about, he offered to show me a copy of a new film which had just arrived from the USSR. Thus I first saw Turin's *Turksib*, which was to impress and influence all British documentarists, projected on to a lavatory wall by a hand-turned projector. The copy had flash-titles[1] in German and

[1] Foreign silent films were imported with their printed sub-titles, or captions, reduced to two or three frames so as to reduce the film's total length and thus lessen import tax based on footage length.

later, when I saw the version which Grierson helped Turin re-title in English, I realized how great was Grierson's contribution.

How the few months were spent before I joined the EMB Unit is not important, probably in trying to get articles about films accepted, and selling a few drawings. Quite a lot of the time was spent in the Coffee Room, where you could make a single coffee and one digestive biscuit last almost two hours. With its austere, cane-back chairs, its tiled tables, its net curtains, the Coffee Room was ruled over with much dignity by a charming white-haired lady known to all only as Madame. Her biscuits stood in many a time for lunch. She once bet me £5 that I wouldn't have a film of my own showing in the West End within five years. I was able to give her two tickets for the Press Show of *Contact* at the Rialto Cinema in 1933, but I did not collect my bet.

Other frequenters of this haven of idleness and talk were Adrian Brunel, the feature director and ever humorous, Miles Mander, writer/director/actor with whom a good friendship was formed, Oswell Blakeston, poet, writer, painter, occasional film-maker, Elliot Stannard, scriptwriter always in work, Vernon Clancey, scriptwriter and journalist, Shayle Gardner, actor, and Aubrey Flanagan, friendly columnist of *Today's Cinema*, one of Wardour Street's trade journals. Blakeston recalls that, 'One of my happiest moments was when Madame chased some females who had entered her Coffee Room. "Oh, Lord!" cried Madame, raising herself from behind her curved counter, "Out, out, OUT".'

At the end of March, as a result of a telephone message, I went to see Grierson, in a sparsely furnished basement room he then occupied in the EMB offices in Queen Anne's Gate Building, near Parliament Square. He talked a great deal, of which I understood little. Then he fired, 'What do you find in cinema?' I replied, 'Drama.' 'What is drama?' he demanded. 'Beauty,' I said. That stopped him. I was told to report to the Wardour Street cutting-room the next week.

The squalor of Dansey Yard had been replaced in 1931 by two rooms at the very top floor of No. 175 Wardour Street, where there was an outer office shared by all, a cutting-room of course, larger than before, and of the greatest importance, silent projection equipment. The early so-called Poster films were made in the cutting-room at night when no official fire inspector was around. When I had been at work for a few days joining reels of someone else's film by hand, I asked Grierson for a letter of employment. He grinned and scribbled some twenty words on a piece of dirty EMB paper. 'It's not worth the paper it's written on,' he said. He proved to be right five months later.

Soon Evelyn Spice, a journalist friend of Grierson's from Canada, joined us, and Donald Taylor, a young man just fired from Jonathan Cape, the publisher of *The Film Till Now*, was added to the little group. I recall Donald Taylor's interview with Grierson because I was in the same room. Grierson asked him what *his* main interest in the cinema was? Influenced no doubt by my book, on which he had done some publicity, Taylor spoke ecstatically about the great German Art films. 'Good God!' cried Grierson, 'the only things that matter in the cinema are newsreels.' It was just a Grierson act. Nevertheless, Taylor got the job of carrying film-tins up and down those endless flights of stairs at thirty shillings a week. Not long after, in May 1931, the Unit moved again, this time to occupy two floors at No. 37 Oxford Street, opposite Frascati's gilded restaurant.

The first chance given me to go out and actually shoot some film was in May. On fine mornings, Sir Stephen Tallents was in the habit of walking from his office in Queen Anne's Gate Building across St James's Park and so to the Film Unit in Oxford Street. He suggested to Grierson that the magnificent display of British tulips in the Park might make a nice very short film. For some reason known only to himself, Grierson thought I was right for the job. So Jimmie Davidson, as cameraman, John Taylor as humper and I as director were ordered the next fine day to go film the tulips. We got to the Park by bus, the conductor swearing at our bulky equipment. Perhaps influenced, like Donald Taylor, by early German films, I saw at once that the tulips must be shot with their swaying heads against the sky. After an argument with a park-keeper, a small pit was dug in the grass beside a tulip bed and the camera

– the one and only hand-turned Debrie – was placed in the hole. By this time, the sun had gone. Davidson and I went to a local pub leaving young John Taylor to guard the equipment. Later it was found that he had got bored and had gone off to watch the pelicans. An hour or two afterwards, the sun shone, Davidson and I quickly returned and, we took the required shots.

When Grierson came to show the week's work to Tallents and other members of the Board, the tulips were the success of the screening. But there was also a sharp reprimand from Tallents. It seemed that while John Taylor had been watching the pelicans and Davidson and I had been waiting for the sun, Tallents had passed by on his usual walk. At that time the leather casings of the camera equipment were emblazoned with a large blue EMB. Tallents just said that the Unit's precious equipment should not be left unattended in a public place. Those few shots of tulips (only 400 ft of film) were the only footage made by me, other than some of the Poster films, while at the EMB Film Unit.

At that time we all became familiar with the backstreets and alleyways in Soho, some of which are there today. A small but cheap Italian restaurant in Greek Street run by Mr Castano (he appeared later in *Today We Live* as a café proprietor), whose hobby was pony-trotting, was much used. Upstairs was the Star Club with a bar-billiards table and a one-arm bandit on which Flaherty, when he came to London, always lost money at two-shillings-and-sixpence a time. Apart from ourselves, the club was a hang-out for some of the shadiest Soho characters. We got on very well with each other.

By all normal reckoning in the film trade, the EMB Film Unit had an absurdly small budget on which to function, and ludicrously inadequate equipment and premises. In the early months, the Unit had no editing-machine or film-splicer; film was read by eye and cut and joined by hand. Camera equipment consisted of an old hand-turned silent Debrie and two small hand-held cameras, a DeVry and an Eyemo, both of which scratched negative like – well, like what? When a move was made from one premises to the next, this was done on a handcart with the Unit taking it in turn to push and pull.

Tallents recalled, after giving a description of the premises in Oxford Street,

This is an optimistic picture of a small cluster of rooms which I often visited with pride but were treated with ribald disdain by such members of the commercial film world as dropped in out of curiosity, or in search of a seagull shot from *Drifters*. Cedric Belfrage, at that time film-critic at the BBC and for the *Sunday Express*, wrote that we were working under laughably primitive conditions. No matter, films were made if only in the hard way.[1]

A member of the Unit that year, Edgar Anstey (writing in *Sight and Sound*, April–June 1952) recalled:

Grierson was disinclined to encourage such disabilitising activities as reading or going to the theatre on the grounds that such natural cultural matters should have been taken care of in earlier youth. If one were obliged to understand some cultural review, to reread Plato or Trotsky, it must take place in secret and rather shamefully.[2] In spite of this, or possibly because of it, the whole atmosphere of the Unit was the most stimulating I have ever known, with the creative urge always socially purposive and never dilettante. I remember working at the cutting-bench alongside Grierson on the editing of *Industrial Britain* and concluding that his instinct for the value and function of a scene could only be explained by his genius.

Tallents also remembered:

Grierson fused and welded his eager and miscellaneous team – internally and often an argumentative crew but in their outward front united – into an enthusiastic, hard-working and single-minded Unit. Of their hard work, lights burning late in the windows of No. 37 Oxford Street were the outward token. Their fundamental unity soon began to bear fruit outside that modest base. They began to build up, out of practical

[1] *The Listener*, 31 December 1931.

[2] On the contrary, the author was encouraged by Grierson to read Veblen, Merriam, Kant and other writers, as well as to see every entertainment film within reach. All extra-Unit activity was urged. In some notes to me (27 December 1970) Grierson wrote: 'I doubt if we missed a single big theatre or film event in the 1930s and I just can't believe that I would discourage the reading of Trotsky (as Anstey suggests) when I have read almost everything he wrote. Why, once when Ralph Bond was out of work, we hired him privately to sharpen up our reading of Marx. At Merrick Square it was, and weekly, and there was Stuart Legg among others in attendance.' I recall that someone once scrawled on the cutting-room wall, 'Grierson plus Flaherty equals Marx', but this was to encourage the CID man attached to the Unit. – PR

experiment and endless discussion, a body of informed and coherent criticism. They attracted too outside visitors of distinction.[1]

Among those who came to see the Unit's work were H. G. Wells, Julian Huxley, Walter Elliot, Malcolm MacDonald, Sir William Furse, Lord Pethwick Lawrence, Sir Edward Marsh and Mrs Alfred Lyttleton.

Grierson wrote in hindsight,

The documentary film was . . . an essentially British development. Its characteristic was the idea of social use, and there, I believe, is the only reason why our British documentary persisted when other aesthetic or aestheticky movements in the same direction were either fitful or failed. The key to our persistence is that the documentary film was created to fill a need, and it has prospered because that need was not only real but wide. If it came to develop in England there were three good reasons for it. It permitted the national talent for emotional understatement to operate in a medium not given to understatement. It allowed an adventure in the arts to assume the respectability of a public service. The third reason was the Empire Marketing Board and a man called Tallents.[2]

Grierson should, of course, if modesty had allowed him, have added his own unique talent and vision. He went on:

The film with its documentary possibilities was, indeed, just one among the magic pointers against the blackboard. But I liked the idea of a simple dramatic art based on authentic information. I liked the idea of an art where the dramatic factor depended exactly on the depth with which information was interpreted. I liked the notion that, in making films of man in his modern environment, one would be articulating the corporate character of that environment again, after a long period of sloppy romanticism and the person in private, an aesthetic of the person in public.[3] But the initiative lay with Tallents. Without him, we would have been driven exhausted by this time into the arms of Hollywood or into the practice of a less expensive art. Tallents marked out the habitation and the place for our new teaching of citizenship and gave it a chance to expand. In relating it to the art so variously called 'cultural

[1] Cobb Lecture, 27 November 1946.

[2] 'Story of the Documentary Film,' *Fortnightly Review*, August 1938.

[3] It is worth the record that the EMB's most used poster wa snot of Britannia or John Bull or even the Wembley Lion but a steel-worker with his face and torso red against the furnace glow.

relations', 'public relations' and 'propaganda', he joined it with one of the driving forces of the time and guaranteed it patronage . . . His need, and our purpose, coincided so precisely that an alliance between public relations and the documentary film was struck which was capable of withstanding all later temptations to commercialise our skill.[1] It was a strange alliance for Whitehall. The intangibles of art – whether of propaganda or of film – were hardly 'to be packed into the narrow act' of a Treasury file; and Tallents's contribution at that time deserves to go down among the more curious feats of Civil Service bravery.[2]

With his usual courtesy, perhaps Grierson here gives too much emphasis to Tallents's energies and foresight, which of course existed strongly, but they were continually stimulated and given an urgency by Grierson's long-range policy and purpose for education in democratic thinking, living and working. Grierson's theories on the need for wide education in citizenship and democratic participation therein, as found in his essays and lectures, go far beyond anything envisaged by Tallents.[3]

During 1930 and 1931, there was no problem in finding staff for the new Unit. Some came from the field of amateur film-making, some from those who were frustrated by the state of the commercial studios, while others had no film experience at all. An advertisement in *The Times* brought a spate of replies. Grierson gave Tallents an entertaining account of the rush. 'Of the 1,500 tyros who have applied for jobs in the EMB Film Unit, 1,500 have expressed their enthusiasm for cinema, for art, for self-expression and the other beautiful whatnots of a youthful and simply vague existence.'[4] Not one of them, declared Grierson, understood that the EMB was working within the terms of a definite commission with financial resources limited to that commission. Nevertheless by careful selection, Grierson enlisted a handful of trainees, most of whom became film-makers in their own right in due course. For the record, the majority of

[1] At the demise of the EMB Film Unit, the Ostrer Brothers through their big GB Corporation made an offer to Grierson to buy the Unit and its Empire Film Library. They were interested to develop the educational film market as a potential customer for its manufacture of sub-standard projectors and not for any integral educational purpose.

[2] Op. cit.

[3] Vide: *Grierson on Documentary*, edited by H. Forsyth Hardy, revised edition, Faber, 1966.

[4] Tallents' MS referred to earlier.

them had a public school and university (Oxbridge) education and stemmed from what are called middle-class families. Of the group, only three had had previous film experience: J. D. Davidson had been a professional cameraman, Arthur Elton had worked at the Gainsborough Studios, and the author's inept activity at the Elstree studios has already been described. But like Flaherty when he went out to make *Nanook* and Grierson when he made *Drifters*, we were, let us confess, amateurs and had to learn by error. Maybe it was not such a bad thing. Basil Wright, when Grierson hired him, had made a film on 16 mm, but Grierson 'didn't know one lens from another'.

The following were taken on at the Unit in this order: J. D. Davidson (as cameraman and general production manager), Basil Wright, John Taylor (handyman), the author, Evelyn Spice (from Canada), Donald Taylor, Arthur Elton, Edgar Anstey, Stuart Legg and J. N. G. Davidson (from Ireland). Also to be noted as valuable full-time helpers at the Unit were Marion Grierson (John's sister) and Margaret Grierson (John's wife).

We were far from adequately paid (£5 per week was top), we had divergent points of view and disparate backgrounds but for perhaps the longest span in film history up to that time we kept a unified front to the outside world and followed a common purpose. Although working long hours, often through the night – there were no union rules then – some of us found time to write articles and even books about our documentary beliefs in particular and cinema in general, and lecture dates were never passed up, whether remunerative or not.[1] We gave a good deal of help to a new journal, *Cinema Quarterly*, edited by Norman Wilson and H. Forsyth Hardy, of the progressive Edinburgh Film Guild. It was started in the autumn of 1932 and published from Edinburgh. We realized that a steady flow of writing and lecturing about the documentary idea was the next best operation to film-making itself. It is probably true to record that the British documentary movement would not have gained its national and, later, international reputation so fast if its films had not been backed by this continuous output of

[1] *Celluloid: The Film Today*, Longmans, Green, 1931, was wholly written at nights or over weekends.

journalism and lecturing. Within a short time our work also became known to such intelligent film critics as Cedric Belfrage, Ernest Dyer, Cyril Ray, Aubrey Flanagan, Leslie Duckworth, Ernest Betts and C. A. Lejeune (who had her reservations, as has been seen). They supported us nobly, both in their newspaper columns and over the air. From the beginning, *The Times* fathered us, thanks to the vision of W. A. J. Lawrence. Ritchie-Calder, at that time on the *Daily Herald*, was another firm believer in our work, while H. Forsyth Hardy at *The Scotsman* was a staunch ally. Where Wardour Street and Elstree spent thousands trying to buy Press publicity for its mediocre pictures, documentary had it for the dropping of a hat. But the films had to be worth it.

In the lecture field, the growing number of film societies following in the lead of the pioneer one in London, and the interest being shown in the universities, kept us all too busy. I myself can remember going to more than twenty-five major cities in the United Kingdom to talk to enthusiastic audiences, not always about documentary but it was never omitted. Grierson, Wright and the others did the same elsewhere. At the inaugural meeting of the Glasgow Scientific Film Society, Elton gave an appropriate introduction. When he appeared, a reporter on the *Glasgow Herald* noted, he had long wanted to meet the missing link between Art and Science. Now he had. A Trade Union branch meeting in North London one bitterly cold winter night came up with an audience of around ten persons; my suggestion that we hold the lecture in the nearest local pub was a great success. So was documentary.

One other factor deserves this record: that is what may be called the movement's 'social' background. During the early 1930s, both at the EMB and subsequent units, documentary makers would meet most evenings in one or other of the pubs around Soho Square to talk about work in progress, about entertainment films currently showing in London, about politics and world events. The pubs we used in turn were *The George*, at the corner of Wardour Street and D'Arblay Street, administered by the genial Bessie, *The Coronet* (now rebuilt and renamed) in Soho Street, and lastly *The Highlander* at the corner of Dean Street and Carlisle Street (also rebuilt and renamed) where the Galloway family presided. It was in the latter that the *March of Time* in later years shot a sequence about British documentary and where Flaherty would spend hours on a pintable losing money. Long's Wine Bar in Hanley Street was also used by those who could afford its sherry on Fridays. Lyons Corner House at the corner of Tottenham Court Road, and which was open all night, was a rendezvous for breakfast after all-night shooting on the Poster Films at 175 Wardour Street. Sometimes one was asked down to Merrick Square, Southwark, to Grierson's house hear the River. There we shared a meal and a bottle of whisky. Parties in the conventional sense were very rare, but an exception was a rum occasion held by BasilWright on his return from making his West Indian films.

The documentary film-makers drank their fair share in those days but it was mostly a part of discussion and argument, or to entertain a distinguished visitor – Flaherty and his wife, Cavalcanti, Captain Badgeley of the Canadian Motion Picture Bureau, and Al Lewin, a Hollywood producer friend of Flaherty's. In afterthought, I am satisfied that this intermixing was of importance in keeping the documentary people together as a unified group, especially when, in the mid-1930s, units such as Strand and Realist were set up. Also of great value around that time were what were called the Friday night shows at No. 21 Soho Square, when old feature films, our own new work and sometimes films of would-be film-makers were screened and discussed. When still at Cambridge, Donald Alexander's short 16 mm film of a miners' strike in South Wales created a strong impression; he shortly after joined my Unit and later became a very good director. Personal disagreements there certainly were, but this homogeneous social contact should be remembered from this first decade of British documentary. It has had no later substitute.[1]

With its specific brief to 'bring the Empire alive', and using public money in doing so, it could hardly have been possible for the work of the EMB Unit to have reflected world events between 1929 and 1933, but during its three-and-a-half years at least it gave a picture, however modest, of some aspects of

[1] Compare how I found the exact opposite in New York in 1937, vide: Chapter 9.

British life and work. In later years, Grierson was to write significantly to me about this.

It was because of the Empire and Commonwealth purpose that we had at the Imperial Institute the first cinema devoted to 'people in many lands'; and, not least important, to a display of workmen at their work in many lands. This idea must ring a special bell for you. It was among the first of my interests that we should get the British workmen on the screen. Apart from our answer to Flaherty with our local fishermen *et al* in place of exotic types from the far beyond, more significant of the larger approach was that primitive approach to the international cinema of workers at the Imperial Institute. Another aspect of this Window on the World is worth noting internationally. Where did the working-class documentary traditions in the Socialist countries come from? You don't need much of a memory to remember that the Russians never could do anything with workmen filmically once they got separated from the dramatic and melodramatic stances of the Revolution. You will certainly not find it in Dziga-Vertov, who thought of seeing every which way and round about but never from the inside. Pudovkin's *A Simple Case* was a warning that they didn't know how to dramatize the working people. You have only to ask in the Socialist countries and not only in Europe, and there will be a very proper acknowledgement to Joris Ivens but also an acknowledgement will be to British documentary continuously between 1930 and the War. Date it from your own *Shipyard* in the 1930s and from *Housing Problems*. As for getting inside cinematically, we were close to a sense of not only recording movement but getting inside that movement from the beginning.[1]

World events made their impact. The American economic collapse foreseen by most of us, the resulting vast growth in unemployment at home and overseas, the evacuation of the Rhineland and its inevitable occupation by the Nazis, Japan's invasion of Manchuria, the burning of the Reichstag, the corrupt coming into being of the Third Reich, the anti-Jewish and anti-Trade Union suppression, the supine behaviour of the upper-class British, these were clear in front of us as we drank our pints of bitter. And all the time the commercial studios made films like *The Ghost Train*, *The Lyons Mail* and *The Skin Game*, while the film of the year in 1931 was Asquith's *Tell England*.

---

[1] In notes to the author, 26 December 1970. There will be found a good deal more along similar lines in *Documentary Film* (3rd edition, 1952.)

Tell it what? Alexander Korda had arrived to make British films in the American way.

The work output of the EMB Film Unit between 1930 and 1933 fell into several types of film. The first picture was designed for schools. Called *Conquest*, it was almost wholly a job of editing, using stock footage from American westerns such as *The Covered Wagon*. Copyright problems inhibited its distribution. With the establishment of the Empire Film Library at the Imperial Institute, the need was immediate for a supply of films far in excess of what the Unit could afford. Grierson obtained already-made film footage from many sources, including a large output mostly of travel films from the Canadian Motion Picture Bureau. This material was broken down and edited and often re-edited by the tyros at the Unit to make wholly new films. How many times a frozen Niagara and its spring thaw was arranged and rearranged by various hands is not on the record. The point was that Grierson rightly believed that film-making began in the editing process, and re-editing other people's films was an admirable exercise in which you put yourself in the would-be position of how *you* would have shot the film in the first place. Another reel that appeared regularly for the Library was an Empire Journal film magazine, for which Grierson's sister, Marion, was responsible.

Then there were the Poster films; endless loops of film (about 30 ft long) intended for use on continuous daylight projectors at EMB exhibitions and in shop-windows. They were made out of trick titles, what ingenious devices could be thought up, abstract effects and models. A new one had to be made from a drawn script to a completed film in one week at a cost of not more than £25. Basil Wright and I took it in turns to make them. Typical subjects were Scottish Tomatoes, Empire Timber, Australian Wine, Wool and Butter. They were photographed by Davidson with the old hand-turned Debrie. They demanded imagination and a strict economy over costs. Every frame, let alone foot, of film had to make its effect. It was a wonderful discipline for beginners. These Poster films were in some ways the forerunners of today's TV commercials, but without such luscious high budgets and expensive technical devices. Wright

49

and I would maybe sweat at the chores but it was excellent training. Above all, it made us realize the value of our materials. It was making films the hard way but all the time one learnt.

During the summer of 1931 by some miracle worked by Tallents, the Treasury made available a small amount of money to make several new, freshly-shot films which were to be a first testing ground. Wright and Elton were chosen to be the director/writer/editor of four of them. But before they reached beyond idea and script stage, an important event took place at the Unit.

One summer evening a few of us were, as was the custom, drinking over the day's work in *The Coronet*. Jimmie Davidson appeared out of breath and said to Grierson, 'There's a Mrs Flaherty on the telephone from Berlin for you up in the office'. As a result of this call, Robert J. Flaherty, fabulous maker of *Nanook* and *Moana*, came to work at the EMB Unit for a few not uneventful months.[1]

Flaherty, it appeared, after his not too successful collaboration in Tahiti in 1929–30 with the German director F. W. Murnau, which resulted in the hybrid film *Tabu*, had joined his wife Frances in Germany, where he had hoped to conclude negotiations to make a film in the Soviet Union. After months of delay, the deal fell through and, with funds running low, Mrs Flaherty had thought of calling Grierson in England to see what prospects there might be for Bob in this country. In his inimitable way, Grierson at once grasped the fact that to have the great Flaherty working at the EMB Film Unit would not only add lustre but would give a unique chance for the young tyros to see something at first hand of Flaherty's instinctive handling of the film camera and of his wonderful powers of observation. The next day Grierson put the proposal to Tallents. For financial reasons alone, the latter accepted the idea with some reserve, but his way was helped by the Imperial Conference in the previous year having widened the EMB's terms of reference to include Empire markets overseas as well as inside Britain. In

---

[1] The following account appeared in the original MS of the Flaherty biography written in 1958–59 based on research by Paul Rotha and Basil Wright. This was used only in part in *The Innocent Eye*, by Arthur Calder-Marshall, W. H. Allen, 1963.

addition, some other money had been granted for Anthony Asquith to make a film at the Unit, but the offer had not been accepted. The Flahertys checked in at a hotel near the Unit's offices. I remember vividly the Grandfather of Documentary being conducted around the shabby two floors of the Unit's offices and cutting-rooms. I remember, too, going to their hotel to look at the superb photographs Frances Flaherty had taken in Savaii where *Moana* was made. Bob told us how most of his film had been shot when the sun was either rising or setting, thus throwing long shadows, the light shining underneath the foliage to give a stereoscopic quality. In 1924, *Moana* had been the first film to be shot wholly on the new panchromatic film stock. I recall his delight, almost childish, in discovering the English-made, spring-driven Newman-Sinclair camera, with its quickly interchangeable magazines and its wide range of lenses. He liked its long-focus lens, which he was to use with such wonderful effect in *Man of Aran*.[1] A gyrohead tripod which the resourceful Jimmie Davidson hired from the Gaumont-British studios especially pleased him by its potentialities for smooth camera movement.

The Unit was still operating on the tautest of shoestrings. Money for wages, for film stock, for transport and hotels was minimal. Tallents, however, with his subtle powers of persuasion, had contrived to convince his finance officers and hence the Treasury to employ Flaherty at an undisclosed fee, as well as to find £2,500 for the cost of the film he was to make in England. This was a budget hitherto unknown by the Unit. (It should be realized that this production cost, like those given later, should be roughly quadrupled to equate with costs today.) How Tallents conjured up this money for Flaherty was one of those mysteries best left undisturbed. The upshot was that it was agreed between Grierson, Tallents and Flaherty that he should go off and bring back material for a short film that would

---

[1] The various models of the Newman-Sinclair camera, with many refinements and improvements, played an important role in the technical story of the British documentary film. It was such a simple camera to work that many young directors soon learned to use it without resort to a professional cameraman. Basil Wright, for example, shot his West Indian films single-handed and with John Taylor shot all of *Song of Ceylon*. It was widely used during World War II.

reveal the craftsmanship which stubbornly persisted in even the most up-to-date of British industries, even behind the smoke and steam and grime and slums of the industrial Midlands, although at that time Flaherty did not show much interest in the slums.

An early achievement of the Unit had been to destroy the fallacy widely held in British film studios that British weather was a deterrent to exterior film photography. For economic reasons alone, EMB films had to be shot in *any* kind of weather. Some remarkably good cinematography was the result. Hence Tallents was rather unfair when he wrote,

There remained to be destroyed the belief that the industrial life of Britain and her grey city atmosphere could never be portrayed on the screen. The real point of bringing Flaherty to England at this moment was to destroy that fallacy.[1]

It was not the *main* reason for Grierson wanting Flaherty to work at the Unit. It may have been one reason advanced by Grierson in his persuasions to Tallents to employ Flaherty, but it was the latter's use of the camera as a medium of observation that the tiros were to watch. Nevertheless, Flaherty was to bring back later some wonderfully photographed footage of industrial landscapes in which he captured the contrast of white steam, black smoke and grey overall atmosphere by including all three in one shot.

Grierson now explained patiently to Flaherty that someone down in Whitehall would need to see a script of the film he was about to make. Flaherty point blank refused. He had never written a script in his life and he wasn't going to start to please some civil servant at a desk. Grierson became very firm. No script, no money. Outraged, Flaherty retired to his hotel and kept a hermit-like silence. For three days he did not even appear in the pub. Then he called at the Unit and handed Grierson a thick wadge of paper. On the top sheet in Flaherty's heavy handwriting was written: INDUSTRIAL BRITAIN, a Film about Craftsmen, by Robert J. Flaherty. On the next page was: A Scenario: Scenes of Industrial Britain. The remainder of the wadge of pages was blank. It is quite certain that if Tallents, or

[1] Cobb Lecture, 27 November 1946.

anyone else at the EMB or in Whitehall, ever read a script for the Unit's new film, that script was not written by the maker of *Nanook* and *Moana*.

The Unit's humble operation obviously would not allow Flaherty to pursue his by then established method of film-making by digging himself into a location before starting to make any of the film except what he called a 'notebook'. Grierson, of course, was well aware of this danger; the £2,500 could be swallowed before Flaherty brought in one usable sequence of film. At the same time, Grierson knew the importance of Flaherty becoming acclimatized, even if briefly, to the British scene. Basil Wright was about to start on his first real film (apart from some Poster films), later known as *The Country Comes to Town*, some of which was to be shot in Devonshire. His cameraman, James Burger, not a staff member, was paid about three times as much as the director. The latter admits to having been both excited and excessively nervous of his first assignment. Grierson decided that it would be a mutually rewarding experience if Flaherty should accompany Wright to see something of the English countryside, while Wright would benefit from Flaherty's wisdom and advice in the initial stages of his film. What happened on the occasion has been described by Wright and need not be retold.[1]

When Flaherty returned to London, he found that Grierson had hired a production manager for him. J. P. R. Golightly, who was destined to become a bastion of the British documentary group, had been an estate manager in the West of England. Now unemployed, he had met Dr Anthony Grierson, John's younger brother, who had suggested that there might be a job at the EMB Unit. After an interview, and before he knew what had happened, Golightly found himself signed on as what he described as a 'man of all work' for Flaherty's film to be. He had no prior experience of films or film-making, such was Grierson's impetuosity.[2]

Flaherty and his production manager set out in a very old

[1] It is part of the Flaherty story, not that of the EMB, and may be found in Arthur Calder-Marshall's *The Innocent Eye*.

[2] For this information and most of the following account of Flaherty's location adventures in England, I am indebted to an interview with Mr Golightly on 26 March 1958. He died 29 January 1967.

Austin car, Golightly at the wheel, with a Newman-Sinclair camera and what for the Unit was a very generous amount of film stock. They were supposed to spend a day filming Saltash Bridge in Devonshire, and then head for the Midlands. For a few days no news came from them. It was the routine at the Unit each morning to screen 'rushes' of any film that might be in production at the moment for Grierson to see. One morning there were thrown on the screen, without any identification, several reels of shipping scenes and of cranes loading and unloading at some unidentified docks. Then a few shots, very nice, of Saltash Bridge. We at once knew that this was the first batch of Flaherty's material. There followed many erratic shots taken from what appeared to be a railway-coach window, quite unusable because of the train's vibration. After the reels were finished, we were all very shocked. A good deal of precious film had been used on scenes which were either unusable or not remotely related to Flaherty's brief. Matters were not made easier when, after a great deal of delay, Flaherty was located in some hotel in Devonshire and Grierson cautioned him about the amount of film stock he was using. Flaherty, no doubt hurt, explained that what he had shot so far were only 'tests' which he had made just to 'get the feel of things'.

The two-man unit proceeded on its way. The trouble was, recalled Golightly, that Flaherty wanted to film almost everything he saw. 'We would be going along in the old Austin and suddenly Bob would see a string of electricity pylons striding across the landscape. Immediately he would order me to make a detour. The windmill shots with which the film finally opened were made just like this, by chance.'[1] Golightly himself was not a little worried. Knowing nothing about films, he could not himself have been expected to have held Flaherty in awe, but he was aware of the vast respect with which all at the EMB Unit regarded him. At the same time, his new employer had urged the need for strict economy, especially in the use of film stock. As quite a proportion of the total amount of stock allocated for the *whole* film had now been used on what Flaherty still called

[1] I recall similar experiences while making *The Face of Britain* in 1934 while on journeys up and down the country ostensibly to make the film *Shipyard* at Barrow in Furness in Lancashire.

his 'tests', Golightly's anxiety grew. At his urgent request, the two-man unit returned to base in London where a serious and no doubt stormy meeting took place between Flaherty and Grierson.

After this angry interlude, and loaded up with two 2 kw lamps and appropriate cable to light interior scenes, the Austin and its crew set out again for the Midlands. Golightly's job was to make contacts at places where Flaherty wanted to film, fix the hotels (Bob always wanted the best), arrange for the electricity supply for the lamps when needed, shift the latter around at Flaherty's command, pay the bills, keep the accounts and drive the car. In time, Flaherty observed that even a man of Golightly's great resources could not cope with such a multitude of tasks. After a word with London, the young John Taylor, aged 17, was sent to join the unit as dogsbody number two at Stoke-on-Trent.

Golightly relates that Flaherty would watch a process, such as glass-blowing or pottery-making, for a long time and with deep concentration. He would observe every movement of the workers on the job so that when he came to use his camera, he could anticipate their every action. Such a method was later to make a deep impression on the documentary makers at the EMB. Among the industrial processes to be shot was steel-making. Here Golightly had some difficulty in obtaining permission for Flaherty to film at a particular works near Birmingham. 'He could be very irritable,' said Mr Golightly, 'if permission to shoot was not given at once. He was surprised that factory-managers had not heard of him and his films; he thought they should have felt honoured that he, Flaherty, wanted to film in their works.' Finally, permission was agreed but certain areas of the steel plant were banned to them, unfortunately some of the best from a filmic point of view. This ruling was accepted with bad grace by Flaherty.

That evening Grierson and Jimmie Davidson showed up un-expectedly at the same hotel in Birmingham. Grierson was in good form. It seemed that on their way that afternoon they had shot some spectacular steel scenes which they happened to see by chance. The more lyrical Grierson's description waxed, the more apprehensive became Golightly, because it soon became clear that the steel works where Grierson had filmed had been the same that Bob had shot that morning. And moreover, Grierson had filmed in the very areas which had been forbidden to Flaherty. When he grasped the situation, it is understood that Flaherty's rage was as sensational as had been Grierson's account of the filming. As he saw it, quite untruly, Flaherty felt that he had been deliberately outwitted by Grierson. Didn't these goddamned steel people and these goddamned civil servants in Whitehall, didn't he – John Grierson – realize that Robert Flaherty couldn't be treated like this? Grierson gave a characteristic goading reply, 'Why, Bob, down in Whitehall they think you're just a bloody beach-photographer.' According to Golightly, Flaherty drew himself up out of his chair to his full height and girth, raised his fists to the ceiling of the crowded hotel lounge, and cried, 'F—— them! F—— them! F—— them!' They were asked to leave the hotel.

The Flaherty–Golightly unit next moved across to Northern Ireland where they were to shoot in Harland & Wolff's shipyard. It was there that Flaherty managed to get his bulky form wedged in a gantry high up over the stocks. 'It took half-a-dozen men to free him,' recalled Golightly. 'He was a very scared man and had to stay in the hotel several days to get over the shock although he wasn't hurt in any way.' It was in Belfast that they again ran out of film stock and money. Golightly sent telegram after telegram to London to which there was no reply. Now, Flaherty became very angry and telegraphed Grierson that unless some money and more film stock came by return he would sell the camera. 'The money and film came,' Golightly said laconically.

When Flaherty finished shooting, or rather when money and film stock were finally exhausted, they returned to London. It was clear that there was some wonderful footage, notably the glass-blowing and pottery-making, but to Grierson as producer there was no unified film. In some unrecorded and doubtless tactful way, it was agreed that Flaherty himself should not edit the film. This Grierson pledged he would do himself. Flaherty departed from the Unit to start negotiations to make *Man of Aran* for Michael Balcon at Gaumont-British.

A screening of all Flaherty's material at once suggested that more filming was needed. The stock library was raided. Basil

Wright was sent off to shoot some inland waterways and flying-boat material; Arthur Elton went down a coal mine. Grierson appointed Edgar Anstey as his assistant and all the footage was moved to a room in Grierson's house which had been fitted up with primitive but workable editing equipment.

Anstey remembered that in all there were about 12,000 ft of Flaherty material, which was far from excessive when one recalls the immense footage used on *Nanook* and *Moana*. It spoke well for Mr Golightly's stewardship. There was, of course, no script from which to edit, and Anstey stated that at no time did he have anything on paper from which to work.[1] Part of the time Grierson was unwell and confined to bed where he would edit the film by eye. It was completed as a silent film and when Anstey left it (to go off on HMS *Challenger*), it was about two reels long, about 30 minutes. It had much the same shape as we were to know later as *Industrial Britain*. Flaherty had no part in all this; indeed one wonders if he ever saw the finished film.

All next year, 1932, the film lay fallow. Then the EMB concluded a distribution deal with Gaumont-British Distributors for the release of a series of EMB films to be known as The Imperial Six. Part of the deal was that the GB Company put up some money so that the films could have a sound track added, thus making them suitable for ordinary cinema release. As a result, *Industrial Britain* did not have its first showing until the summer of 1933, when it played with great success in London and throughout the country.

The film was notable for its continual use of big close-ups with very simple lighting; for its sensitive camera movements anticipating action; and for its industrial landscapes already mentioned. The wonderful faces, caught in all their concentration on the job in hand, linger in one's memory for many years. If *Industrial Britain* was significant for no other reason, it put the real faces of British workpeople on the screen in a manner not seen before, except for *Drifters*. They were given their natural dignity. On the other hand, the film had sentimental overtones stressed by Donald Calthrop's emotional narration which irritated some critics, especially in America.

In addition to the main picture, a silent one-reel film called

[1] In an interview, 9 July 1969.

The English Potter, destined for school use, was edited by Marion Grierson from the Flaherty material. 'It is,' wrote Grierson, 'thank God, still silent and, except for a synthetic ending, a lovely thing to see.'[1]

Of the parent film, Tallents was to write,

I always thought the magnificently photographed *Industrial Britain*, with its vivid shots of steel-workers and potters and glass-blowers, and its closing portrayal of a ship outward bound with the exports of Britain, as moving as any that the Unit in those days yielded.

There is no question but that, with *Drifters*, *Industrial Britain* was the most successful and widely liked film to come out of the EMB Unit. It is to be noted that it was still in circulation years after World War II in countries outside Britain. In a private letter to Tallents about the Memorial Performance of Flaherty films held by the New London Film Society (March 1952), Grierson again wrote of the film:

I wonder if it will give you a guide to the good Bob? It was made in spite of him. Its manner and mood were not his. On the other hand, it is true that it was the combination of Flaherty's approach and our's – different as they eventually proved to be – that set the line for a decade of documentary film-making – here and abroad.[1]

In September 1931 my employment at the EMB Unit was ended on the grounds of economy. No one else was fired. On the contrary, during that summer several new people were taken on, Arthur Elton, Stuart Legg and Edgar Anstey among them. One night in *The Coronet* Grierson accused me of being what he called 'in the Courtly tradition'. When it is recalled that I had neither been to a university nor come from any part of the Establishment, I always think he must have confused me with Arthur (now Sir Arthur) Elton.

That autumn the two-reelers were begun which were eventually to make up the series called the Imperial Six. Basil Wright made *The Country Comes to Town*, which showed the bringing of London's food and milk supplies from the countryside to the

---

[1] In a letter to Tallents, 31 December 1951

city overnight, and *O'er Hill and Dale*, a Scots shepherd's life in the lambing season. Arthur Elton made *The Shadow on the Mountain* about research into grass-breeding in Wales, and *Upstream* about salmon breeding in Scotland. Flaherty's film would make the fifth in the series, while the sixth had to be a compilation of Canadian footage, *King Log*, with music by Dennis Arundell. They all were given a good cinema distribution, by GB-Distributors.

There was then to come the first film to be made for an outside body, the Gramophone Company. Produced by Grierson and directed by Elton, *The Voice of the World* (1932) was made through New Era, and had its first showing at the Radio Exhibition, Olympia. It pursued the impressionist style. Grierson wrote of it:

The film is interesting for its large-scale combination of processes. Gets across excellently the size of the industry and the variety of radio performance. But too symphonic a treatment (after the fashion of *Berlin*), to indicate the dramatic character of the most revolutionary instrument of culture and opinion in the modern world. Concentration on movement and rhythmic good looks obscure *importance* of the instrument. The building and *delivery* of the instrument, the key to the situation, not dramatized sufficiently. The result powerful but less heroic. Elton possibly unappreciative of radio's social significance and therefore lacking in proper (aesthetic) affection for subject. This point important as affecting almost all the tiros of documentary. Too damned arty and post-war to get their noses into public issues. Miss accordingly the larger dramatic themes possible to the medium.[1]

Stuart Legg's first film, *The New Generation*, in 1932, photographed by Gerald Gibbs, was again made through New Era for the Chesterfield Educational Authority. It was a simple, well-made, straightforward film. Thus it can already be noted that Grierson's capacities as a producer and adviser were getting known wider than the confines of the EMB Unit. Several Government departments, official bodies and industrial firms

[1] *Cinema Quarterly*, Vol. I, No. 2, Winter, 1932. Thus Grierson the producer becomes critic of a director working under his *diktat*. This quirk to criticize what was partially his own work found odd expression some years later when Grierson reviewed (*Sight and Sound*, Vol. 22, New Quarterly Series, No. 2, October-December, 1952,) the third edition of *Documentary Film* although he had contributed a fulsome Preface to the book!

sought his help. Always alert to get a new film made if it would follow the documentary purpose, he advised the Travel and Industrial Association, and the Ministries of Labour and Agriculture on their film activity. In this way were made *Lancashire at Work and Play* (1933) and *Spring Comes to England* (1934) by Donald Taylor, and superior travel pictures such as *So This is London* (1933) and *For All Eternity* (1934) by Marion Grierson. From his trip to Labrador Edgar Anstey brought back *Eskimo Village* and *Uncharted Waters* (1933), while J. Norris Davidson directed an unfinished semi-story film called *The Hen Woman.* Evelyn Spice made a series of school films covering the English seasons and the economic areas of the country. The Post Office made use of the Unit in Stuart Legg's two films, *The New Operator* (1932) and *Telephone Workers* (1933).

The impression must not be given that all or any of these EMB films were small masterpieces. They were doubtless overpraised at the time in our own propagandist campaign for documentary ideas.

In 1933, the EMB sent Basil Wright to the West Indies. His mission was to make the first of a series of films for specialized use under the general title of *The Eyes of Science*, a title borrowed later by Grierson from an American film made for Kodak by Dr Watson. They were to be made mainly at the Imperial College of Tropical Agriculture in Trinidad. Subjects to be covered were such matters as research into Panama disease in bananas, Witchbroom disease in Cacao, Shifting Cultivation, Forestry and so on. The main film was rough-cut by Wright on his return to England, but the negative was mislaid in the change-over to come between the EMB and its successor. What was finished, however, were two beautiful short films that Wright shot 'on the side', as it were, because they established his special approach and style to film-making. *Cargo from Jamaica* was a film of the banana plantations, a challenging comment on the heavy, manual loading methods used by native labour in Jamaica in comparison with the easy, mechanized unloading of the freight at the London docks. *Windmill in Barbados* was a picture of the sugar fields, the contrast between old and new methods and labour conditions. Both short films were photographed as well as directed and edited by Wright, to be forerunners of the lyrical, poetic style of movement that was to come to fruition in *Song of Ceylon*. They were of course shot silent. But both are memorable films.

In complete contrast was Arthur Elton's *Aero-Engine*, finished in 1934. In six reels the whole construction of aeroplane engines was covered in detail – the raw materials, their shaping into component parts, the assembly and the testing, and finally their performance in flight. Concentration was not only on the machines but on the men whose skill made them possible. It was finely photographed by George Noble, whose work was to be associated with many early documentaries. The film epitomized Elton's absorption in the precision of engineering and mechanics, an absorption that was to occupy most, but not all, of his later work. It had none of Wright's emotional, poetic quality but instead a respect for and understanding of the film medium's capacity to explain and inform.

If in the above account of the EMB output more attention has been paid to *Industrial Britain*, with its uneven making by more than one pair of eyes and hands, than to other films it is because it was more typical, if also a little more extravagant, than the other works. First, it typified the need for economy in working methods, a unit plus camera equipment usually travelling by public transport and its crew normally lodging in a cheap hotel. Second, although *Industrial Britain* drew in the main from Flaherty's lovely footage, it was the first of what may be called the 'group' films, that is several people – Grierson, Wright, Elton, Anstey *et al* – having worked on it in addition to Flaherty. This method, which Grierson was to follow closely, was in direct opposition to that of Wright in his West Indian films and Elton in his *Aero-Engine* picture. This will be expanded on later.

Grierson liked to switch around production personnel even when a film was in the making, to bring what he thought might be a fresh approach. I was not in sympathy with this method. *Contact*, *Shipyard* and *The Face of Britain* were essentially individually made films, and maybe the worse for that. This is perhaps the reason why Grierson asked me to leave the EMB Unit after only a few months' work. He may have realized that I did not fit in with the group method of working. It will be seen that he regarded what later came to be called the *auteur* conception of film-making as a romantic harkback. At the same time, the Unit's overall work gained attention, but this divergence of creative contribution could cause confusion about who did what on any particular film. *Night Mail* was a case in point. Examples were known, as at Strand a few years later, when a producer contributed a great deal to a film's script and possibly even did the final editing, but was content to let his whole work be grouped under the overall title of producer. *Today We Live* and *The Future's in the Air* were instances.[1] Individual styles were, of course, developed, especially in the case of Wright, as his work was to show over the next three decades. Elton, on the other hand, was as the years went on to become more and more a producer and administrator, while Legg's skill was to mature in the compilation film and journalistic approach, as his work in Canada would reveal.

In the summer of 1933 a report came from the Imperial Committee on Economic Consultation and Cooperation recommending that the Empire Marketing Board as a body should be disbanded, with its Film Unit and by now quite extensive Film Library at the Imperial Institute. The dissolution of the Board was determined in September of that year. It was an unwise and shortsighted Government decision. The Editor of *Cinema Quarterly*, Norman Wilson, wrote:

The EMB is an intricate organisation with wide ramifications, and we cannot but deplore its possible demise in so far as it would effect its Film Unit, the disappearance of which would be a serious blow not only to the interests it serves but to the cinema as a whole. Apart from its work of 'bringing the Empire alive', its documentary work for industry and science, its service to education the value of which is cumulative and can be assessed only after the passage of considerable time, perhaps the greatest achievement of the EMB has been the training of a number of young men as film directors, free from the trammels and inhibitions of commercialism. Working in a unity of spirit and effort their talents have nevertheless been allowed to develop along distinctively individual lines. It may be that one day the influence

---

[1] Vide: Chapter 7

The Empire Marketing Board Film Unit (1933–30)

of the spirit that has been created at the EMB Film Unit will have been its most valuable gift to the cinema.

With the widening applications of the cinema as a means of instruction and demonstration, and the gradual realization of its value as an influence and means of propaganda for social and industrial purposes, it would be little short of tragedy if this group of specialized workers – the only one of its kind outside Russia – should be dispersed. It is safe to say that the Government will find increasing use for the cinema in the future, and whatever the fate of the EMB as such, it is to be hoped that every effort will be made to retain the services of its Film Unit, whose real work, after its initial period of experiment, only now should be commencing.[1]

It is unlikely that the journal in which this wisdom appeared was read outside film society circles, certainly not by members of the Select Committee on Estimates which heard evidence on the EMB Unit in the following year. In *The Observer*, Miss C. A. Lejeune was more cautious but nevertheless discerning.

With the disestablishment of the EMB in September we are likely to lose a very valuable department of British films, and one that has done a great deal in the past few years to stabilise the motion picture camera as the servant of education.

The EMB Film unit has never been ostentatious; it has suffered, on the whole, from lop-sided publicity.[2] A number of interested people up and down the country – students of the cinema mostly, and educationists – have been aware of the work that John Grierson and his little band of enthusiastic craftsmen have been turning out from their workshop in Oxford Street . . . But on the whole the reputation of the Film Unit has not been built up on its most important work. Just a handful of the EMB films have got, or will soon be getting, into the theatres.

She then listed the titles of the Imperial Six.

The films represent the most spectacular of the EMB's product. But they are few and experimental, while all the time, week in and week out, the Unit is operating in another and more important field.

She went on to describe the work of the Empire Film Library and its free loan of films to schools and other educational bodies and added,

[1] Vol. I, No. 4, 1933.
[2] For which Miss Lejeune herself was largely responsible.

63

. . . their value as a collection is unquestionable. Indeed, so great is the demand for them that schools often have to wait weeks for a delivery. They represent a world of information which cannot easily be re-assembled . . . What is to happen to this Library when the EMB is disbanded . . . This dispersal of patiently-gathered knowledge is surely something that should be prevented, whatever may happen to the Unit itself.

Now there came the nub of the case, which will be elucidated later.

Miss Lejeune continued,

If the Government will not undertake to preserve the Library intact as a national possession under the auspices of the Imperial Institute, here is a chance for one of the commercial firms to jump in and combine altruism with profit. The owners of 16mm projectors, such as RCA and British Acoustic,[1] are dependent for their future on the speedy compilation of a good library, and the chance of acquiring several hundred genuine educational films that have passed the tests by educational authorities is not to be despised.

It will be a bad blunder if the EMB Film Unit is disbanded . . . But if the Unit must go, as a Government department, do let us preserve its assets. One of these assets is good will among industrialists and educational and civic authorities.[2]

This could be read as an omen of the Film Trade's evidence to the Select Committee on Estimates to be held the next year. It is possible that the manufacturers of film projector equipment were not so much interested in the creative potential of the Unit which Tallents and Grierson had built up as they were in buying a ready-made film library to stimulate the sale of their projectors in the educational market. Grierson went on record as saying that the GB Corporation offered to take over the EMB Film Unit and its Library.[3] The offer was not accepted.

The Tallents–Grierson relationship had proved several constructive things. First, that the film as a medium of creative potential could be used in the public service in a field other than that of entertainment. Second, that its economics of production,

---

[1] An associate company of the Gaumont-British Corporation. By 'owners', Miss Lejeune means of course 'manufacturers'.

[2] 13 August 1933.

[3] Cf. p. 44 footnote.

distribution and exhibition could be found from Government as an alternative to commercial interests. Third, that the film medium could be a powerful instrument of communication between peoples. And last, that its creative opportunities could attract to it talent for good film-making that otherwise would have had no outlet. When the EMB Film Unit was finally disbanded in 1933, the main reputation of British films overseas rested on the slender output of that Unit. It was no small achievement in four years for a sum of money less than that spent on any one big entertainment film of the time.

4. *Making* Contact *(1932–33)*

After I left the EMB there followed a year's semi-employment. I rented a cheap furnished room in Manchester Street, off Baker Street, which was possible in those days. In the house was a *ménage* of theatre and film people: Miles Mander, Madeleine Carroll, Lydia Sherwood, Elizabeth Allan and the veteran actor Stewart Rome. Miles Mander, also mostly out of work, obtained an occasional script assignment for a feature film and asked me to collaborate with him. Some, like *The Mystery of the Marie Celeste* and *The Actor Manager* (from Leonard Merrick's novel) were abortive, but others, including *Fascination* (for which we wrote in a minute part for Merle Oberon – then Merle Thompson), a remake of *The Lodger* and *Don Quixote*, later made by Pabst with Chaliapine, reached the screen. Sometimes Miles Mander and I got paid but often we didn't.

It was Miles Mander who introduced me to an unpleasant character, John Amery, a son of L. S. Amery, then Secretary of State for Dominion Affairs and, ironically, Chairman of the Empire Marketing Board. In some way young John Amery had found some money, hired a cameraman, and shot thousands of feet of almost useless film of wild-life in East Africa. He now wanted a story invented to be shot in a studio in England so that his so-called 'wild animals' could be interpolated. It was to be called *Jungle Skies*. I wrote an appalling script which Amery much liked. His cheque for £50, however, did not materialize. After many broken promises, I decided to go and get the money. I needed it. His vast office was in Long Acre. On a huge desk were photographs of Mussolini and Al Capone. He at once gave me a cheque. I slipped it in my pocket and went to the door. He called me to turn round. He had a gun in his hand. He demanded the cheque. I left the room. The cheque was of course returned

66

by my bank. With reluctance I went to see his father. He was embarrassed but not surprised by my story, but at once gave me his own cheque for the amount due. I did not mention the Empire Marketing Board. Young John Amery was hanged in 1945 for his collaboration with the Nazis during the war.

Another odd introduction by Miles Mander was to a peculiar middle-aged woman named Dinah Shurey. She had bird's nest hair. Like Harry Bruce Woolfe, she was an upstanding Empire loyalist. She had some money from an undisclosed source and a film production company called Britannia Films Ltd which had made some quite atrocious films, such as *Every Mother's Son*, *Carry On* and *Afraid Of Love*. I failed to grasp why Miles Mander had given me the introduction. Then she said that she had heard about a German film called *Kameradschaft*, about a mine disaster. She wanted to buy the British rights. Would I like to go to Berlin with her and while she negotiated with the producers, Nerofilm, I could make suggestions for English sub-titles. It was, of course, the great film by Pabst, destined to become a classic. Why this strange woman wanted to acquire the British rights puzzled me and I never solved the puzzle. Although reluctant to be associated with Miss Shurey, I could not refuse the chance of going to Berlin again, meeting perhaps Pabst, and exploring the German film world for possible work.

In Berlin, Miss Shurey was shamefully double-crossed by the German producer, Seymour Nebenzal, who had practically sold the British rights to someone else. But poor Miss Shurey did not find this out for two weeks, during which time I wrote English sub-titles for the film. Pabst himself was in North Africa preparing to make the exteriors for *Atlantis*, which was to be made in German, French and English. Nebenzal promised that I would be asked to return to Berlin and work with Pabst on the English version. It never transpired. Although I did not meet Pabst, I did meet his architect-designer, Ernö Metzner, who had done the sets for *Kameradschaft* and was now designing the studio sets for *Atlantis*. Metzner and his Chinese wife were highly intelligent people; he had directed the *avant-garde* film *Überfall* which impressed many people. Later he came to England, where he was very unhappy in the studios, and went on to America.

Making Contact (*1932–33*)

It was the Berlin of 1931, with the depravity which repulsed Flaherty so much. I had little time to experience very much, being occupied at the laboratory with the sub-titles, but I was not sorry to return to England and regretted that Miss Shurey had been defrauded out of her good intentions. On later occasions when I talked with Pabst, he told me much about Nebenzal's activities; so also did Fritz Lang, who had made *M* for Nerofilm. Such contacts as I had again in London and Berlin with the world of feature films reaffirmed my reactions at Elstree to this rat race, of which there is only one worse, the second-hand car market. I am not interested in cars, but I am in films.

I became convinced more and more that the only answer lay in the documentary method of finding film finance. Grierson had complete control over the Government's interest in documentary production. There might be the possibility of finding money in industry. I approached a big department store – Selfridges – to try and get them to sponsor a film of a day-in-the-life of a big shop, but before I had any response, I had a fortunate meeting.

If *The Film Till Now* had brought about no recognition in the film industry, it did bring contacts outside. Among these was Ralph Keene, then assistant manager at Tooth's Art Gallery in New Bond Street. As an outsider he was passionately interested in films but realized the need for economic sponsorship. A frequent visitor and occasional buyer of modern art at Tooth's Gallery, Keene told me, was J. L. Beddington, who was in charge of publicity and advertising for the giant Shell-Mex and BP oil company. Quite apart from his later interest in films, Jack Beddington used Shell money in the 1930s to sponsor many young painters and writers, some established but many unknown at that time outside a small circle. Among those who benefited from Beddington's patronage and who later gained success were, in no special order: Peter Quennell, Nicolas Bentley, John Piper, John Minchendon, E. McKnight Kauffer, Barnet Freedman, Rex Whistler, Michael Ayrton, Paul Nash, Edward Bawden, Leonard Rosamon, Graham Sutherland, Robert Byron, Edward Ardizzone and, of course, John Betjeman who edited the admirable Shell Guides to British counties. This list of outstanding painters and writers shows Beddington's judgement in finding

Making Contact (1932-33)

potential as well as established ability and then backing it with sponsorship by a big industry. Since his death in 1959, no one so far as I know has followed in such a vital role of industrial patron.

Having heard my ideas about documentary, Ralph Keene said he would fix for us to meet Beddington, who had, Keene thought, commissioned one film to be made, *Liquid History*, which had not been a success. Keene had an idea for a short trick film to be based on the motif of seashells which he reckoned might seduce Beddington. Although far from my kind of filmmaking (except for the EMB Poster films), I helped Keene prepare a kind of script which was sent to Beddington. A meeting with the latter was arranged for discussion. For some reason I do not recall, Keene could not be present. Beddington in his charming but frank way had misgivings about the script, which I shared. But it was clear that he wanted to do something with the film medium. I was about to talk about the whole documentary idea when his telephone rang.

A cryptic dialogue ensued, of which of course I heard only one end. Then Beddington put a hand over the phone mouthpiece and turned to me with a grin. 'What about making a film with Imperial Airways about their overseas air-routes? They will provide free travel and facilities if Shell will put up some hard cash?' That was exactly how I came to make my first documentary film.

Beddington commissioned me to write what could be written of a script for a modest sum. When I explained to Ralph Keene what had happened, he took up a most generous attitude. He could not, he said, leave his good job at Tooth's Gallery for such a pipe-dream. He would like to contribute any ideas he might have in conceiving a script, but after that I should be on my own with the film. It was a handsome gesture that I have never forgotten.

After further discussion, talks with C. F. Snowden Gamble, the publicity manager of Imperial Airways, and visits to Croydon Airport which was then the main London air-terminal, I submitted a kind of brief outline for the film (it could not be a script) to Beddington. He approved it at once. Shell were prepared to find a total sum of £2,500, which was to cover

69

everything except cost of air travel. Film stock, wages, hotel accommodation abroad, laboratory charges and all the many items of film production were to be found for this figure. Then arose a problem. Shell could not contract with me as an individual to produce the film. A contract must be made with a company. I could have proposed New Era Films but because of its EMB relations decided against it. Looking around the industry, I could find only one company which had some kind of an honest reputation and which would give me services without any control over the making of the film. It was Bruce Woolfe's British Instructional Films, at Welwyn Garden City. It had been the producer of Asquith's feature films and also had its reputation for the *Secrets of Nature* series. I did not know then what I came to know about Bruce Woolfe in later days, but if I had, it would not have made any difference. I had complete control over the film on Beddington's insistence. A contract was drawn up between the Shell Company and British Instructional Films, by which they provided technical services for the production in return for 10 per cent of the contract price. My own fee was agreed at £200 for what eventually came to be a year's work of direction and editing. But it was my first film and much could result from it for the future.

For the record, because it has some importance later, Bruce Woolfe and his brother Willie, who was studio manager at Welwyn, began in the business as exhibitors in an East End cinema. Their spectacular success was when they booked a French film about the life of Christ. At the same time *The Miracle* was being staged at the Albert Hall and being widely advertised all over London. The Woolfe Brothers toured the town very early one morning in a taxi and fixed small stickers billing their own picture and cinema's name across the huge posters for *The Miracle*. They did fantastic business.[1] But Bruce Woolfe was a reasonably honest man in film industry terms. Among his co-directors at BIF at Welwyn were Lord Tweedsmuir (John Buchan, the novelist) and A. E. Bundy, the theatrical impresario. If Bruce Woolfe is to be remembered in cinema history as a whole, it is because he did back the amazing Percy Smith with the *Secrets of Nature* series. Percy Smith was an

[1] He told me this story himself while I was editing *Contact*.

amateur who operated from a small house with a greenhouse attached in North London. For £10 a week he delivered a small amount of film he had made in his greenhouse or garden of plant and insect life to Bruce Woolfe, whereupon the material was 'put together' by Mary Field who, as time went by, added a banal commentary. She drew £50 a week. In its small, petty way this was typical of the exploitation methods of the industry, except that its end product was good.

No proper script could be written for *Contact* any more than Flaherty could write one for *Industrial Britain*, or Wright for *Song of Ceylon*. To write a script you must know what you are writing about. It was obvious that I knew nothing or very little about the countries over which the air-routes sped or the places at which planes stopped. To have researched into the backgrounds of air-routes between London and Karachi on the one hand, and Cairo to Cape Town on the other, could hardly have been possible in the time before our departure date was fixed. Even the latter did not depend on my choice. It was a matter of when Imperial Airways, already an overbooked airline, could carry our free-riding passengers. What was made very clear to me by the traffic department of Imperial Airways was that once we left London with a book of ticket reservations over three months, any variation from this schedule would mean endless delays which the film's budget would not stand. What I could not foresee was the lack of adequate coordination between personnel in London and personnel out on various places along the air-routes. In many places when we arrived, station staff had not heard that a film was being made and that a film unit would arrive expecting certain facilities to have been arranged.

For Beddington's sake as well as for my own, I wrote a kind of outline around which the film that I would shoot could be assembled. It spoke of Man's new Conquest of Space and Time with emphasis laid on the closer communication between peoples being made possible by air travel, especially by airmail.[1] In a letter to Eric Knight at the time, I set out a skeleton of headings:

[1] This Outline, for what it is worth, is deposited at the University of California, Los Angeles, with much of the rest of my Archive.

Making Contact (*1932–33*)

Themes: 1. Poetry of the New World of the Air.
            2. Prophecy for Future of Air Transport.

Sequences: 1. Conquest of Space on Land, Sea and Air (statement of fact).
            2. Building of an Aircraft (the Machine) (descriptive).
            3. Ground organization at airports on three continents. (descriptive documentary).
            4. A big Airport (London): Airmail, People, Freight.
            5. Interlude: romantic, poetic visuals of aerial impressions. A new world of being in and above the clouds.
            6. The actual Air-Routes. Trans-Asia. Trans-Africa. Linking the City to the Desert, the Old to the New, and the Present to the Future.
            7. Home. The return of the symbolic aircraft at dusk in England. Symphony of floodlit welcome at airport. Perhaps a fantasy of crowds as the aeroplane draws up on the tarmac having flown 14,000 miles and arriving dead on time.

Beddington, bless him, grasped my aim from this highfalutin' piece of work and his blessing was given to go ahead. He must have felt as Tallents did when Grierson started off to shoot *Drifters*, except that the risks were greater. Grierson at least knew the sea from his minesweeper days; I had never been in an aeroplane before. But we had one thing in common. Neither Grierson nor I knew one lens from another. He had the North Sea to dramatize; I had some 35,000 miles of unknown air-routes.

Only one thing Beddington insisted on. There must be in the film no direct reference to Shell, although they were footing the bill. If an air-stocking at some God-forsaken air-strip had on it the name SHELL, then I couldn't help but film it. But he emphasized that in no way at all was it to be considered a piece of advertisement. It was a deep gesture to be made in the early 1930s and it was to have its successors as, when the Orient Line sponsored *Shipyard*, there was to be no mention that the S.S. *Orion* was an Orient Line ship. This was public relations at its best and most imaginative.

Problems began almost at once. At the EMB Film Unit, Elton had just made his *Aero-Engine* picture with, in the last reel, some remarkable aerial photography by George Noble.

72

Making Contact (*1932–33*)

Noble would be ideal for *Contact*. He agreed to take on the assignment and up till within a few days of our time for departure was keen to go. He had all innoculations done and passport ready. Then he abruptly said that he had been 'talked into staying at the EMB'. I have often, I must confess, wondered if that was sabotage. It was not George Noble's own choice; of that I am sure. The fact remained that, with less than 48 hours to go, I was without a cameraman. The flight could not be postponed. I knew of no other cameramen who were free and had to rely on one suggested by Bruce Woolfe at the studio. Horace Wheddon was a man of about 40, who came to see me wearing a bowler hat, all honey and smiles. I saw some of his exterior filming in Palestine, which was of very good quality. He could not have been a worse choice for this assignment. The bowler hat should have warned me.

Two weeks' shooting had already been done in England at Coventry of aircraft designing and construction, of the ground organization at Croydon Airport, of planes arriving and departing and so forth. For this a BIF staff-cameraman, Jack Parker, did admirable work, but he was too valuable to the studio for him to come with me. For my equipment, about which I knew little, the studio provided me with an old hand-turned Debrie with a tripod which was only turned by twisting handles. Subsequently, it was found that the spindle in the head was broken before we left. They also provided me with a very old Newman-Sinclair camera used by Cherry Kearton in ancient days for his animal films. This had no tripod and only one 35 mm lens. Thus we had two cameras almost incapable of any camera movement, something I did not realize until too late. Some years later, when George Pocknall, who was in charge of the camera department at the studio which equipped me, came to do some filming for me, he confessed that he had had instructions from Bruce Woolfe not to 'take any kind of trouble over what equipment was supplied to Rotha'. In other words, Shell and I were given the left-overs of the camera department; it was something I did not forgive Bruce Woolfe for many years. But then, he was interested only in his Company's 10 per cent cut on the contract price, not in what kind of a picture emerged. That was, and still is, the film business.

73

Making Contact (*1932–33*)

For aerial filming, no outside mounting of a camera was permitted on any aircraft. Insurance companies prohibited it. Any aerial shots would therefore have to be made through a very small sliding window in the Captain's cockpit. 30,000 ft of film stock was allocated for the journey, most of it having been sent ahead to await our arrival at stops along the route. In most cases, when we arrived, I found that it had not been cleared through customs by the local airport officials because they had had no orders from London to do so. Over and over again, it came to light that no organization at all had been pre-arranged from London before our flight. We might as well have been ordinary passengers travelling as amateurs with an 8 mm home-movie camera. Everything organized by the Shell people, such as local transport, worked efficiently all through. Almost everything that fell to Imperial Airways in London was a failure. Today I keep as a souvenir a bill for tea at a hotel in Khartoum which was not allowed for in our schedule; it pursued me from address to address for many years.

As film was exposed by us, it was to be sent back by air to London for laboratory processing. Bruce Woolfe was then to screen it and send me a report by cable as to its photographic quality. In my three months away from England, he sent me only one cable some half way through the 35,000-mile journey and that was to tell me that the Newman-Sinclair camera, which I had used a lot because of its portability, was giving gate-trouble which produced a jitter on the screen that could not be corrected. The camera had not been adjusted before leaving to take the kind of stock we were using. Thus most of the film taken on that camera was useless.

Somewhere along the way, however, Beddington did send me a letter in which he wrote that Bruce Woolfe had screened for him some of my material and that he had never seen such 'wonderful aerial camerawork'. This at least was some encouragement.

The unit of three (my then wife came with us and was of great help note-taking and otherwise) left London on 5 November 1932, to fly some 35,000 miles in $3\frac{1}{2}$ months, with no chance to break the journey except at prescribed stops as per ticket book. None of us had ever been in an aeroplane before. We

74

flew from Croydon to Paris, by train to Brindisi because the Italians would not permit Imperial Airways to fly over their territory, by flying-boat to Lake Tiberias in Palestine, by Heracles-type biplane to Baghdad, to Sharjah on the Persian Gulf for a night-stop in the desert, and so to Karachi which was as far as the air-route went in those days. Then back the same way, but at Tiberias we missed the change-over plane to Cairo. At the time only a weekly service operated so we had an enforced wait for a week and even then we had to get to Cairo by train. Money was very short, so we travelled third class, which was an experience. From Cairo down Africa – the Sudan, Uganda, Nyasaland, Rhodesia to Cape Town. After Christmas, back up the same route but with stop-overs for filming at Kampala and Assiut of a week each, and thence to Athens. Two hundred and forty flying hours in $12\frac{1}{2}$ weeks.

Troubles with Horace Wheddon began early. Had I been surer of myself or had more money at my disposal, I should have changed the whole schedule, sent him back to England and waited for a substitute cameraman. But this was impossible; Imperial Airways had been adamant before I left England that in no circumstances was I to diverge from the agreed flight schedule. Near Baghdad Wheddon point blank refused to take a shot because I wanted the camera slightly tilted. He finally agreed, but only if I gave him a letter absolving him from any responsibility, which I did with pleasure. I sat up most of that night typing out dozens of such letters for future use. Next he spent his time at nights in hotel bars telling his newly-found friends that I was a wealthy amateur and that he, Wheddon, was really making the film. This stopped when I refused to honour his bar bills. Then I found that he would not shake hands or share the same table with anyone not his own colour. Finally he fell ill with phlebitis on the return trip up Africa and I parted with him in Egypt. A substitute cameraman, Frank Goodliffe, was sent out to meet me in Athens. He proved as cooperative as Wheddon had proved difficult. Before leaving Wheddon in Assiut, I made him give me some rudimentary lessons in using the Newman-Sinclair; I was determined not to lose the opportunities of filming between Egypt and Greece. More by luck than skill, my footage was usable.

Making Contact (*1932–33*)

A detailed diary was kept during the three months and many letters written. The diary entries were a day-to-day reaction to people and places, especially problems of production on a hazardous series of locations with very inadequate equipment; there were no hand-held cameras available then. My camera equipment weighed around 125 lbs. One thing does come clear from reading the diaries today and that is the dislike I formed for most of the white people with whom contact was made in Rhodesia and South Africa. A few exceptions were met: David Schrire, with whom a long friendship was begun and whose letters are quoted in this book; Volodya Meyerowitz, a Russian-born sculptor and brilliant still-photographer, working in Cape Town and who committed suicide so tragically in London; and a game-warden or two in Kenya and Uganda whose names I do not recall.

But some extracts between 5 November 1932 and 1 February 1933 can speak for themselves.

Over the Persian Gulf

A strange place from which to write a letter, just over 3,000 ft above the Persian Gulf and the plane batting along at 95 mph. Below are pearl-fishers, said to be slaves of the King of Muscat, with rows of nets. On the other side of the cabin is a Quetta colonel, in shorts and with a monocle. 'Way back in the 80s, my lad.' So far have only used the Newman camera from the plane. Have seen some lovely things but am scared to shoot too much from the air because the vibration is so great. Castelrosso was an enchanting small, brightly-painted harbour nestling under a mountain on the route between Athens and Galilee. The Governor tried to confiscate our camera and refused permission to film. As evidence of his authority he showed us a volume which dealt with the taking of daguerreotypes. Remarkable how this hostility has been met all the time so far. No one welcomes a film camera. Permission to shoot in Athens on the return journey is going to take almost a month to obtain.

Baghdad was disappointing – a dirty, dusty city with no magic or charm, only stench. Another disappointment was the desert fort at Rutbah Wells, quite modern and without interest. On the other hand, last night was spent under canvas in a barbed-wire compound outside Sharjah, a small town on the Musseldam Peninsula. We met the sheikh, a powerful man, who until recently was bitter against the British. Now he is more tolerant and received us with coffee and sweetmeats. On either side his falconers, some superb white horses, and a lot of white baby camels. With the aid of several interpreters, we made it clear that we wanted to shoot film next week on the return journey and he regally gave permission provided that he was photographed first.

Karachi

Arriving here had one spot of excitement. A key shot in the film is to be of an aircraft taking off from an overseas airport. But how to do this when there is only one plane and you are in it? A cooperative pilot (they all are so far) suggested that he made a landing in the usual way, dropped me and camera off (Wheddon refused to do this), then he would take off again so that it could be filmed. All went well. I lay in the grass at the perimeter of the airfield, camera on ground, no tripod. I got the shot okay and walked leisurely across the grass to the airport buildings. I was met by an excited group of officials. Hadn't I been warned that the airfield was alive with snakes? I saw no snake.

Wheddon more than difficult again. Typically British in that he dislikes any but the most conventional camerawork. Essentially of the picture postcard school. The most disheartening thing is the number of marvellous shots one sees but cannot get. Whether you haven't got permission to film, or the sun is in the wrong place, or you haven't the time. When a plane only stops at a place for ten minutes to refuel, there's no time to think of your script or your eventual editing. It's really newsreel work. The allocation of film stock is difficult. You shoot some cloud shots, say, between Galilee and Baghdad and later see something much better but you have no film stock left. It is not possible to carry much stock with us because of its weight and the customs duty to pay from country to country. Imperial Airways in London could have done so much to help in advance.

Sharjah

The guard which the Sheikh has ordered to surround the camp and the plane has been told that if anything is stolen or anything should happen to any of the passengers, then the eyes of the whole guard will be put out. Nothing happened.

Shaibah (Basra)

Have stopped for the night at a RAF aerodrome. The bar full of airforce types jokingly telling each other how they 'bombed up' a village that afternoon. I asked them why. I was told, 'Just to let them know we're here, old boy.'

One of the big difficulties of this task is that obviously during the day the aircraft is in the air and we are in it. We start at dawn and land at sunset. There is no real chance to film anything on the ground.

Basra–Baghdad

Very early 3.0 am start. Along rows of flares. Dawn did not break until we were near Baghdad. From the air it is clear to see the shifting course of the river and the foundations of old buildings. Wonderful luxurious banks of the Tigris. In the plane it is easy to throw oneself back into the past.

A filthy dirty hotel. Drove in a car to try and get some shots of the gaudy mosque at Khazimain. Pursued in the bazaars by mobs. Smells and dirt and heat. A knife fight in the bazaar. But typical of this city, one of the first things seen was a shoe-shop wholly furnished with modern steel fittings as if in Regent Street or Fifth Avenue. On the way back shot the tomb of Haroun-el-Raschid's wife – shades of Leni's *Waxworks*. More argument with Wheddon over camera set-ups. Everything here is decaying. Deep impression of past glories but today they all look degenerate.

Spent a day out in the desert at the splendid Arch of Ctesiphon. A great span of bricks rising up out of the sand. Shot it from all angles with an inch lens. Next day went by interminable dusty road to Babylon. Donkeys looking like haystacks, camels, oxen and absurd goats. Stopped on way to take some shots of windblown sand. May find better examples later but that is one of the problems, you do not know if you will find better later on. Unlike Baghdad, Babylon was far from a disappointment. I had not expected it to be so large or in such a fine state of preservation. Wandered all over the ruins and got some good material of broken columns, animal bas-reliefs on the Ishtar Gate and the famous Lion. Had what could be a good idea when I saw some of masonry crumble and fall of its own accord. In all shots thereafter I had our guide kick dust and stones down, he himself being out of picture of course. Perhaps in this way I can get the effect of the past crumbling before the future. The present being, of course, the airplane. Shot some stuff in nearby village of Kuwairish of palm trees and so on. Wheddon grunbling because I inevitably seem to select the local public lavatory as my favourite place to set up the camera. Nicknames the driver's boy Peter; he would make an excellent camera assistant back home. He soon got to know one lens from another. Found a two-domed mosque covered with blue tiles. The sun was going rapidly and the camera jammed. Wheddon contrived to join the film with one of my wife's hairpins but I doubt if the stuff will be usable.

Making Contact (*1932–33*)

Still Baghdad. Discouraging and hopeless day trying to get shots in the bazaars. The material is admirable: every available type of person, stalls and produce. Rich, gorgeous coloured fruit, silks and fabrics, metal workers, and a gallery of types – Arabs, Jews, Persians, Baghdadi, and a host of local tribes. But the moment we produce a camera a crowd of hundreds collects, swarming like flies around us, jeering, laughing, mocking, pushing, touching – anything to stop us filming. My God, to have a hidden camera! We tried on both sides of the Tigris but impossible. Wheddon slow and indifferent as to results. Iraqui policemen did their best to help. Then we saw a cockfight which added to my dislike of this foul place.

Saw a minute but attractive mosque. No decoration about it; plain white adobe dome and walls against a dark blue sky. So simple to contrast with all the gaudy mosques. But Wheddon like the bloody fool he is runs out of film after one shot! Back to the hotel to reload camera and of course I see a dozen things I want to shoot. We leave for Tiberias tomorrow morning. Glad to leave this godamned place where no one does anything except hang around for money. The dirty foul-smelling hotel bill far too high and everyone hanging around for tips. Hell take them all! You can have Baghdad!

Baghdad–Tiberias

On a small, three-engined plane, an Avro 10, heading for Rutbah Wells. The normal Imperial Airways service could not carry us. Passed three RAF machines patrolling the desert. Watched the shadow of our plane on the sand below until my eyes ached. After Rutbah, we struck the mountainous country in Jordan. The small plane could not fly very high and thus avoid the airpockets. I was very sick and just hated flying and airplanes more than anything else in the world, not a good mood for someone making a film about the wonder of air travel. Stood in a thimble-size lavatory and was sick and sick and sick. Some compensation to find that the pilot of the little plane was being sick himself.

Learned at Simakh, the airport at the South end of the Sea of Galilee, that they had had strong storms. Saw the wreck of a Hannibal class aircraft minus wings, which had been blown to pieces on the ground. Imperial Airways had been smart enough to have its name and their name obliterated before we arrived in case we might film it. Flying-boat from Athens now 48 hours late due to weather, so no film stock for us. It will not arrive until the end of the week so we must hang around waiting to shoot. From the bedroom balcony one can see half of Tiberias. It looks clean and enchanting in the warm afternoon sunlight, the sea indigo, the houses pink and yellow. At last cleanliness and no smell. What a contrast with Baghdad!

A friendly and efficient guide called Nichole, born and bred in Tiberias. Have found much to shoot when the stock comes. And always the indigo sea in the background. Ploughing with oxen and donkeys, superb cypresses, fig trees, cacti, all green and luxuriant when compared with the barrenness of what we left in the East. The lateness of the film stock arriving will cut our schedule here, just when there is so much to shoot. Admired the craftsmanship of a man making wooden ploughs with the simplest of tools.

Everything here looks very beautiful but now I have seen something of the cruelty that lies beneath the surface. How can they be so diabolically cruel to their animals? Chickens tied together with wire, donkeys being worked covered in sores, and while we were shooting at a mosque a small boy was playing with a decapitated sparrow. Their whole aim in life seems to be cruelty amid this lovely environment of graceful hills, whispering eucalyptus trees and white and blue walled houses.

Away early down to Samakh to shoot the old man making wooden ploughs. Pin broke in the Debrie camera. How Flaherty would have liked the craftsmanship of this ploughmaker. His father and grandfather made ploughs and he hopes his two sons will also make ploughs.

He uses only two or three tools – a thing like a chopper, a drill worked like a violin bow and a saw.

Went to the little seaport town of Acca, of Crusades memories. Wonderful stretch of golden sand with fishermen dragging in their nets. Leave Tiberias tomorrow for Cairo. By train. No aeroplane available. Have just about got enough money for three third-class tickets. Could have done much more here if there had been time.

Cairo

At El Kantara on the Suez Canal they demanded £300 deposit on each camera. As I did not have this sort of money, they impounded the cameras, which we can claim in Cairo. To the latter, again by train. None of this need have happened if Imperial Airways had not let us down. At some places even the ground staff had not been told of our coming and this is supposed to be a film to publicize air travel! Cable here from the Cape Town Film Society welcoming me to Africa, which was nice of them.

Cairo has been a dead loss to the film. Took two days to clear the equipment through customs and then we got fined, I've forgotten how many hundred piastres, for not declaring a camelhair brush bought at

Making Contact (*1932–33*)

Woolworths for a shilling. It is an offence to import camelhair into Egypt. Then the (English) bank refused to honour my cheque because I could not prove who I was! My passport was insufficient. Wasted a whole day trying to get a statement out of British consular official that I was me when he did not know me from Adam. By then the bank was closed. Shall just have time on Monday morning to get money needed for the flight down Africa. I did get a few dreary shots of the Sphinx and the Pyramids, the most overrated things in the world. Am depressed and despondent about the whole film.

Juba–Nairobi

Again a dawn start. Everyone getting tired of it all. One tries hard to sleep in the plane but the iron-frame chairs which some designer thought up are as hard as hell and the so-called headrest projects forward instead of back. Had breakfast at Kampala in Uganda. Should be wonderful stuff to shoot on the return. Rich foliage, giant trees, masses of brilliantly coloured flowers. The so-called *Trader Horn* country because MGM shot their film around here. Some entertaining stories about Van Dyke (who directed the picture) from a Captain Drysdale who arranged transport for the huge MGM unit. The extravagance of it all; calling for 200 pygmies at one hour's notice. After all I wrote about *Trader Horn* in my book,[1] this is amusing. This Drysdale, a guide and a hunter, has arranged a trip for us to the Murchison Falls on our return. Here is real enthusiastic cooperation but nothing to do with Imperial Airways. Then away along the edge of the lake low down over tropical forest with crocodiles basking in the sun. At last things look interesting. At Kisumu changed into a land machine and had a very bumpy flight to Nairobi. Seems odd being here after John Amery's *Jungle Skies*! Too late to film, but we are here for a week.

Next morning arranging transport with the Shell people and seeing the game-warden of the Masai Game Reserve to get permission to film. He lives in a kind of bungalow in a grove of lemon gums and curved cactus. He was like Haggard's Allan Quatermain, in green corduroy shooting-jacket and huge padded pith helmet. A man smelling of rifles and dead animals and campfires. Very courteous and will fix anything we like but not to carry guns, which we do not wish to do anyway. Got some good stuff in the afternoon – lovely clouded sky and beautiful foliage, Guatemala cypress, lemon gums and paw-paw.

Away in the early morning by car into the Masai Game Reserve.

[1] *Celluloid: The Film Today*, pp. 196–211.

Over the Ngong Hills and down along a dirt road on to a seemingly huge plain on which from high up could be seen groups of game – giraffe, gazelle and buck. Got some shots of vultures and carcases of cows. Everything very dry near a Masai bomba; sheep dying of hunger. To film them the Masai demanded money, even here so far from anywhere. They demanded a shilling for each sheep. Wonderful tree forms again – candelabras and thorn bushes. Superb cloud effects on way back but Wheddon too slow to get out camera.

On Sunday headed for the Rift Valley and the Escarpment and beyond to Lake Naivasha. Flamingoes, wildebeeste, impala, Grant and Thompson's gazelle and the world's most wonderful small creature – the dikdik. Back to Nairobi in the moonlight.

Spent all Monday at the airport getting shots of aircraft being refuelled. Burnt my left arm on an outside exhaust pipe of a Shell Moth. Dislike the hotel in Nairobi with its strict colour bar. But it suits Wheddon. Next day up the Fort Hall Road. Shots of sisal growing. On to Thika for the waterfall and also to Fourteen Falls. On way back stopped at another coffee shamba owned by a Dane and saw process through. They work the native boys hard – 6 am to 6 pm and no break for meals.

Raining all next day. Received first cable from Bruce Woolfe. Gate-trouble with the Newman camera. Very upsetting because so much footage has been shot on it. Impossible to repair here. All that can be done is to use the clumsy old Debrie and hope that the Newman can be repaired when we reach Cape Town. Leaving tomorrow.

Still in Nairobi. Typical Imperial Aiways day. Hanging around the dreary airport (if so it can be called) because the plane won't start. Loading and then unloading all the baggage. Back to the hotel for lunch. Back to the airport. Plane still won't fly. Back to the hotel again. Why the hell didn't they send for a machine from Kisumu where we know there is a relief?

In the hotel found the following informative Japanese leaflet.

'At the rise of the hand of a policeman, stop rapidly. Do not pass him or otherwise disrespect him. When a passenger of the foot hoves into sight, tootle the horn-trumpet melodiously at first. If he still obstacles your way, tootle him with vigour and express with the word of the mouth the warning, Hi! Hi!

'Beware of the wandering horse that he shall not take fright as you pass him. Do not exploit the exhaust-box at him. Go soothingly by.

'Give space to the festive dog that makes sport in the roadway. Avoid entanglement of dog with your wheel-spokes.

'Go smoothingly on the grease mud as there lies the skid demon. Press the brake of the foot as you role [*sic*] around the corners to save the collapse and timing.'

Mpika–Johannesburg

This has been the worst flying day of all from 3 am this morning until touchdown at 7.45 pm at Germiston, stopping at Broken Hill, Salisbury, Bulawayo and Pietersburg. Far too much to fly in one day in a small aircraft like this and all for Imperial Airways prestige to say that the mail arrives on time. While changing planes at Broken Hill my still-camera was lost. Impossible to see anything of Jo'burg, far too tired.

Johannesbury–Touew's River

5 am start after usual trouble of overloading. The Big Hole of Kimberley looks very big from the air. Engine trouble all the afternoon. Landed here, 100 miles from Cape Town, and the passengers all revolted against going on in the dark. Too rough. Pilot gave in, so we stay night. This in spite of the fact that we have on board a newsreel of the Stribling-MacQuorcadale fight and the usual mails. Notice in cabin of plane: 'SAFETY CHAINS FOR LADIES TRAVELLING ALONE.'

(Note: Of the week in Cape Town little need be recorded. My diary's main entries reveal my disgust at the European behaviour to the African. We had Christmas there and more drunkenness among white people I have never seen. My wife was warned not to sit in the sun in case she got sunburnt and might be mistaken for a native. She said 'That would be nice.' Tried to film in the notorious District Six area but the police stopped it. The city and surrounding country are beautiful, but it is a keg of dynamite waiting for the match. The Shell people gave a party and were upset that I hadn't got a dinner-jacket with me. Hell, flying some 35,000 miles with one suitcase!)

Cape Town–Johannesburg

By train; Imperial Airways could not carry us. It is more comfortable at least. Rolling veldt until the first white slagheaps of the Rand Valley. A 35-year-old city build on gold. Pretentious and lacking in any kind of good taste. A gimcrack city. Gold runs through the whole place and yet all talk is of the crisis whether to come off the gold standard or not! Next day at the Crown mine filming. They work the Africans hard. We watched them coming up in cages after an $8\frac{1}{2}$ hour shift. Each with a brass bangle bearing his number. They live in a compound (which we were not allowed to visit) and are shown old Hollywood westerns once a week as a treat. Many of the miners were bleeding and bruised as they came up blinking into the sunlight. They looked utterly exhausted. The Manager was with us the whole time and very strict as to what we filmed. Shall not be sorry to leave this hell-hole behind tomorrow. From my hotel window all I can see are the signs flashing out FORD, SHELL, DODGE, CASTLE BEERS, HAIG. The whole place is shoddy.

(Note: the journey north was uninteresting until after leaving Dodoma we had a crash landing)

Kigwe

It would seem that this is the first time the pilot has flown over this part of the route, so he lost his way and ran out of petrol. Made a beautiful landing in the thorn trees near a small railway station with a single-track line that goes God knows where. One train goes once a week and that was yesterday. But at least there is a telephone and a very excited African in charge. This is obviously the great moment in his life, a crashed aeroplane. Against all orders from Imperial Airways before leaving England, I filmed the landing in the thorn bushes from the cockpit window. Both wings and engines were ripped off, leaving the fuselage suspended in the trees. It was a very skilful landing. No one hurt, no fire. Just a long wait in the sun until a relief train can be sent in heaven knows how many hours' time. The only food and drink are what was on the plane. A fat American woman has a box of peaches she had brought with her. She does not offer to share them out. I persuade Wheddon to take some shots I wanted but he is reluctant, so 'shaken by the crash'. Eventually in the early evening the train shows up, an engine and one carriage. Someone had thoughtfully stocked it with food and bottles of beer. Made Dodoma just after nightfall. New Year's Eve. We shack up in a dreary little 'hotel' run by a Greek. Some Englishmen, locals I assume, in their moth-eaten dinner-jackets, are trying to start a party. Charles Nichols, a young American who is a passenger on the plane, and I do our best to break up the party without success. The Englishmen just look at us fishlike. So Nichols and I end up the evening driving the train up and down the line with its searchlight full on. Kid stuff but it breaks the monotony.

Dodoma–Nairobi

A relief plane sent down from Nairobi but with no seats in it because it was assumed that the ones in the crashed plane could be transferred. They were wrong. So they put into the relief plane some dining-room chairs which obviously slide all over the place. Sitting on the floor of the plane is preferable. Flew very low over bush country. The relief Captain has a hangover. After all it was New Year's Eve last night. A memorable crossing of the Escarpment down into Moshi. Kilimanjaro covered in cloud. Almost thought we would hit the hills. Then over the Athie Plains, flying very low over scattering game – zebra, giraffe and buck – should be good film if Wheddon has done his job well. The sun casting long shadows over the plain. Nairobi again and its usual crowd of bar-loafers. They will make Wheddon happy. Now he *has* a story to tell. The crash in the bush!

Nairobi–Kampala

The plane heavily overloaded so we must take a Wilson Airways Moth as far as Kisumu. More like real flying in a small aircraft. Then into the flying-boat and over the lake to Kampala. We are a day late owing to the forced landing. Drysdale, as promised, has everything laid on. We go straight to the Murchison Falls. Hurried loading of the cameras in hotel and then a 168-mile car ride through the night to Buiaba. Several leopards in the car headlights. Transferred on board the S.S. *Livingstone*, like a small tug, and away up the choppy lake.

Kampala–Murchison Falls

After a restless night because of the rolling boat, woke to see the banks of the Nile with papyrus, and the tug steaming slowly up the middle of the Nile. All morning we sat on deck with cameras ready and got what I hope will be good shots of crocodiles and hippos. Many wonderful strange birds and buck on the river banks. The place is teaming with game, but then it is rightly a game reserve. After the many almost unbelievable stories of the *Trader Horn* unit, with all its expensive equipment and big-time team of technicians, I hope to do better with my two unreliable cameras and a reluctant cameraman. Spotted fine bull elephant meandering around the shore. We put off in a small whale boat to stalk it. The river banks here are made up of ribs of hilly bush and shallow but thickly wooded valleys. So long as we stick to the ribs we shall be out of the elephant's way but can get close to him. Drysdale, Wheddon (with Newman camera), two native boys and myself, in single file climb one of the ribs of hill. The thorn bushes are alive with spikes and one must go carefully. We are very near the elephant now. He is peacefully eating leaves off a tree. Suddenly from just in front of us there is a roar which I shall never forget.

85

We saw a magnificent lion about ten yards away. Drysdale shouted, 'Run like hell!' We did. Wheddon promptly dropped the camera. Lion or no lion, I picked it up. Down that hill, which had taken so long to climb, we pelted irrespective of the thorn bushes. The lion did not follow us. It was Drysdale's theory that it was guarding its cubs. We reached the whale boat and were on board the tug in a matter of minutes. Drysdale insisted we were washed down with iodine, which was more painful than the thorn scratches. Poor Wheddon was so scared, I almost felt sorry for him and then remembered how he threw away the camera. Later we continued on our way towards the foot of the Falls. That night I slept with a lion's roar in my ears; it must have been MGM's which Van Dyke had left behind. Crocodiles and hippos bump against the side of the tug all night.

Early next morning, after a breakfast of fried bacon and pineapple, we put off in the whale boat for the foot of the Falls. The tropical vegetation and clouds are magnificent. We put ashore in a little bay since known as the *Trader Horn* crocodile pool. Drysdale remembers that the MGM unit were very cruel to the animals in order to 'get a performance' out of them. Here Wheddon made an announcement. He was not going to land without adequate armed protection. Drysdale, who had by now summed up the situation, quietly said, 'All right, Mr Wheddon, you sit in the sun all day. It will be very hot, I will leave one boy with you to guard you.' There were, of course, no firearms with the party. So I had Wheddon set the exposure on the Newman camera for me and Drysdale, my wife and I, with two boys, set off up the narrow path that led up to the top of the Falls. It was rather like being on Hampstead Heath except for the foliage. At the head of the Falls the drama was fantastic. The Nile tears and twists itself through a gorge about 20 ft wide to cascade down into the main river. Deafening and awe-inspiring. I shot a 200 ft magazine of film, all I had with me. Then we retraced our way down the path.

About three hundred yards from the shore where the whale boat was moored, in the middle of the track, was a big elephant spoor. It had not been there when we climbed the track a few hours before. Then we saw him, the same bull as the the previous day, again peacefully eating at a tree. Drysdale said, 'We'd better wait for a while. He'll make off soon'. The boys lit a fire so that the smoke would drift in the elephant's direction. We sat under a tree. My wife said, 'It's rather like waiting for a No. 53 bus.' She then looked up into the tree and above us was coiled a big snake. It was not moving. By then the elephant had ambled away and we made the whale boat safely. Wheddon was sitting in his shirt sleeves, a bottle of whisky in one hand. I gave him the camera. He calmly told me that the exposure was wrong and that I must have altered it. So all that possibly magnificent material of the Falls is wasted. I would swear for ever that the lens stop had been deliberately set wrong.

Exquisite quietness as the boat sailed along the Nile in the half-light, forest fires burning on the banks. Drysdale talked about his dream project of making a film about the River Nile, tracing it from its source in the Mountains of the Moon to the moment when it meets the Mediterranean. I suggest that it is called *The River of Life*.

(Note: Back in England later, I tried for several years to get this project set-up. I drew up an outline, with maps and detailed notes, and a costing based on Drysdale's estimates. No British company would hear of it.)

Kampala

Wheddon in local bar tonight, I am told, trying to get a letter stating that he has been in dangerous territory without proper protection.

Regret leaving Uganda, a country I should like to come back to, with a proper cameraman and more time. The colour is superb.

(Note: The air journey North was without event, until Assuan. The Governor at Wadi-Halfa had laid on a small party for us but when he heard that I had no dinner-jacket, the party was called off.)

Assouan

Several wasted days here in thick mist. The Shell man a very intelligent Egyptian most interested in cinema. Wheddon goes sick, acting theatrically as if drunk. Then some sun so we go, minus Wheddon, out into the desert on camels. If my exposure and focus are right, it could be good stuff. Wish now that I had had some elementary training in using a camera before leaving England, but never foresaw a cameraman like Horace Wheddon. Called a doctor for him. He must stay in bed for several weeks. I cable Bruce Woolfe to send me another cameraman but the earliest he can meet up with us is at Athens. That means that between here and there if there is any shooting to do, I must do it. Had a try at the great Assouan Dam today. Fine material if only my work is okay. At the airfield the incoming plane brought mail from England. An invitation to Eric Knight's wedding in Philadelphia.

Athens

Little of any event took place on the way back to England. Frank Goodliffe, a good and cooperative cameraman, met us in Athens.

Making Contact (*1932–33*)

Much time lost in getting permits to film on the Acropolis, permits that Imperial Airways had been asked to obtain two months ago. When we did get them, in a method reminiscent of Réné Clair, we were dogged by bad weather. Snow in Athens! The last thing I expected. In one week only two hours of sun.

Piraeus–Brindisi

So, 30,000 ft of film stock. 24,000 miles. 240 flying hours. 3 months' journey. Wish it had taken twice as long, had three times the amount of film stock, had an intelligent cooperative cameraman and that the whole journey had been far better planned in advance by Imperial Airways in the London head-office.

To all intents and purposes, my diaries and letters end there· If the above extracts are overlong, they are used to show some of the problems of the early documentary film-makers. But the difficulties helped in one way. When in 1936 Alexander Shaw, Ralph Keene, John Taylor and George Noble set off from England to Australia to make several films for Imperial Airways, I made it my business to see that their organization was far more fully prepared and that they got proper producership from London while they were away. Their negative came back to England quickly, I screened a print in London at once and sent detailed cables the same day as to its quality, and actual frame-clips from the shots the next day. They were hardly out of touch with me for more than two weeks at a time even when in the Dutch East Indies and Australia. It was rather different from the service provided by Bruce Woolfe and his British Instructional Films in 1932–33.

On returning to England, a screening of all the footage was the first step. It revealed that about one quarter of what I had shot was unusable as a result of the camera fault, for which the staff at the studio was wholly responsible. But it must be said that the actual photographic quality of Horace Wheddon's work was excellent. That is only fair to say. Now there was to come the editing of what film was usable down to the agreed final length of 4 reels, about 45 minutes of screen time. Here I quote from my letters to Eric Knight, in America.

Making Contact (1932–33)

This studio is like a morgue; no films of any size have been made here since Asquith's *Tell England* three years ago. But one good thing; as it is not British Instructional's film, I am left wholly to myself. No interference, but no assistance either. I am doing every foot of my own cutting, joining and all that. It brings me down to the guts of things. It is only by editing material that you have shot yourself that you realize your mistakes. All the same, I know that if I had had proper equipment overseas, I would have shot it differently. There would have been, for one thing, a great deal more camera movement. I know that I shan't produce a masterpiece but hope to make a workmanlike picture that may lead to more films to make.

I can already see that the film will suffer by being too static for two reasons. First, my training at the Slade as a painter did not influence me to appreciate the importance of movement. Second, the single tripod I had with me allowed for no kind of real camera movement; every shot had to be conceived statically. No amount of skilful editing can achieve movement on the screen if the movement is not there already in the shot.

I've a campbed installed in the cutting-room so that I can live with the film.

10 *April* 1933

Contact grows apace. But very slowly. Sometimes I take what must seem like a ridiculous length of time about a sequence of shots when most technicians would see the way to cut it at once. But I have to sit and think it out for myself. You must remember that, apart from the little Poster films at the EMB, this is the first film I have edited and it's got to run four reels. People at the studio constantly ask, 'When will your picture be ready?', to which I can only reply, 'There are sixteen frames to a foot of film, and my film will be 4,000 ft long. Every foot of film is worth thinking about for ten minutes. Work it out for yourself.' And they walk away thinking I am mad. Happily Beddington at Shell is content to be patient and tells me to take my time. But as I am being paid a single fee for the whole job, it makes living difficult.

19 *April* 1933

Have just finished a rough-cut of the first three reels of the picture. I wonder if I have cut it too fast? It's all very well to cut fast for your friends who know film, but will the ordinary public follow it? I've just edited an impression of an Eastern town – the muck and filth and cruelty contrasted with the gilded mosques and lovely foliage of the trees. Just any mid-Eastern town unnamed. Then later will come a similar kind of town in Africa. Over each flies the airliner disturbing man and beast as they watch it travel overhead. But the machine itself is not shown; we hear only the increasing and then decreasing sound of its engines.

Editing was finished by the end of April. Now came the sound track. I decided to have no spoken commentary but where absolutely necessary a minimum of sub-titles, very short ones. Clarence Raybould, a conductor working at the BBC but also a composer, was brought in to write an original music score but in the time available (Bruce Woolfe was urging me to get finished) he only wrote music for the first reel. For the other 3 reels he adapted music from other sources, Mozart, Rossini and Tchaikovsky. For reasons of economy, the whole 45 minutes of music had to be recorded in one day. It was put on Tobis-Klangfilm, a German system.

10 *May* 1933

To all intents the film is finished. The negative is now being cut. There is little I can do but wait. Now I realize that the film should have been shot in colour but where would the extra cost have come from? There is talk that the film may be given a premiere at a so-called gala performance which our patriotic Film Trade is giving to the delegates from God knows how many countries soon about to meet in London for the World Economic Conference. Before sending the picture for negative cutting, I showed it to Beddington and with his agreement asked Grierson too. They were both kind about it, especially Beddington. What the hell! I've done a job in rough conditions and I haven't the slightest idea of what I shall do next.

That was the first time that Beddington met Grierson and like so many others came under his spell of persuasive talk. (Only one man in the film industry could talk more persuasively than Grierson – Alexander Korda, but then he was a Hungarian.) From that meeting over *Contact* there later came a request to Grierson to write a report for the Shell Company as to how it could use films in the widest sense, and eventually from the report came the setting-up of the Shell Film Unit. I had the impression that Grierson came rather to deprecate Beddington for his concern with aesthetics, for at that time the mere mention of the word was anathema to Grierson.

July 1933

The film still has not had its first showing. The gala performance I wrote about earlier is now fixed for one night next week, after a slap-up dinner at the Dorchester Hotel. The audience, we are told, will include the Prince of Wales, all the overseas delegates at the Conference who want to attend, and the foreign and British Press. Aw, hell take them all, say I.

16 *July* 1933

The picture has had its stuffed-shirt showing to an audience of ministers and their wives, economists and their wives, and a herd of newspapermen, the lot filled up with liquor and food. In name the performance was put on by the Film Industry as a whole, but in fact Gaumont-British muscled in for themselves. The Ostrer Brothers saw a fine opportunity for publicity. The bloody Prime Minister and sundry members of the Cabinet were also there. At the dinner, one of the Ostrer Brothers rose and welcomed the guests in the name not of the British Film Industry as was expected but of Gaumont-British. Their rival studio company, British International Pictures, looked pretty sick. After the stuffing and drinking, everyone adjourned to the New Victoria Cinema, London's newest and most garish theatre, where the stage was set with the flags of all the nations except Germany and the USSR.

The programme began with the usual newsreel (Gaumont-British), went on to a poor travelogue of Windsor Castle (produced by C. A. Lejeune's husband now at GB in charge of the Gainsborough Miniatures series of shorts) and then to an extract from a Movietone reel of the Derby and Trooping the Colour. By now the well-fed, cigar-smoking audience was ripe for a musical or some such entertainment. Instead they got *Contact*.

They watched in silence. At the end of the first reel, after we have seen the building of the aircraft accompanied by Raybould's fugue, they gave it a hand. Half a reel later, they gave it a bigger hand. About 300 ft from the end, when the airliner comes in to land in the dusk, they began applauding again and kept it up until the end.

After the interval, Gaumont-British presented their feature, a comedy. It was a complete flop. As it showed, the audience dribbled up to the foyer to drink GB's champagne. Everyone said what a wonderful evening it was and how the British Film Industry was doing so well. I went to a pub I know in those parts and puked in the toilet.

23 July 1933

Complications have now arisen over the film's release. While I was editing the film, British International bought out British Instructional. They (British International) are very angry that my film was shown at all as the performance turned out to be a bonanza staged by Gaumont-British. Bruce Woolfe tells me that they were annoyed that the Selection Committee chose *Contact*. It would seem that Wardour Films, who are the BIP distribution company, are doubtful if they want to release the film at all. There is, however, a contract guaranteeing release signed between Shell and Wardour.

30 July 1933

It is now clear that Wardour dislike the film and all it stands for because it is a new kind of film-making which they are incompetent to market. They fear for its success, says Bruce Woolfe, and are doing all in their power to shelve it. The matter came to a head last week at a meeting of salesmen when the managing-director of Wardour Films, Arthur Dent, said, I am told, that, 'Me and the boys have seen this lousy tripe called *Contact*. It's about 90 per cent stock-library material, dull and dreary, with no real story. It might make a small return if cut down to one reel with a running commentary added.' This in spite of the film's undisputed success at the gala performance and in face of the Prime Minister of Canada sending a letter saying that it was one of the best films he had ever seen (Imperial Airways were delighted by this) and the *Evening Standard* writing a 'remarkable achievement in filmcraft'. After Dent had made his statement, Bruce Woolfe handed in his resignation. It was about the only decent thing he did during the whole picture.

Now it seems the problem is to get the film away from Wardour. The bastards won't give it up to another distributor. They are holding a Trade Show for exhibitors at the lousiest and smallest projection theatre in Wardour Street and are issuing no Press invitations. Both Shell and Imperial Airways are angry at the whole situation. They even talk of suing Wardour for breach of contract.

30 November 1933

The film has now been running for a week at the big Regal Cinema at

Making Contact (*1932–33*)

Marble Arch as a second feature to a shocking George Arliss picture, *The Working Man*. The manager of the theatre tells me that *Contact* gets a hand at every performance and that he will play it for another three weeks. I also hear that despite Wardour's attitude, it is being booked well all over the country. At the Regal it is being shown on a newly-installed wide- screen which means that the top and bottom of the picture frame are cut off. Thus all the carefully composed close-ups, especially of faces, are castrated. On complaining to the manager, a Mr Pepper, he told me to mind my own business; it was his affair to know how a film should be projected. He's very proud of his wide screen.

Later I was able to write to Knight that *Contact* had been booked for a further five weeks at another West End cinema, after which it played at three other cinemas in central London.

5 February 1934

In spite of Wardour's vulgar advertising, *Contact* has now been booked to more than 1,500 cinemas in the United Kingdom. This should mean a gross revenue of more than £12,000. Allowing for cost of prints, advertising and other what are called 'exploitation' costs, this should mean some return to Shell for their £2,500 investment although it was not their intention to make money out of the film. All they wanted were showings.

The arguments, horse-trading, double-dealing and crooked box-office returns arising from the distribution of *Contact* revealed to me the corruption of the Film Trade, perhaps not so much today as in the 1930s. All I found out confirmed what I once wrote, that the film business ranks only second to the second-hand car market for crookedness.

Beddington told me later that Shell never saw a shilling from Wardour for the cinema takings. They would have sued but for the dignity of a big Corporation. But they were more than satisfied by the prestige gained. On 15 November, Beddington wrote to me from Shell-Mex House, 'I can't help writing to tell you that I have heard this week from two completely independent sources what a very good film *Contact* is; in both cases friends of mine have been to the Rialto Cinema and said that the film had an extraordinarily good reception.'

In general the film had mixed reviews in the Trade Press

but very enthusiastic ones in the general lay Press. Here only one is given because it was revealing:

This description of Imperial Airways is Rotha's first film, and shows him more mature in criticism than in production. The film is never quite permitted to get off the ground. Always the critical mind of Rotha seems to be jibbing and hedging and taking care lest the mistakes he has recognized in others' work appear to damn his own. The photography is too careful, the editing too studied, and sequences of the film too altogether cerebral. A careless rapture or two would have made his airplanes fly higher and faster, would have supplied a necessary breeze to his photography, and made the contacts between continents warmer and more exciting. These criticisms are noted only because Rotha is coming into the first line of documentary and calls for all the heavy weather we can make for him. Even if the photography were not as beautiful as it is, the size and scope of *Contact* would make it important in this year's documentary account. The trouble with Rotha is that he doesn't think about cinema (like Eisenstein), nor does he patently enjoy making it (like Elton): he worries about it. If, in his next, he forgets half of what he knows, doesn't care so much about the other half, and sets out to enjoy his material as well as shoot it, he will do something very exciting indeed.[1]

In fairness to Grierson, he did see the film a second time at the Tatler Cinema and in the columns of *New Britain* wholly retracted his criticism. He wrote that the film 'marched'.

Unknown to me, Bruce Woolfe entered the film for the Venice Film Festival in 1934. To Richard Griffith I wrote:

4 *August* 1934

I've just had a clipping from an Italian newspaper saying that *Contact* evoked cheers from the Venice Festival audience. What the hell, who would ask that when the great mass of Italian people are suffering under the Mussolini lash? I am ashamed that the film was shown there and want no part of it. Bruce Woolfe, who was there, was given some kind of phony gilt medal which he now hangs on his office wall.

There had, of course, been many examples of publicity and advertising films being previously made for industrial firms in Britain but these were far from the documentary conception.

[1] *Cinema Quarterly*, Autumn 1933, review by John Grierson.

Making Contact(*1932-33*)

Contact, however, was not the first British documentary film to find its economics for production in sponsorship. *Drifters* must have been the first but that sponsorship was by a Government using public money. Elton's *Voice of the World* was probably the first documentary to use industrial backing for prestige for the Gramophone Company. *Contact* for Shell was the second. They took no credit on the titles of the film, but it soon became widely known who had backed it. With Elton's film, it was to set the road for many such financed films in the 1930s and subsequent years. If the facts about *Contact*'s release have been set out at some length, it is because it is important even today for a film-maker to know how much his work is at the mercy of the often ill-equipped distributor and exhibitor. There are, of course, exceptions but the wholesale and retail sides of the industry are in my long experience gravely lacking in all but a kind of very vulgar and often inefficient showmanship.

5. *Shipyard* and *The Face of Britain* (1934-35)

While *Contact* was waiting for its release, Bruce Woolfe had formed a company, British Independent Films, to make one film for non-theatrical release which he asked me to direct. It was sponsored by the BSA–Lanchester–Daimler group of automobile manufacturers. There was little to it other than that it gave me more experience of industrial shooting. It took five weeks to make including editing. It was called *Roadwards* and must surely be lost. At the same time, in 1933, Bruce Woolfe was concluding negotiations with the Gaumont-British Corporation to set up a subsidiary company for the making of instructional films. Miss C. A. Lejeune's ear must have been close to the ground when she suggested, as has been quoted, that a big opportunity might lie with a commercial company taking over the threatened Empire Film Library.

Almost all cinemas in the United Kingdom had by now been equipped with sound systems, mainly by the two big American companies of RCA and Western Electric. For equipment manufacturers of both recording apparatus and projection machines there lay a bonanza ahead in the unexploited non-theatrical market – schools, adult educational bodies, industrial firms, clubs and the like, in fact anywhere where there was room for an audience, a projector and a screen. The GB Corporation had its subsidiary, G.B. Equipments, for marketing projectors made by another subsidiary, British Acoustic Films. The newly-set-up company with Bruce Woolfe as its head, GB-Instructional, would make films for this market and if they could be films sponsored from the outside, so much the better. Hence their close association with the British Film Institute.[1] Western

---

[1] Illuminating evidence dealing with this emerged at the hearing of the Film Trade case before the Select Committee on Estimates, Vide: Chapter 6.

Shipyard and *The Face of Britain* (*1934–35*)

Electric concentrated on the industrial field, linking up with the manufacturers of advertising films, such as Publicity Films at Merton Park Studios, part-owned by the London Press Exchange.

Bruce Woolfe and Mary Field became well-paid directors of the new company, which was to build a small studio in Cleveland Street, off Tottenham Court Road, in the West End. The studio, however, earned its upkeep mainly by recording radio commercial programmes for European transmission. The fruitful relationship with Percy Smith was continued; *Secrets of Nature* became *Secrets of Life*. Bruce Woolfe also maintained his useful contacts with the War Office through the Government Film Adviser. I was engaged on a menial fee basis. It may be asked why I did not transfer my custom elsewhere. The answer was that there was no other suitable company except for those making advertising films, and even GBI was preferable to that. My best move would have been to have set up my own unit but that would have meant capital, to which I had no access.

During 1934–35, I made four films at GB-Instructional. Each depended for at least half its cost on outside sponsorship, gained through the success of *Contact*. My relationship with Bruce Woolfe remained as before. He was in no sense a producer; rather his company provided production facilities and found a minimum amount of money to add to that from sponsors. In return, GBI had the sole ownership of the films in the cinemas and later in the non-theatrical market. On some occasions I would smuggle out the cutting-copy (the penultimate stage in a film) of my films at night and screen it to Grierson at the EMB, who would always give me his reaction and advice.

Rising Tide was a hotchpotch affair. At the expense of the Southern Railway, someone had shot some 5,000 ft of film of the building of the new quay and graving-dock at Southampton. It was beautifully photographed by George Pocknall, that veteran cameraman who was unmatched in his shooting of exteriors, but directed with no imagination. This raw material was turned over to me. A theme was thought up which touched on unemployment, on industry in the North, and on what Bruce Woolfe called the 'economic interdependence between the Empire and Britain'. An ill-conceived affair, it still gave me more

97

opportunities for shooting on location and for experiments with editing. Its total cost was around £1,500, of which I was paid £100 as fee. It had a West End screening at the Curzon Cinema but what happened to it after that is not known. A shortened version, not by me, was later shown in all the GB theatres under the title of *Great Cargoes*.

During the location work in Lancashire and Yorkshire, I wrote many letters to Eric Knight in America, some of which may stand recording.

London, January 1934

Have just returned from two weeks shooting in the Industrial North– papermills, cotton, glass-making and steel. This is for an impressionist sequence to contrast with the agricultural sequence from the Commonwealth which will be stock footage. The sequence is treated symphonically – spinning bobbins, pouring moulds, stream of white hot glass, pulp baths shot with side-lighting so they look like icefloes. My cameraman was Jimmie Rogers, who shot Cavalcanti's two memorable films in France. He is only too keen to experiment, with his hand-turned Eclair, a beautiful instrument which he owns and treasures. Exciting stuff to shoot, although I am the first to confess that it is the easiest way of putting industry on the screen. The whole sequence throbs with rhythm. But there are no people in it. It is superficial without getting beneath the skin of what industry really means, but so was Flaherty's *Industrial Britain*. But such a human aim would be beyond the scope of this modest ragbag.

Sheffield, 23 January 1934

This is mealtime and the unit is resting prior to shooting at midnight. Three steel furnaces are being tapped to pour for a 150-ton ingot. I have spent all day just observing. The steel-workers are splendid, great tall muscular men who wield shovels like cricket-bats. Superb faces running with sweat and screwed up like devils in the fierce heat of the furnace. I am wearing a mask and the camera will be swathed in wet rags. Little artificial lighting is needed because the molten steel itself gives off a fantastic glare. One thing I especially like, when a furnace is nearing the exact temperature to be tapped – and this is of course all important for the quality of the steel – little men (they looked little anyway) appeared in white coats to take samples of the steel from the furnace and vanished into their laboratory to make tests.

Shipyard and *The Face of Britain* (*1934–35*)

The big guy in charge of the furnace took a look at the flames through a blue glass shield and did not worry to wait for the laboratory report. By years of experience he knew, maybe by instinct, the colour of the molten metal for the exact moment the furnace should be tapped. Old skills and instincts, Knight, against the little men in white coats. But enquiry showed that the little men got paid far more than the big guy.

Vickers is one of the three firms which combine to form the English Steel Corporation, one of the biggest steel combines in the country. These days they are working overtime producing steel for guns, steel for torpedoes, steel for crankshafts for submarines and boilers for battleships, all weapons of war. They make no secret of it. Inside the main entrance to the general offices is an elaborately enscribed war memorial. Beside it stand two monster shells. They are now supplying armaments to Japan for use against the Chinese. They would sell armaments to anyone who will buy them. The publicity manager of the company tells me over lunch nonchalantly that the company expects to have forty fatal accidents a year in the works. Men killed in the making of steel to kill other men. What irony, and here am I trying to make a film ostensibly about unemployment and internationalism.

The smoke and dirt of these industrial towns of England are unbelievable. Drabness and squalor everywhere. The centre of the town is invariably Victorian, big official buildings, but in the worst possible style. Otherwise the city centre is filled with cheap smart tailors' shops and cut-price food stores and gaudy picture palaces and dance halls. The slum areas are appalling. The main streets are choked with clanging trams and swerving trolley-buses. Above all is a permanent pall of smoke. The noise everywhere is deafening. Off to shoot now.

Days later. Pleased so far with the shooting. The furnace tapping was spectacular. Streams of molten metal and giant cascades of sparks. Fettling and riddling the furnaces gave fine action stuff with an ever-swinging camera. I did the camera-operating myself. My shirt was scorched with the heat. Drop-forging will give good material for the cutting-bench. Armour-plating was sensational in its lurid glare of flames. Finally some exteriors of chimneys belching smoke.

Shipyard was to be wholly different. The film had a unity. It had a valid central theme.[1] Its origins lay in the fact that Sir Stephen Tallent's younger brother was the Public Relations

---

[1] After endless searching, no copy seems to exist. This I regret as it was one of my favourite films.

Officer for the Orient Shipping Company. He had been taken up by the documentary idea by the enthusiasm of his brother. He had also seen *Contact*. The keel for a new liner had just been laid at the Barrow-in-Furness, Lancashire, yard of the Vickers Armstrong Company. He persuaded Vickers to find half the money with Orient finding the other half to sponsor a film of 30 minutes at £2,000. He asked me to make it, using GBI facilities. GB also guaranteed a release for the film in its theatres.

Very soon I was in Barrow to make the all-important first-hand survey of the subject. I had already made up my mind that a film merely showing the building of a liner stage by stage would be dull. In Barrow the theme became immediately obvious. There was a great deal of unemployment there. There was only one ship on the stocks, where there should have been six or seven. This was a sister ship, for the P & O, to the one I was to use. Happily the building of this other P & O ship was three months in advance of *Orion*, my ship. To all intents and purposes, they were identical. Therefore when I came to shoot, I could use the two ships alternately and match them together into one in the film. The two ships meant some employment for the town, until they came to be launched at the end of a year's work. My theme was thus not just the building of *Orion* but its effect on the social life of the town.

I spent a good deal of time in people's homes, in their kitchens mostly, at their favourite sport of whippet racing, in pubs and clubs, at the Employment Exchange, and at the Labour Party committee room, as well, of course, as in the yard itself. There side by side were the two ships, No. 696 rising three months ahead of No. 697, the about-to-be-born *Orion*. My script was brief, just the description of a liner being built.

So for nearly a year I paid monthly visits to Barrow for a few days each time. I lodged at a fly-blown commercial hotel which had no hot water and poor food. The ship grew and the film grew with it. Cameramen on these trips varied according to who was available at the studio. Frank Bundy, George Pocknall and Frank Goodliffe did most of it and served well, but young Harry Rignold was there all the time and did some shooting on his own with me. The film was shot wholly on a Newman-Sinclair, using a 16 mm friction-head tripod that was always falling over. A slow-motion Newman was hired for the whippet-racing scenes. Each visit to Barrow built up to the final day, the day of the launch. When *Orion* went sliding down the slipway, it would be a day of triumph for the shipbuilders who had created her, from draftboard designer to plater and riveter, but at the same time a tragedy, because again there would be unemployment in Barrow. That is something I tried hard to bring across in the final sequence of the film: the despair of those men watching her slide away, hands in their pockets, and then turning off to the Employment Exchange. That was a sequence that critics, such as Calder-Marshall, wholly missed when they attacked British documentary for its avoidance of social reality.[1]

Only one incident during the many weeks of shooting was memorable. It was the critical day of the launch towards which all had built up. A ship can obviously only be launched once. I had bullied GBI into allowing me five cameramen, including myself. The night before, after filming a sequence of driving out the chocks that held the ship up till the last moment, I held a kind of military briefing. Each cameraman was allocated his position and told exactly what to shoot. Each had to be in his place two hours before the launching time. One had to cover the arrival of the launching party, the Establishment in their bowler hats and their ladies in their tocques. A second had to catch the moment when the propellers touched the water and started to turn, a third had to cover an overall long shot, panning with the ship as it slid down to the sea. I myself took a hand camera up on to the bow of the ship so that I could shoot from high up down directly on to the heads of the notables performing the ceremony on the platform below; and then continue shooting down on to the slipway with the chains pulling tight as the *Orion* slid away. They covered me with a tarpaulin and tied it down with ropes. The main danger, apart from dropping the camera, would be from snapped steel cables that could come lashing across the boat. None did.

It was raining heavily that November morning, as it had been the two previous days. I had much wanted to get some shots of

---

[1] How tragic it is to record as I write today, almost 40 years later, that there is again grave unemployment in Barrow-in-Furness.

the bows of the ship, with her name proudly displayed in the sunlight, the result of twelve months' work by several thousand men and our small camera crew. It was impossible. The light was hopeless. She just looked like a giant brown slug. But, as I lay up there in the bow looking down at the hundreds of workers like ants who had assembled to watch the launch, the sun came out in fitful moments, a few seconds at a time. It was too late for me to get off the ship. My cameramen were all in their stated positions. Then I saw below me a cameraman wandering around, camera on his arm, waiting for the launching party to arrive. Obviously he was a newsreel man. I hastily scribbled on a page of my notebook, 'Please shoot 50 ft now of the ship while sun is out. Will amply reward.' I wrapped it in some coins and threw it down. He picked it up, signalled okay, and I saw him take the one shot I so badly wanted. Later, in the pub after the launch, I gave him £10 for his help. He was a Pathé cameraman.

As usual, all the day's negative, including the precious shots of *Orion* in the sun, was sent that night down to London for processing by the laboratory. A report would come through by telephone at eight the next morning. It did. The precious shot had been destroyed. A breakage had occurred in the negative processing-room. Later, I was able to have one static frame of the shot extended (step-printed) and so made do with the best possible. That's the way filming goes.

Early during the monthly journeys by small car (an AC belonging to Harry Rignold) from London to Barrow-in-Furness and back, it occurred to me that an opportunity was being wasted. I had just read Priestley's book *English Journey*, published in parts in the *Daily Herald*, and had also been interested in a series of articles about the changing pattern of the British countryside in the *Architectural Review*. I suggested to Bruce Woolfe that as well as the Orient film, at small extra expense, I could shoot material up and down the country for a second film to be called *The Face of Britain*. He agreed to find the cost of the film stock but only if a sponsor could be found. It was at that time that parts of the national electricity grid system for rural electricity was under construction. Someone introduced me to Hugh Quigley, that very intelligent and eccentric character among whose duties was a kind of publicity for the Central Electricity Board. We at once saw eye to eye about a film on the possibilities of replanning Britain, both industrial and rural, based on the flexible power of the national grid. Electricity was spreading its pylons, overhead lines and power stations all over the landscape. It implied a cleaner and better planned country. It was to be an over-ambitious film trying to say too much in too short a screentime and with not enough resources. But it was worth trying.

The journeys by car through the industrial Midlands, the North and Scotland during 1934 showed me at first hand the grim poverty of the British people, so many of whom were existing on what was then called the dole. The appalling legacy of the rape of so much of the natural wealth which had made Britain famous as the workshop of the world sharpened my social conscience, a sharpening that was permanent. I quote from a letter to Eric Knight written from Scotland.

Kinloch Rannoch, Scotland, 18 *July* 1934
On the way here everything was marked by tragedy. All through the industrial Midlands and Lancashire, the terrible slums of Glasgow and the Clyde Valley, you could see the scarred mess that greedy men have made of this handsome country. So much of it is now derelict and polluted. Great slabs of countryside are mutilated by rusting factories and smokeless chimneys. Refuse from another age when some men, a few, trampled upon everything including human beings to get wealthy. The twelve miles of valley from Glasgow are said to be the most thickly industrialized area in the world. It is certainly the biggest example of exploitation and destruction. Today two thirds of the chimneys no longer smoke. The gaunt bones of factories reflect their drab images in filthy motionless canals. Men sit around on the grass verges of the new by-pass roads and play cards. Now and then the police in fast cars pay them a visit and arrest them for gambling and their dole money is forfeited. This is the great century of commerce in which we so proudly live. Where are the men who have made the money out of this prostitution? That is what I should like to know. Safe in their mansions away from the smoke and filth, safe in their clubs and board-rooms and grouse moors. A barman in a local pub in Motherwell in the Lanark Valley said, 'It's just the natural course of events, man. Nobody can be blamed. It'll all come out right in the

103

end.' That is the biggest lie of all. The newspapers say there is industrial recovery, that Britain again leads the world, that there is now stability and all is set fair for the future. But seeing at first hand as I have been doing is to believe. Maybe the industrialists are again making their profits, their balance sheets read fine, maybe they are selling more than a year or two back, but the whole blasted fabric is rotten through and through, Eric. It can only be torn down and rebuilt on a firm and well-planned economic basis. What is more, it is the youth who'll have to do it. The young men and women have got to get down to rebuilding a new Britain where everyone can lead a decent life and share in all the land can give.

In *English Journey* Priestley had a chapter describing the mining village of Shotton in East Durham that took me to this place of horror. Priestley's description cannot be equalled. It was just as he wrote. A monstrous, giant, smouldering slagheap towering over a shabby street of slum houses, hovels fallen into ruin with one lavatory for fifty persons. But inhabited. Rent for a house was 25 shillings per week. All the property belonged to the company that owned the mine. Few men were in work. I watched the rent collectors at their disgusting job; wringing a few shillings from women some of whose men were bloodying their hands and shoulders in the earth hundreds of feet below where we stood, or standing on the street corners. From some petty cash I had with me, I paid the rent for some families and bought beer in the pub for some of the miners. It gave me pleasure that the profits of Gaumont-British should be so used. How I justified it in my accounts when I got back to London is neither remembered nor important. I shot some film there but it was with a heavy heart. So this was Britain in the 1930s.

Both films were edited during 1935, *Shipyard* first. GBI had no portable sound equipment for recording on location. To have taken a sound truck (the size of a bus) up to Barrow-in-Furness would have been far too costly. So the sound tracks for both films, apart from a minimum of music, were fabricated in the studio, or rather in the spacious carpenter's shop at the back. With the imaginative help of the recordist W. F. Elliott, every kind of sound effect was conjured up by synthetic means, including a waterfall (the toilet was useful here), a flashover of a million-volt spark, shipyard riveting and so on. We bought a number of old disused cisterns and water-tanks; they made a wonderful variety of sounds. A rawlplug driller made an excellent riveting sound. And so on. How this was done has been described in detail elsewhere.[1] It might have been better if we had had available today's tape-recorders but at the same time such synthetic fabrication of sound and the intermixing and overlaying of the sound tracks (for some sequences six separate tracks were mixed together into one master track, to be remixed again with voices) were imaginative, stimulating and provided amusement. To speak the sparse narration for *Shipyard*, I used a man from the yard at Barrow with his native dialect; for *The Face of Britain*, I used A. J. Cummings, the political columnist of the *Daily Chronicle*.

The salesmen of GB-Distributors disliked both the films intensely. They had never seen anything quite like them before, being used to the normal travelogue type of film. No effort was put into trying to distribute them. The national Press was most enthusiastic; both films got far more coverage than they deserved. Oddly enough, the Trade press was also very warm, especially about *Shipyard*. But this made no difference to the GB salesmen; they were determined to give the films as small a showing as possible. Bruce Woolfe sent *Shipyard* to the Venice Festival and *The Face of Britain* to the Brussels Festival. Both won awards which later decorated his office. He made no contribution to either film, other than take his cut on the production cost.

Of the many things written about *Shipyard*, especially Basil Wright's appreciative review in *Cinema Quarterly*,[2] the most valuable to me were Grierson's references in the same journal under the heading *Two Paths to Poetry*.

The most interesting event in recent months was, for many of us, Rotha's *Shipyard*. I shall not pretend to review it for I am too close to these films to worry about the particular value of this or that. What concerns me, and I hope some others, is where they are leading. In documentary we are in course of making not individual films or

[1] *Documentary Film*, Faber, 1936, and *Sound Recording for Films*, W. F. Elliott, Pitman, 1937.
[2] Vol. III, No. 3, 1935.

individual reputations, but new ways of looking at the life about us. Movements, and schools of approach, are everything. And there is something sufficiently distinct in Rotha's work to mark it as a separate tendency: distinct at once from the romanticism of Flaherty, which all the young men have now respectfully discarded, and from the hard-boiled and certainly more academic realism of the GPO group. I shall try and analyse this Rotha quality and estimate it.

Forget all about Rotha's writing when you consider him as a film-maker. He is, as every student of film appreciates, our film historian; and he is the keeper of our conscience as much as the keeper of our records. On questions of film movements and film influences of the past he is an analyst of quality.

As a creator of film he happens to be none of these things. The history of his subject-matter does not concern him nearly so deeply as its good looks in still and tempo. Analysis of his subject matter – of the influences which affect it and the perspectives of social and other importance which attend it – is not so important to him as the general impression it gives. For lack of a better title I should call him an *impressionist*.

He then dealt with what he called the information tendency in the GPO directors and went on:

So much for the informationists and what they represent. Rotha's *Shipyard* brings us back with something like full measure to the old position – for impressionism and against analysis, for art and against information, and no one will say his case is not finely made. The other people were critical and had no creative power to back them. Rotha is certainly creative. He comes equipped with a great splendour of camerawork. He has a force and fervour of tempo'd description better than anything before him, for he has known how to use sound to intensify his impressions. He joins with the other school in his industrial background and sociological implications and, if he had freedom, his sociological implication would be even plainer than was permitted in *Shipyard*. In these matters Rotha is certainly on the side of the gods.

Yet, when the splendid flurry is done, are the bones of the ship in the film? Are the wash and the width of the sea it will sail? Is the man who planned her there? – are the orders he gave? – is the shaping of the ship to the blueprint of his knowledge and purpose? Does the fo'c'sle head rise high with purpose willed and form made to a purpose? Is it enough to make a poem of men hammering and building and forget the precision of a rivet?

The energies are certainly there, caught, indeed shimmering, among the rising ribs of the colossus. The voices are there, in broken scraps of calls and conversation. The tools are there in hot bursts of riveting and beating and turning. Something out of the town behind them is there and the houses they came from, and the unemployment they will go back to when the job is done, and something too of their thoughts. A great deal is there: shimmering all of it as the sunlight of fine photography flashes across plate and hammer and screw. But – and I ask this detachedly that the case may be understood – is it a ship that really goes down to the sea or only a hunk of art? The case of the others (the informationists) is that the art is better if it is also a ship.

In any case it is of the greatest value that Rotha should reach out separately in this way, and of the geatest importance that his growing point should prosper. It may be that two separate arts are involved and that we must look for the development of both. The one is cold and, with power, may yet be classical; the other is rhetorical and may yet, with power, be romantic. But this is certain: in our realistic cinema, all roads lead by one hill or another to poetry. Poets they must all be – or stay for ever journalists.[1]

Two further pictures were edited from the leftover footage from my films. For these I was allowed to engage Stanley Hawes, later to distinguish himself as a director/producer both in England and overseas. After I left GBI, some unknown editor cut down *Shipyard* to one reel, removed all credit titles, took off the Lancashire voice commentary and substituted the GB Movietonews commentator, E. V. H. Emmett, and the result had a showing in newsreel cinemas. In its full and proper version, however, the film was presented at the Film Society on 13 May 1935, and later shown at many film societies. For me, its most memorable showing was at a midnight performance in the town in which it was made. Shipyard workers and their families crowded the Palace Theatre. They knew what their film tried to express. That indeed was a reward, if a bitter one.

Later that year the popular Sunday newspaper *The News of the World* sponsored a short film about road safety, *Death on the Roads*, which I made for GB-Instructional quickly and cheaply but was given a nation-wide showing. I recall little about it

---

[1] *Cinema Quarterly*, Vol. III, No. 4, 1935.

Shipyard and The Face of Britain (1934–35)

except that it called for some staged accidents that fooled the
Herts police, and used a very beautiful model called Nina
Keech. It also involved a keeper of a signal-box who rode a
bicycle dangerously in a fog off the Watford bypass. It was cut
very fast like a gangster film and much pleased the Minister of
Transport, at that time Leslie Hore-Belisha, who appeared in
the picture. In what spare time was left during 1934–35, I wrote
Documentary Film, to review which Miss C. A. Lejeune
strangely forgot all about her Documentary Fetish.

In *The Observer* (9 February 1936) she wrote:

'I am glad,' says John Grierson in his preface to Mr Rotha's book,
'that the documentary method has been promoted to the fuller consideration of a book.' He is right. It may seem a very big book for a
very small contemporary output, but the omens are with it. Documentary film, the film with a social thesis and no footlights, is a vital
and growing force in the cinema of today.

'It has the growing consideration of many young men of ability
who have come in from poetry, painting, music, journalism and
academics, to serve it,' Mr Grierson goes on. He himself came in
from journalism. Mr Rotha comes in from painting. Both are ac-
claimed today among the sapient as leaders of the new, or newish
movement, Grierson as the monastic head, Rotha more as the lay
preacher; Grierson dry, academic, ruthless, Rotha a little more con-
templative and inchoate. Both knew how to work as well as how to
talk, and both, in their kind, talk well.

Rotha's present book is in every way the most important thing he
has yet done in the cinema. He has grown up by a generation since his
last work. His worst fault, perhaps, is a high seriousness that makes
the pages rather heavy reading; the material is to him so rich in
implication that he does not always stop to touch or cajole or stimulate
us into sympathy.

But when all is said, *Documentary Film* is a real book – a book about
things that matter by a man who has thought about and achieved them.
Since *The Film Till Now* and *Celluloid* Mr Rotha has become a skilled
practitioner. There is no more loose throwing about of theories, no
more garnering of spent information. He speaks like a man with
authority, a man who *can*, and almost everything he says is right and
sensible. Nor could he have chosen a more apt time for saying it,
when the imminence of television, and the increasing interest of the
education authorities in film teaching, is bringing the documentary
film into the front rank of pressing social affairs.

108

Shipyard and The Face of Britain (1934–35)

Something here should be said, if briefly, about the social and political background against which these films were made. More quotes from my letters to Eric Knight in America are relevant because they were written on the spot at the time.

London, 1 *August* 1933

Yesterday I went into Hyde Park to mix among some 15,000 people (Police estimate) who gathered to attend an anti-war demonstration. They were obviously mostly so-called Left-wing of one kind or another. Among the speakers were Ellen Wilkinson, Beverley Nichols, Tom Mann and Jimmie Maxton. They spoke some fine, strong outspoken words. The fiery red-haired Ellen was especially good. What a fine speaker she is! A group of strikers from the Firestone Tyre factory were there, on strike because of their working conditions. Will you believe this, Eric? They have an 11-hour day for 27s/6d a week, 10 minutes for breakfast, and a ½ hour midday break. These break-times have to include a long walk to and from the canteen. There was little doubt about their militancy and unity.

Meanwhile the big industrialists like Sir William Morris, the automobile king, reveal their liking for the methods and politics of Hitler and Mussolini. Lord Beaverbrook, owner of the powerful *Express* newspaper interests, does not disguise his liking for the Nazis and is one of the most ardent supporters of the new military principles begun in our own Police Force. All the old type of executive is being cleared out of the Force to make way for their successors of the Army type. The armaments companies like Vickers (where I made *Shipyard*) are spoiling for another war. How else can they sell their product? I suppose that as they have won against Manchuria, the Japs aren't buying any more. Some people I meet believe that there will never be another free general election in this country. This I cannot believe. But it is terrible that people can even think like this. It would be the end of our democracy, such as it is, but it is still the best in the world. But there are frightening injustices, social and economic, in this country that must be put straight if England is to have any real future.

A wealthy young man of the dilettante kind who once wrote a film book called *This Film Business* has recently started a production group using 16 mm.[1] His intentions are admirable and his honesty not to be doubted. He has money of his own from oil, it is said, an Oxford background and a 'sympathy for the working-classes.' He is seriously trying to make films with a Socialist purpose, and has so far made two

[1] Rudolph Messel.

109

– *The Road to Hell* and *What the Newsreels Do Not Show*. I have seen both and declare them amateur and immature. What he has actually produced can only be called 'wheel montage' which does nobody any good. He uses a few friends with cultured accents to speak dialogue for factory workers. It reminds me of what was once called the fashionable habit of slumming. In other words, they stink.

3 September 1933

The newspapers are full of the German atrocities. Hitler and his entourage of Goering, Goebbels, Himmler and the others read like a gang of sadistic thugs. Some of the stories from the refugees are too horrible to repeat. Some of these Nazis are those who ran popular schools of sadism in Germany in the 1920s. Atrocities on small girls, rape matches, whippings in human cages, anything to make a profit out of a naturally sadistic nation. Now they are being put into a position of unlimited power by the big Ruhr industrialists because of the fear of Communism. They will get help from certain classes in England, who have the same fear.

8 January 1934

Lord Rothermere has leaders in his *Daily Mail* headed 'Put the Nation into Blackshirts' and 'Give the Fascists a Helping Hand.' The *Morning Post*, a Tory paper of old standing, is running a series of articles said to be written by Goering under the heading 'How to Construct a Fascist State'. Maybe the shrewd thing to do these days is to go into the shirt-making business. But it is not funny.

6 March 1934

Last week the Hunger Marchers came to town and were very orderly and organized. Seventeen of them gained admission to the public gallery in the House of Commons and at regular intervals one after another rose to their feet and shouted, 'We think this Government is lousy. Ramsay MacDonald is a traitor to his class. We want fair play for all. We demand a real Socialist state'. After each had said his piece, he quietly left the House. Ten thousand of them met and paraded in Hyde Park, again orderly and peaceful. Twenty thousand police, so the newspapers report, stood around with drawn truncheons. There were some skirmishes and the police were very rough. Men don't walk from Scotland, from Wales, from Yorkshire and the North for nothing. What they said on their way to London was their own affair. Reports are that in many places they were met with food and shelter. They were for the most part fine-looking men, bronzed, with fair hair, wide muscular chests and powerful arms. Such men mean business. One night last week seven of them entered one of London's smartest hotels (The Savoy, I think). Waiters tried to usher them out. The men walked on. The commissionaires and foreign waiters tactfully withdrew. No one sent for the police. The smart set, with orchids and white waistcoats, stopped dancing, rather at a loss. The men made no fuss. They just drew up chairs around the band and asked for cups of tea. These they were given. There was dead silence in the restaurant. The men sat there for twenty minutes, drank their tea, paid for it, and walked out. For a few minutes maybe some of London's smart set saw what could happen to them unless something is done, and done soon, about unemployment and living conditions in Britain. This story is absolutely true. I had it from an eye-witness. Little was said in the newspapers.

17 March 1934

The other night I was drinking with Grierson in the usual pub and he spilt me the idea that a cooperative should be formed among the documentary people. He is going to ask all those who formed the original EMB Film Unit to join together into a kind of guild, to pay five per cent of their earnings into a common pool against unemployment, and to draw up a draft contract of employment for each member of the group no matter where employed. After the credit titles on the screen, each member of the group will be entitled to put the initials of whatever name the guild will select. I think the idea is excellent.[1]

25 March 1934

Current affairs are occupied by the £31 million surplus on the budget. Tuesday will see what the Government will do with it. Some papers demand an end to the hated 'means test' for the dole. Others a restoration of the sixpence off the income tax. The most sensible suggestion is that some £20 million should be spent on a wholesale campaign to destroy the slums which litter this benighted land and let the unemployed rebuild properly planned housing. But without doubt much of it will be spent on armaments. That is the only reason why the Beaverbrook and Rothermere newspapers have called the dogs off the Prime Minister and the Cabinet. I think I am right in saying that both the Press Lords have considerable shares in armament companies. Meanwhile some parts of the country begin to do a little better but other areas are getting steadily worse. These are the so-called Black

---

[1] This was eventually the basis of the Associated Realist Film Producers formed in 1935 of which, however, Grierson himself did not become a member. Vide: p. 160.

Areas. This revival of trade is ephemeral. War is still in many minds here. Most newspapers carry articles about the need to rearm now, not to be caught napping as in 1914. It is just taken for granted in many quarters that there *will* be a war in Europe shortly. Various bodies are working among the ordinary people getting statements signed that they will not fight if there is a call to arms. This is strong among women. Odhams, the big newspaper and magazine group with trade union links, have brought out the *New Clarion*, a frankly Socialist paper, and launched it with national advertising. I am told that it is selling well. It is outspoken against all forms of capitalism and especially the dangers of militant fascism.

15 April 1934

Over the last few weeks I have had talks with Alexander Korda. He is very sick with the supporting films that United Artists, who distribute his films, provide for his pictures such as *Private Life of Henry VIII* and *Catherine the Great*. I have suggested that he sponsors a modest documentary unit of his own to make four films a year with his own sponsorship and four sponsored from outside, like *Shipyard*. In this way, he would be assured of good-quality pictures to go with his features and some rental. He is almost sympathetic to the proposal. The drawback is that he admits he is very short on production money. He says he drew even on his first two films but has lost since then.

While working at the Cleveland Hall studio of GB-Instructional there occurred a typical example of newsreel political bias. In 1935 there was a general election coming up. The leader of each party was to be given a camera interview, separately of course, for insertion in the newsreels. For Stanley Baldwin, leader of the Conservative Party, they built a sumptuous set, with pillars and impressive mahogany furniture and old master reproductions on the walls and a world globe on the desk next to a great bowl of flowers. When Mr Baldwin was 'done', the set was cleared away and rapidly it was the turn of Sir Archibald Sinclair, leader of the Liberals. For him they built a mousy, middle-class suburban room with chintz curtains and a basket armchair. Next came Mr Attlee of the Labour Party. They brought in what looked like the corner of the workmen's canteen from a nearby factory. They took two hours to 'do' Mr Baldwin, half-an-hour to 'do' Sinclair, and Attlee they polished off in a few minutes. This was done by Movietone a week prior to the election.

Towards the end of 1935 several potential sponsors approached me with projects for films. They included Imperial Airways again, the National Book Council and London Transport. It was now time to make a break with Bruce Woolfe and his group. Why should they go on having 10 per cent on the contracts I brought to them? They gave little in return except material services which I could get elsewhere. The way was set for a new Unit. But before we progress to that, we must return to the fate of the EMB Film Unit.

6. *The GPO Film Unit (1933-37)*

During 1933, two events took place of which one was to have a big impact on the story of the British documentary film, and the other happily small. We have seen that the EMB Film Unit with its library of films was officially dissolved in September of that year. Sir Stephen Tallents, however, was to move from the Board to the General Post Office public relations department, and he persuaded Sir Kingsley Wood, then Post Master General, and a member of the Conservative Government, to be allowed to take the Film Unit and its library with him. It has also been seen that Grierson's abilities had been recognized outside the sphere of the EMB and his advice had been sought by other Government departments including the Post Office. The latter's officers, therefore, did not come fresh to the use of documentary films, although up till then only for instructional purposes. In the memorandum submitted by the GPO to the Select Committee already referred to, it was stated that six months prior to the break-up of the EMB Film Unit, the GPO had decided in March to acquire sound-recording equipment to be installed in a small studio and to be managed by the EMB. 'When, therefore,' the memorandum stated, 'the dissolution of the EMB was decided upon . . . it was of great importance to the continuity of Post Office publicity policy that the EMB Film Unit and Film Library should be preserved.' Immediately after the transfer, Sir Kingsley Wood appointed a Film Committee, among its members being Walter Elliot, Malcolm MacDonald, Clement Attlee, Humbert Woolfe and of course Tallents as Chairman. The GPO Film Unit officially came into being and was installed at offices in Soho Square.

In his Preface to the GPO Film Catalogue (November 1933), Kingsley Wood laid great stress on the communications value of the Post Office and EMB films. The technique of communications, even before the EMB, had been a Grierson preoccupation and it was soon to become clear that he would interpret the word in its widest sense. It is of note that this was a good many years before the United Nations with its Specialized Agencies. The earlier indoctrination of Professor Merriam and Walter Lippmann was to bear fruit under auspices as wide, if not wider, than at the Empire Marketing Board.

From *Drifters* onward, the British documentary movement was resented on two fronts, each of which would collaborate with the other. First, there was the Film Trade which had two reasons for antagonism. It regarded Government film production – unless put out to tender to the Trade – as unfair competition, and it had its eyes, as has been said, on the potentially profitable non-theatrical distribution and exhibition fields in education and industry. Through its three affiliated companies – GB-Instructional for production, GB-Equipments for sales of projectors etc. and British Acoustic Films for the manufacture of same – the big Gaumont-British Corporation was the major trade interest concerned. It should be remembered that Bruce Woolfe was now the managing-director of the GB-I company. Second, there existed a feeling among some politicians on the Right of the Conservative Party that documentary film-makers were subversively suspect. Bruce Woolfe was the liaison man between the two fronts; he had made the war reconstruction films referred to earlier which had been distributed through Sir Edward Gordon Craig's New Era company, the Craig who had tried abortively to get the making of *Drifters* stopped. The Trade now made use of the second front in an attempt to prevent the GPO Film Unit and its Film Library from functioning as the EMB Unit had functioned. And in this pregnant situation, the newly-formed British Film Institute was to be induced to play what could only be described as a shady role.

Although not an integral part of this documentary story, some record of the Institute's infant years are needed here. Its relations with the documentary movement for the next ten years are relevant. The Institute was set up in 1933 as a result of the publication of *The Film in National Life*, a report with recommendations conducted by the Commission on Educational and Cultural Films to enquire into 'The Service which the Cinematograph may render to Education and Social Progress'.[1] The Commission was mainly financed by the Carnegie United Kingdom Trustees. When set up, the Institute itself was at first financed by a levy imposed on Sunday cinema box-office revenue. It was to have a chequered life in the 1930s and 1940s, to say the least.

One of the Institute's main aims was to explore and develop the educational film market in Britain. It was a field ripe for development in more ways than one. It was no surprise that among its first Board of Governors was a powerful figure, C. M. Woolf of the Gaumont-British Corporation. The Institute's reputation was not helped by its becoming entangled with a general manager who embezzled its furniture, and a governor who became involved in a much-publicized lawsuit known at the time as 'The Talking Mongoose'. It was an unhappy, misguided body. At the outset, for the sake of appearance, it paid a brief, superficial, lip-service to the British documentary movement. It actually set up a Documentary Panel, of which this writer was asked to be a member. The Panel never held a meeting. Then, under inspiration from the Trade, the Institute became actively hostile to the documentary group. Its evidence to the Select Committee on Estimates to be given later was all revealing. Its personnel stopped not far short of slander. A one-time Director, the late Oliver Bell, ex-Press Officer of the Conservative Office, stated in the Manchester Press Club that it was common knowledge that senior members of the British documentary group were in receipt of funds from the Soviet Union. No slander action was taken; it was not thought worth it. It should be noted, however, that as a result of pressure and evidence just after World War II, and an official enquiry, the Institute was reconstituted and largely restaffed. This was due mainly to the publication in 1947 of the Arts Enquiry report on 'The Factual Film', the work of a then-anonymous group invited by the Trustees of Dartington Hall, which gravely criticized the Institute's record to that date.[2] The Institute has

[1] Allen and Unwin, 1932.   [2] Vide: p. xvii.

116

subsequently come in for further criticisms but it is without denial a better organized body than it was in the years with which we are now dealing.

The attack on the documentary group, and in particular on the GPO Film Unit, culminated in the evidence given to the Select Committee, published as a Blue Book, on 2 July 1934. It will be quoted from at some length. The Committee was made up of 28 members, none of them versed in film matters. Its Chairman was Sir Vivian Henderson, of a distinguished military background. There is no doubt that the enquiry was prompted by the Film Trade, the British Film Institute and Conservative Party interests. Representing the Trade was Miss Mary Field, a director of GB-Instructional Ltd and a maker of educational films, who was backed up by Mr Neville Kearney, head of the film industry branch of the Federation of British Industry, an ex-Foreign Office official, and by Mr R. S. Lambert, at that time Editor of the BBC publication, *The Listener*, as well as a governor of the Film Institute. It was the latter who had been involved in 'The Talking Mongoose' affair. Evidence given in support of both the EMB Film Unit's past record and the GPO Unit's current activities was given by, naturally, Sir Stephen Tallents, and Sir Henry Bunbury, Comptroller and Accountant General for the Post Office, according to Grierson a kind friend to the documentary movement.

The main allegations against the two Units were, as expected, based on the fact that they could produce films more cheaply than the Trade, although it should be remembered that the New Era Company did not exactly make a loss out of its service and distribution charges to both Units. Today, nearly forty years later, the evidence makes fascinating reading in relation to the story of British documentary. Some of the findings of the Committee provide startling comment. No political slant was shown; it was strictly an economic enquiry. No reference was made to the fact that the films made by the EMB had gained an international reputation for their quality and outlook, a reputation secretly envied by the Trade.

The new GPO Unit had continued its service relations with the New Era Company but all production control now rested

with Grierson whom the Report described as its Films Officer.
Of this, it said,

. . . it became clear that the relations between the Post Office and a
commercial concern were not those usually in force between a Government department and a commercial concern. Your Committee does
not think this is a desirable arrangement.

After some detailed figures relating to the upkeep of the
Unit which reveal on what a slender shoestring it operated, the
Report continued:

Your Committee are not convinced that all expenditure incurred by
the Post Office has been included in its figures, or that the comparison
with Trade prices is very reliable, particularly as no tenders appear
to have been asked for from any other firm than the one actually
employed.

Then came the following revealing statement,

Your Committee visited demonstrations of both Post Office and
Trade films and . . . they were impressed with the quality of the
instructional and advertising films produced by commercial firms, and
with the fact there would be no difficulty in procuring suitable films
of the nature from the Trade.

Your Committee consider that, however desirable it may be to use
cinematograph films for the technical staff of the Department [the
Post Office], expenditure for that purpose is not at present authorised
by Parliament. . . . They recommend, therefore, that the purposes
for which films may be produced by or on behalf of the Post Office
should be limited to the advertisement of definite Post Services
services. . . . Your Committee consider that the Post Office should
cease to take part directly or indirectly in the production of films
of this kind, and that Post Office officials should in no way influence
the placing of contracts by other bodies with any particular firm.
Your Committee also consider that the production of films for the
Post Office service should not be entrusted to a single firm without
resort to competition. They recommend that, in accordance with the
usual principles of public service, all suitable firms be given an
opportunity of tendering for this work.

It may be noted that if the Committee's recommendations
for production had been adopted, which is what the Trade

desired, there would certainly have been no *Night Mail* or *North Sea*, and it is very doubtful if there would have been a Crown Film Unit to serve the national interest in World War II.

Turning from production to distribution, the Report went on,

The EMB Film Library, at present in the hands of the Post Office and housed at the Imperial Institute, is under the control of the Films Officer (Mr John Grierson), and managed by two clerks. . . . This Library was taken over by the Post Office because it was regarded as a suitable setting for its films. These consist mainly of views of various parts of the Empire, natural history subjects and agricultural occupations [*sic*]. . . . Your Committee consider that . . . the limits laid down in the Estimate for carrying on the Film Library have been exceeded. They are of the opinion that the distribution of films of an educational and instructional character is no part of the Post Office. . . . They feel also that the best use of the EMB films is not being made if they are used merely as a relief to Post Office publicity.

Under the heading Views of the Film Trade, the Report said,

The Industry objected in principle to the making and distribution of films by Government Departments as being unfair competition with the Trade on account of the added prestige which is possessed by such Departments. . . . The Trade could supply these films equally well. They took particular objection to the activities of the Post Office in . . . giving advice to other Government Departments and public or semi-public bodies. They urged that the recently established British Film Institute, which has been set up *in conjunction with the Industry* [my italics – author], though not itself making films, should co-operate with the Industry in sponsoring the making of certain types of 'cultural' films rather than that a Government Department should enter the field of commercial enterprise.

Note that not one of the nine governors of the Institute had any kind of knowledge or experience of film production at that time. Trade representation on the Board was wholly by distributors and exhibitors of commercial entertainment films.

We now come to the Report's remarks on that interesting official, the Government Film Adviser, attached to the Stationery Office. He and his assistant comprised a staff of two.

The Report said,

The duties of this section, apart from questions of custody and copyright, are now confined to the giving of advice to Government

Departments. Very little contact was made with the EMB Film Unit, and since the Unit has been handed over to the Post Office, there has been no contact whatever.

The Report did not say, however, that the Government Film Adviser's most important task was the assessment of tenders from commercial firms for a film required by a Government Department. This was a method open to abuse. For example, for a number of years in the late 1920s and early 1930s, the War Office had films made for training purposes but its budget to commission production was small. These films were almost always allocated by the Government Film Adviser to Bruce Woolfe, first at British Instructional Films and then at GB-Instructional. Little if any profit could be made out of a production, but the War Office had a good deal of money with which to buy copies of films for which it had contracted. On each copy ordered, a handsome profit could be made, plus a handling charge. It was a comfortable and most respectable arrangement. The Government Film Adviser and his helpmate frequently enjoyed Bruce Woolfe's hospitality at his house in Harpenden.

Apparently mystified by the amount of advice available about film matters to the Government, the Report stated that one of the activities of the British Film Institute 'is giving advice to Government departments,' but how and with what experience was not mentioned. The Committee lamely ended these remarks with,

. . . It will be seen that there is a considerable amount of confusion in regard to the making of films and their use in Government departments. On the question of giving advice, no less than three bodies, all working independently, profess to give advice on film matters. . . . Your Committee are strongly of the opinion that a clear and well-defined policy should be formulated without delay to regulate the use of films by Government departments for publicity and other purposes.

The Report was still not finished with the Institute,

Considering itself a suitable body for the purpose, [it]applied, shortly after its formation, to the Post Master General for the EMB Film Library. This request was not granted. Your Committee explored the possibility of handing over the Library to this body and are of the opinion that . . . it would be suitable for the purpose. . . . As regards adding to the Library, this could only be done by means of gifts, or, if the Institute agreed to this course, by *subsidising the production of suitable films by commercial companies.* (my italics – author).

Two further points from the Report are worth quoting:

The Chairman to Miss Mary Field: 'Have you just made a film by which you teach French?' – 'Yes.' – 'And is it a conversation between one person and another?' – 'No, it is the correct pronunciation of the vocal sounds.' – Chairman: 'There is a big field here for development but we want to ensure that it is developed in the right way.' Mr Neville Kearney: 'In that instance, if the film were made at the suggestion of the British Film Institute and with the cooperation of the Film Trade, the Trade would be paid for its making and they would get their profit. That would satisfy the producer of the picture.' Sir Isadore Salmon: 'Did I understand you to say that the films made by the Trade are better finished, sharper in tone . . . better than those produced by the GPO Film Unit?' – 'Undoubtedly a large film producing company has got greater facilities at its disposal than any Government organization could have unless they invest a very great deal of money in film equipment. . . . That, if I may say so, is one of the reasons why we use the expression that the continuance and the expansion of the GPO Film Unit would practically stultify the British Film Institute and its functions.'

Again:

Sir Isadore Salmon asked Sir Stephen Tallents: 'What effect do you think it would have on your propaganda work if the whole of your activities were limited to that of the Post Office?' – Tallents: 'There is plenty of field in the sphere of the Post Office. But we also attach value to enabling our young directors now and then to get experience outside that field.' – Chairman: 'What do you mean by directors? I thought Mr Grierson had grown!' . . . 'Would you just clear my mind about this Mr John Grierson? Is he a civil servant?' Tallents: 'No.' – 'What is he then from a civil service point of view?' – 'He is a temporary civil servant employed at one month's notice'. – 'Then he is what you call the Films Officer in the Supplementary Estimate?' – 'Yes' – 'Being paid £900 per annum inclusive, for which there is a vote of only £450?'. Mr Hannon: 'I suppose he is a man of undoubted qualifications for his job?' – Tallents: 'His first production experience was when he made the film *Drifters.*'

It is important to realize that against the EMB and GPO Film Units and what they stood for in the 1930s there was woven this skein of intrigue and manoeuvre which most documentary film-makers themselves, intent on their creative work on production, were unaware of. Behind the not very impressive figures of Mr Neville Kearney and Miss Mary Field, there lay a small group of politicians and Film Trade men who were determined to get rid of Tallents and Grierson and their concept of the documentary film. Bruce Woolfe's closest associates among Conservative MPs and Trade characters included Sir Ralph Glyn, Parliamentary Secretary to the Prime Minister from 1931; Sir Joseph Ball, Director of the Conservative Research Department (1929–32) and Deputy Director of the National Publicity Bureau (1934–39), whose film activities will play a remarkable part in this story later; Sir Albert Clavering, Organizing Director of the Conservative Film Association, associated with the Film Trade as an owner of cinemas; and Sir Edward Gordon Craig, of New Era Films, later to become Head of British Movietonews, at that time a widely-booked newsreel which had a close but unofficial connection with the Conservative Central Office. Hovering on the fringe were Mr Neville Kearney, later to become Secretary of the Newsreel Association, and sundry executive staff of the British Film Institute. These gentlemen, who liked to frequent yacht clubs and expensive golf clubs, were probably determined only in their search for social privilege and minor political recognition. I remember an evening at Bruce Woolfe's house at Harpenden where I went out of curiosity when I was editing *Contact*. Most of those named above, and also the Government Film Adviser and his helpmate, had their coats off at a baccarat table. At the end of a long and boring night, Bruce Woolfe said: 'Come into our circle of friends, Rotha, and you will go far in films.' His hobby was growing glass-house tomatoes.

From the negative side to the creative positive side. The GPO Film Unit moved into a fine 18th-century house at No. 21 Soho Square, which, according to Edward Walford's *Old and New London*, 'was absorbed into the pickle-house of Messrs Crosse and Blackwell, having previously been D'Almaine's music repository with grandly proportioned rooms; the same as when the mansion was the townhouse of the Lords of Fauconberg.'[1] At least it gave the cramped Unit more space including a much bigger projection theatre.

Soho Square in the 1930s and 1940s was to be the location for most of the documentary units – Realist, Film Centre, Basic Films, World Wide and my own two Units. About the only intelligent thing that the British Board of Film Censors did in the years leading up to the war was to move from its dim cell in Wardour Street to the very beautiful building known as Carlisle House over on the west side of the Square. Designed by Wren in 1670, it was destroyed by a direct hit from the air in April 1941. A similar house stood at the south-west corner but this was demolished by 20th Century-Fox to erect a hideous block in its stead. A third house of the same period still stands at the south-east corner. It was said that an underground passage linked these three houses. When sheltering in the cellars of *The Highlander*, which stood on the corner of Carlisle Street and Dean Street, about 50 yards from Carlisle House, during a raid in 1941, I found evidence of this.

In addition to the premises in Soho Square, the Unit was to use an old art studio in Blackheath in south-east London which was already being equipped with sound equipment by the GPO before the death of the EMB Unit. As it was bought for a British Government department, the sound system had to be of British make. It was to cause many a heartache and some of the best known of the GPO films suffered from bad-quality sound tracks, such as *Song of Ceylon* and *Night Mail*.[2] At the same time, this almost primitive sound equipment did not hold back exciting experiments.

There was obviously an overlap of product in the takeover from EMB to GPO; films begun at the first being finished at the second. The most important of these was *Song of Ceylon*. Output at the new Unit fell under three heads: films dealing specifically with the Post Office and its communications systems in the public service, such as *Night Mail*, *Cable Ship*, *Six-Thirty Collection* and *Weather Forecast*. Films made for other outside bodies with which either Tallents or Grierson had contacts, the

[1] Vol. III. 1873–1878. p. 190.   [2] Vide: comments in the US, Chapter 9.

best known of which was to be *Song of Ceylon*, made for the Ceylon Tea Propaganda Board. Films which were pure *avant-garde*, such as *Coal Face*, for which obviously the GPO name could not be used and for which Grierson dreamed up a fictitious name, Empo. The last group was wholly experimental, such as the brilliant abstract colour films by Len Lye, followed by those of Norman McLaren. These had a Post Office tag at the end to justify their cost.

As a shop window for some of the films, Grierson used the Sunday performances of the London Film Society, of whose Council he was now a member. This brought prestige and Press attention. Film societies in other parts of Britain were also used, notably those in Edinburgh and Glasgow. And there were always private screenings going on in the theatre at Soho Square. Grierson knew that, no matter how good a film might be, it had to be sold in advance. All this presentation was accompanied by a campaign of journalism and lecturing as had been begun in EMB days. The Unit became a meeting place for visitors from overseas; the Friday night screenings have already been mentioned. The evening pub life now revolved round *The Highlander*, with very occasional more expensive jaunts to the Cafe Royal.

A group of 2-reelers, all of which had cinema release through ABFD, dealt with various Post Office activities. All well made, one or two perhaps a little dull (I am not saying which), they were representative of the impersonal 'group' method of production favoured by Grierson at this time, to be discussed later.[1] They included Stuart Legg's *Cable Ship* (1933), the work of the Post Office in repairing submarine telephone cables, *Weather Forecast* (1934) by Evelyn Spice, the collection and dissemination of news relating to weather conditions, *Six-Thirty Collection* (1934) by Edgar Anstey, the collection, sorting and despatch of a typical evening's mail at a big London Post Office, *Under the City* (1934) by Arthur Elton and Alexander Shaw, the maintenance of telephone cables under London's streets, and *Droitwich* (1934) by Harry Watt, the erection of the tallest radio station mast in Britain. Some of these carried tentative experiments with symbolic sound images under

[1] Vide: Chapter 12.

124

Cavalcanti's influence which were to find full fruition in *Night Mail*.

Basil Wright's *Song of Ceylon* had its origins in this way. In its memorandum submitted to the Select Committee, the Post Office had stated:

An arrangement has been made with Post Office approval between the New Era Film Company and the Ceylon Tea Propaganda Board for the production of some short films in Ceylon. . . . In consideration of this, the Post Office is receiving a percentage on the cost of production, estimated to yield £250. The arrangement was originally negotiated in the days of the EMB, who were approached by the Ceylon Board. It was made clear that the willingness of the Ceylon Board to undertake production of these films was contingent upon a British Government authority being associated with the productions.

It so happened that Gervase Huxley, a member of the EMB Films Committee, was also associated with the Ceylon Board, in much the same way that Tallents's younger brother was the Public Relations Officer for the Orient Line who sponsored *Shipyard*.

The original aim was to make a set of four films on tea production. Basil Wright, after his successful West Indian films, went to Ceylon in 1932, with John Taylor as his assistant. What happened to the short films, for in all good faith they were made, is not on the record; but what mattered was *Song of Ceylon*, one of the most important documentary films of the 1930s, destined to gain the top award at the Brussels International Film Festival in 1935, and to remain world-famous since then. One of the most gentle and poetic films ever made, it lives today, nearly 40 years later, as if it were made today. Only the poor quality of its sound track mars it. Several talents helped to make it possible – those of Grierson, Cavalcanti, Lionel Wendt, Walter Leigh – but more than all, Basil Wright's personal and sensitive approach and his now developed technical style created this beautiful picture.

Graham Greene wrote of the film at the time,

Perfection is not a word one cares to use, but from the opening sequence of the Ceylon forest, the great revolving fans of palms which fill the screen, this film moves with an air of absolute certainty in its object and assurance in its method.

The GPO Film Unit (1933-37)

It is divided into four parts. In the first, *The Buddha*, we watch a long file of pilgrims climb the mountainside to the huge stone effigies of the god. Here, as a priest strikes a bell, Mr Wright uses one of the loveliest visual metaphors I have ever seen on any screen. The sounding of the bell startles a small bird from its branch, and the camera follows the bird's flight and the notes of the bell across the island, down from the mountainside, over forest and plain and sea, the vibration of the tiny wings, the fading sound.

The second part, *The Virgin Island*, is traditional, leading us away from the religious theme by way of the ordinary routine of living to industry. In *The Voices of Commerce* the commentary, which has been ingeniously drawn from a 17th-century traveller's account of the island, gives place to scraps of business talk. As the natives follow the old ways of farming, climbing the palm trees with a fibre loop, guiding their elephants' foreheads against the trees they have to fell, voices dictate bills of lading, close deals over the telephone, announce through loudspeakers the latest market prices. The last reel, *The Apparel of a God*, returns by way of the gaudy gilded dancers in their devil masks to the huge images on the mountain, to a solitary peasant laying his offering at Buddha's feet, and closes again with the huge revolving leaves, so that all we have seen of devotion and dance and the bird's flight and the gentle communal life of harvest seems something sealed away from us between the fans of foliage. We are left outside with the bills of lading and the loudspeakers.[1]

On the production side an article by Lester James Peries,[2] written sometime after Lionel Wendt's death, is of interest when taken in conjunction with Basil Wright's own reflections.

Peries wrote:

He [Wendt] was Basil Wright and John Taylor's guide during the period of shooting in the island. Both by temperament and the range of sensibilities and tastes, Wendt was the last man to take these two on a Cook's Tour of the island. . . . Those vividly caught glimpses of people – ordinary people, peasants and fishermen, dancers and craftsmen, how often they were echoed in Wendt's own still photography.

[1] First printed in *The Spectator* (1934), reprinted in the anthology *Garbo and the Nightwatchmen*, assembled by Alistair Cooke, Cape, 1937; new edition, Secker and Warburg, 1972.

[2] *Indian Film Culture*, journal of the Federation of Indian Film Societies, September 1964. I am indebted to Roger Manvell for drawing my attention to this article.

Among many anecdotes about the shooting of the film, Wendt's favourite was the one of Basil Wright darting out of a rest-house verandah late one evening to catch with his camera a kingfisher on the wing. Little was it realized at the time that it would become the motif of a sequence of incredible loveliness as the kingfisher and the Buddha statue, songs and temple bells orchestrated in London by Wright and Walter Leigh under the inspiration of Grierson, linked past and present to form a timeless symphony. . . .

A poetic commentary was at one stage envisaged but as Wright's images were so poetic in themselves, other ideas were explored. 'One day,' Wendt said, 'I remember vividly that Grierson was in the middle of lunch when he suddenly stopped, fork midway between plate and mouth, saying that some Scotsman by the name of Knox had written a travel book in the 17th-century about Ceylon and that might be the answer.' It was, and Wendt was chosen to speak the narration based on that book. . . . In the remarkably orchestrated sound track, among strands of music, voices, narrative and natural sounds, a good earthy three-letter Sinhala obscenity is faintly but distinctly heard. It must have been Wendt't idea; it was so characteristic of him.

Many years later, Basil Wright himself comments:

As you know, I have never hesitated to express my gratitude to Lionel Wendt for what he did for us; he certainly opened the door on to the *real* Ceylon. Nor have I ever ceased to acknowledge my enormous debt to Grierson as the producer of the film. . . . Writing from memory of Wendt's memories, it is not surprising that Peries got the following facts wrong: Grierson had never heard of Knox's book on Ceylon, I myself stumbled on it quite by chance (when the film was at an advanced stage of editing) in one of those Oriental bookshops near the British Museum. The idea of using Wendt's voice came up more or less jointly at a projection of the film at an advanced stage attended by Walter Leigh, Cavalcanti, Grierson and myself.[1]

In afterthought, writing about 'movement' in our films of the 1930s, Grierson wrote:

As for the movement form in *Song of Ceylon*, we declared it at once as representative of the dialectical approach to film construction; meaning that it gave us a thesis, an antithesis and a synthesis (not to

[1] In a letter to the author, 22 October 1967.

mention a Prologue). I bet you that the real reason was that Wright had got a lot of his shooting in Ceylon so underexposed (and hence dark) that we had to give it a form that allowed for a maximum number of mornings and evenings. (But I must add that apart from the dawn with the birds, the best morning and the best evening shots were made by Wright in Kew Gardens, London.)

Memories differ with the years. Wright in turn comments on Grierson:

For the record, there were three Kew shots only in the film – the first two in Reel One and the last shot of all in the film. And they were even more underexposed than those shot in Ceylon![1]

The total cost of the whole Ceylon project was, discounting overheads, around £3,300. The Ceylon Tea Propaganda Board got an international award-winning film for nothing, as well as four short films for its own use.

Another film to survive the takeover of the EMB by the GPO Unit was *BBC: The Voice of Britain*. Again several people contributed to this long film, including Cavalcanti, Stuart Legg, Harry Watt, Evelyn Spice and of course Grierson, which is perhaps why it lacked the unity possessed by *Song of Ceylon*. The Post Office memorandum to the Select Committee speaks of the film's origins thus:

In 1932 the EMB were approached by the BBC with a view to the making by their Unit of a film of the Corporation's activities. The Corporation were experiencing a wide demand on the part of the public to see behind the scenes of their activities and to view their new building. It was impossible to provide the necessary facilities for even one per cent of those who desired them. The Corporation hoped in part to satisfy the wishes of the other ninety-nine per cent by a film of their work. They informed the EMB that, after an examination of the field, they were satisfied that Mr Grierson and his EMB Film Unit were best qualified to make the particular type of film they desired.

To meet this request, a scenario was prepared at BBC charges and has since been approved. . . . In this, as in the Ceylon case, the financial arrangements are made between the BBC and New Era Films, the Post Office taking a percentage in respect of its overhead charges.

[1] Notes to the author, 29 December 1970

The GPO Film Unit (1933–37)

At the time of production, it was an expensive undertaking. Its final cost was some £7,500 but it was the longest and most elaborate film to be made by the Unit and Grierson more than once told me that he feared it would never achieve fulfilment. Of the many reviews of the film, perhaps that by H. Forsyth Hardy summed it up best:

It would have been easy for a film of the BBC to be a joyless jumble of dull mechanical explanation, self-conscious programme picturization, and a solemn sermon on policy. The GPO film is admittedly diverse; but not only is there a plan behind the diversity but an individual approach is established and maintained. The film dramatizes its material but humanizes it as well, so that its different compartments have vitality and the whole has unity.

Its contents may be described as a chronicle of a day's broadcasting in Britain, although it is hardly as naïve as that might suggest. Certainly it starts with an early morning service conducted by the Rev. Dick Sheppard, but its independent character is immediately established as the camera is released to build up with a few quick strokes the placid picture of a listening countryside. The film is always more of an illumination than a summary, and as it surveys the activities of Broadcasting House – routine, preparation, rehearsal, performance – we are not aware of the timetable as the only link but feel drawn into the drama. . . . It is this seeing eye of the film which is its outstanding virtue. It operates everywhere, inside Broadcasting House as well as outside, ranging the panorama of a listening Britain...[1]

Although as with *Song of Ceylon* more than one creative mind helped on the film, it is probably fair to say that it owed more to Stuart Legg than to any other hand. He had the persistence and patience to probe a big Corporation and in his way 'bring it alive'. But for the very reason of its subject matter, the BBC film had not the lasting lyrical qualities of Basil Wright's picture.

Of this period of the EMB-cum-GPO Units Grierson wrote afterwards,

We could, I think, have done much more for the projection of Britain if the EMB had gone on. . . . But with our newfound relationship between film-making and public affairs, there were so many fields open to us beyond the EMB that the disappointment could only be momentary. The first one that offered itself was the GPO. We grasped it eagerly, for the story of communications was as good as

[1] *Cinema Quarterly*, Vol. III, No. 4, 1935.

any other and in one sense was better. When the EMB Film Unit was invited to go with Tallents to the Post Office – or rather Tallents insisted on it – we had at least the assurance of imaginative backing. It was never easy in the first place to bring a measure of beauty and dramatic significance from materials which no art had ever touched before. Nor is it easy for a merely analytic or literary or publicity mind to follow a process of discovery with which it has little in common. With Tallents behind it, the documentary idea prospered at the Post Office and in surroundings which at the beginning seemed singularly unpromising. . . . Yet the exercise in public communication which we were called upon to perform was challenging and significant of all communication between the individual and his corporate servants. Here was the country's largest organization at outs with its public.[1]

In the years with which we are dealing now, 1933 to 1937, the GPO Unit produced a whole number of films which made their collective mark but four were outstanding and all four were without doubt due in some extent to the professional skill and imaginative ideas of Cavalcanti, who joined the Unit in 1934. Cavalcanti's contribution to the British documentary movement has been a matter of discussion and controversy and even hostility, but perhaps we may now in hindsight try and put the situation into some kind of sensible perspective. That is owed as much to Cavalcanti as to Grierson. Brazilian born, Cavalcanti had worked first in cinema as a designer of sets in the 1920s in France and then himself directed two historically important films – *Rien que les heures* and *En Rade*, both in France. In the early 1930s in Paris he was in the doldrums and had to direct one or two commercial pictures which are best forgotten. He also dubbed American films into French for Paramount at the Joinville Studios, all for a living. He came to London where his friend, Jimmie Rogers, who had been the cameraman on his two important films, introduced him to Grierson. As with Flaherty in 1931, Grierson saw the prestige value of enlisting Cavalcanti to the Unit. There is no doubt (in fact he said so to me at the time), that Cavalcanti, in spite of his sincerity, saw his hiring by the GPO Film Unit as a stepping-stone to entry into the British feature film industry.[2] He did, in fact, do some work

[1] *Fortnightly Review*, August 1938.
[2] Also in an interview with the author, Leipzig, 11 November 1967.

for Alexander Korda on the abortive *Conquest of the Air* fiasco. At the same time, his expertise at the GPO Film Unit is on the record and without dispute. Under Grierson's aegis, Calvacanti made a remarkable contribution to *Song of Ceylon, Coal Face, Night Mail* and the BBC film.

Short as it was, *Coal Face* in 1935 was the springboard from which was to come *Night Mail.* To quote the Film Society programme:

This is presented as a new experiment in sound. A very simple visual band was taken and an attempt made to build up by the use of natural sound, music and chorus, a film oratorio. The usual method of speaking a commentary to a background of music was avoided and commentary and music were composed together. . . . To this foreground of sound were added a recitative chorus of male voices and a choir of male and female voices. The recitative chorus was used to fill out, by suggestion, the direct statement of the commentary. The choir was used to create atmosphere. The poem was sung by the female voices on the return of the miners to the surface and was written by the poet W. H. Auden for the film.[1]

> O lurcher-loving collier, black as night,
> Follow your love across the smokeless hill;
> Your lamp is out and all your cages still;
> Course for her heart and do not miss,
> For Sunday soon is past and, Kate, fly not so fast,
> For Monday comes when none may kiss:
> Be marble to his soot, and to his black be white.

Eric Walter White writes of Auden's introduction to the film world.

. . . His desire to work for the cinema had led him to approach the GPO Film Unit and ask his friend Basil Wright whether there was any way he could be employed. . . . Grierson was delighted to enlist his help; and he was forthwith engaged to write scripts for two films, *Coal Face* and *Night Mail,* that the Unit had in production.[2] As Benjamin Britten had been commissioned to write the music for these films, it was necessary to arrange a meeting between the two collaborators. This took place on 4 July 1935, when Basil Wright drove Britten

[1] 27 October 1935.   [2] Auden actually wrote only the verse.

down to Colwall, near Malvern, where Auden was working as a master at a boys' preparatory school called 'The Downs.'[1]

Britten himself came to be working at the GPO Film Unit as a result of Grierson asking the Royal College of Music if they had 'a bright young student who could write a little incidental music for a forthcoming film'.[2]

Seen again recently, *Coal Face* was a dynamic but also emotional little film, emphasizing the human tragedies of mining labour in the mid-1930s. Its cost must have been negligible. What it had to do with the Post Office is a question not asked. My regret today is that, like so many GPO films, the quality of its experimental sound track is so poor. But the above account will, I hope, dispel the myth that has sometimes been put about that Britten and Auden were established in their respective media when they went to work with the GPO Film Unit. At that time, *Coal Face* did not arouse much critical comment except within the Unit itself.

The next year, 1936, there came the Unit's most talked about work of these years (except for *Song of Ceylon*, which was not strictly a GPO film). Made at a cost of around £1,800, *Night Mail*, unlike *Coal Face*, was to achieve not only wide critical success but also to have a considerable showing in public cinemas through ABFD. Its subject was the nightly ride of the postal special train from London to Scotland. Basil Wright wrote a fairly detailed script. Harry Watt must be credited with the direction. R. Q. McNaughton did most of the editing but the final cutting was by Basil Wright. Again Cavalcanti's fertile imagination contributed much to the elaborate sound track, while Britten and Auden developed their collaboration started on *Coal Face*. Although Britten had sole credit for the music, Grierson remembers that Walter Leigh had many original ideas, especially for what was later called *musique concrète*, while Auden produced the recitative verse that took the train across the border into Scotland. Grierson adds that Vachel Lindsay and Carl Sandberg were inspiring influences.[3]

[1] *Benjamin Britten: A Sketch of His Life and Work*, Eric Walter White, Boosey & Hawkes, 1954, reprinted, Faber, 1970. Basil Wright remembers that Cavalcanti accompanied them to meet Auden (letter to the author, 13 May 1970).

[2] In a letter to the author by Britten, 15 July 1970.

[3] In an interview, 17 June, 1970.

The GPO Film Unit (1933–37)

In addition to the many critical tributes which need not be re-printed here, one of the best came from Lord Carrington, High Commissioner in Australia in 1957. He asked the author, 'Why are films like *Night Mail* not being made any more? After 29 years, it is still in the widest popular demand from our Film Library in Australia.' Why indeed? The question should have been put to the gentleman then in charge of the British Government's information services, and to those in control at the Central Office of Information.[1]

'After *Night Mail*,' wrote Eric Walter White, 'there was some talk of another film with which Auden and Britten were to be jointly concerned – an elaborate experiment about the Negro in Western Civilization – but in the end this was abandoned.'[2]

If a criticism can be made of *Night Mail*, not held by all, it is sentimentality towards the end of the film when the postal-special arrives in Scotland. Its visuals are combined with sob-throated words spoken (and I suspect) written by Grierson himself. This was an echo of the sentimental narration used in *Industrial Britain*, read with heart-throb emotion by the actor Donald Calthrop. These examples of bathos may have been used by Grierson for what he perhaps foresaw as box-office appeal. I prefer to think so because I never found him a sentimental man, but he took offence at my reference to this romanticism in an article I wrote for *Theater Arts Magazine* in New York (March 1938).

A less spectacular and earlier film, much overlooked, demands the record, *Granton Trawler* (1934), a picture of dragnet fishing off the Scottish Coast. It was shot by Grierson himself while on holiday, very well edited by Edgar Anstey and contained some of Cavalcanti's first sound experiments. Herbert Read wrote of it:

The most advanced use of a continuous but disconnected sound track is found in *Granton Trawler*, a simple documentary film shot with a hand camera by Grierson and adapted for the screen with the aid of Cavalcanti. The 'orchestral' means are extremely primitive – a mouth

[1] Further comment, some unfavourable, about *Night Mail* will be found in Chapter 9, when it was shown to many kinds of audience in the US.
[2] Op. cit. They were, however, to collaborate in *The Way to the Sea* at the Strand unit in 1937.

organ, a drum, the conversation of some Scots fishermen, but all combined in a symphonic effect. The *subject* of the conversation, for example, is of no importance – actually it is about football; it is the impressionistic character of the vocal sounds that combine with other sounds to produce an asynchronous reinforcement of the visual effect.[1]

It should be noted that *Granton Trawler* actually predated *Coal Face* by a year and was thus probably Cavalcanti's first experiment in sound.

Looking back now, it is remarkable how much experimental work came out of the small, humbly equipped studio at Blackheath. For those technically interested, the equipment consisted of the old hand-turned Debrie camera (a left-over from EMB days), an early vintage Vinten sound-film studio camera, the Newman-Sinclair camera used by Flaherty, an Editola viewing-machine and a Vinten synchronizer. Sound-recording equipment was the British Visatone (it had no royalty fees) hardly comparable with the American RCA and Western Electric systems used almost exclusively elsewhere.[2] Imagination and enthusiasm replaced technical luxury.

In 1937, two more films stood out from the general output of the Unit – *The Saving of Bill Blewitt*, directed by Harry Watt, and Cavalcanti's *We Live in Two Worlds*. The first, with music by Britten, was a welcome step towards what may be called the 'humanization' of documentary. Set in a Cornish fishing village, it told in story form of a Post Office Savings Bank through the eyes and ears of actual characters. If rather amateur in the handling of its people, it was at least an attempt to bring more life into a fundamentally dull subject. It marked Harry Watt's first approach to human portrayal in documentary which he was to explore more fully in *North Sea*.

We Live in Two Worlds was also a development, an attempt to express the internationalism made possible by modern communications, perhaps the first on this important theme since the Imperial Airways films. It was made in collaboration with the Swiss Post Office. Mr J. B. Priestley, who both compèred the

[1] *Cinema Quarterly*, Vol. III, No. 1. 1934. Similar use of sound was made in *Shipyard*. Vide: p. 104.
[2] Information from Basil Wright. The author never visited the studio.

film and had a good deal to do with its conception, had this to remember about it:

Most films are made by turning a narrative into a series of photographs. This film was made by turning a series of photographs into a narrative. In short, it was created backwards. . . . John Grierson, then head of the GPO Film Unit and the great white chief of British documentary films, came to me and said that after doing a short film for the Swiss Post Office they had a mass of good stuff left over – lovely shots of Swiss peasants in the fields and so on – and perhaps I could see my way into turning this stuff into a good lecture film. They would add a certain amount of new material for me, but it would all have to be done very economically. So on the basis of the list of shots supplied to me, I concocted a little talk about nationalism and the new internationalism of transport and communications, blandly took Switzerland as an example of both – for while it is ringed around with heavily guarded frontiers, it is also an excellent example of this new internationalism – and thanks to a very able director, Alberto Cavalcanti, we ended with an excellent little documentary film, which has, I believe been quite popular. . . .

'Actually we live in many worlds. I entered this new little world when I helped to make this film.[1] I had had some dealings with the ordinary British film industry. But this was quite a different world, this of the documentary film producers, directors and their assistants, whose social headquarters appeared to be a saloon bar just off Soho Square.[2] Even this was a pleasant change from the Savoy Grill, where the other film chiefs could be seen nearly every evening, holding court like caliphs in Baghdad. . . . Enormous sums of money were being handed over by the City . . . to all manner of fantastic Central European characters. . . . Not a penny of this money went to the earnest and enthusiastic young men who were making our documentary films, in which branch of the art we were then leading the world. I had liked what I had seen of their realistic, non-fiction films – *Drifters*, *Song of Ceylon*, *Night Mail*, *The Voice of Britain*, and the rest – and I liked the enthusiasm of these rather solemn young men in high-necked sweaters. Most of them worked like demons for a few pounds a week, for less than some imported film stars were spending on their hair and fingernails. They were rapidly developing a fine technique of their own, so rapidly that if you wanted to see what sound and camera really

[1] Mr Priestley forgot that he met the GPO documentary people first when he appeared in the BBC film a few years earlier.
[2] *The Highlander.*

135

could do, you had to see some little film sponsored by the Post Office. . . .[1]

Two other short films by Cavalcanti came out of the Swiss project, *Line to Tschierva Hut* and *Men of the Alps*, both beautifully made, photographed by John Taylor. Another film about the same time, which is often overlooked, was *Big Money*, produced by Cavalcanti and directed by Harry Watt. Wrote Grierson later, 'It was a unique achievement when documentary made a fine, exciting story of the Accountant-General's Department of the Post Office – surely, on the face of it, one of the dullest subjects on earth.'[2] Opening with a little boy making a big transaction over buying a postage stamp of small value at the counter of a village post office, it told vividly of the machinery behind the Post Office annual estimates, and ended with humour as a senior civil servant, having just made out a cheque for an astronomical sum, grumbled at a junior clerk who asked him for an extra halfpenny for his cup of afternoon tea. Watt was again showing his feeling for human beings.

Grierson's concern with experimental film-making was not only found in the documentary work produced under his supervision. The Poster films in 1931 have been mentioned earlier and Grierson liked to think in hindsight that they were the forerunners of the trick colour films made later by Len Lye and Norman McLaren. He recalled that he bought the rights of a short film of a remarkable abstract light machine constructed by Moholy-Nagy, the Hungarian photographer, of Bauhaus fame. Bits of this film were interpolated in some of the EMB Poster films. Grierson believed that this experimental work began when I joined his Unit in 1931 but I disclaim the responsibility.[3] Basil Wright and I, as has been recorded, each made several of these little Poster films to meet a real need; they were very cheap to make and they met the request of the EMB exhibition department.

Later Grierson found money for and encouraged Len Lye to make short abstract colour films which created a considerable

---

[1] *Rain Upon Godshill*, Heinemann, 1939. For Mr Priestley and this film in the US, vide: Chapter 8.   [2] *World Film News*, November 1938.
[3] Notes to the author, 27 December 1970.

sensation. He had invented a technique of painting patterns on transparent film stock which became animated when the film was projected. *Colour Box* and *Rainbow Dance*, with syncopated sound tracks, entranced audiences of every kind. To justify this engaging experimental work, the films embraced an end-tag linking them to a Post Office slogan of the time. Len Lye's work was taken up and developed widely by Norman McLaren, first at the GPO Film Unit and later at the National Film Board in Canada. McLaren's short films have earned him a world reputation for his personal artistry and ingenuity. He would be the first to say, however, that his work has nothing to do with the documentary story except that its sponsors gave him the opportunity to explore his ideas.

Somewhere in this record of the EMB and GPO Film Units there must be a note of the less luminary people who worked hard and long, young directors and assistants, cameramen, and just dogsbodies who carried the tea-cups – they all helped in their way to build the Units and some of them later became film-makers in their own right. The list may not be complete: memories fade, but among them were Alexander Shaw, Marion Grierson, Donald Taylor, William Coldstream and Ralph Elton. Another talented youngster who edited many films was Frank Sainsbury; among other work, he did the final editing on *Housing Problems*. Of the cameramen, only J. D. Davidson was a permanent employee, but later John Taylor did a fair share of very good camerawork. Others hired on a film-to-film basis included: George Noble, Gerald Gibbs, Jimmie Rogers, A. E. Jeakins, Jack Miller, Osmond Borradaile, Jack Rose, William Shenton, S. Onions and James Burger. F. Gamage and Roy Stocks also contributed to the camera department. Jonah Jones and Chick Fowle began their training with the Unit, to become full-time cameramen, both to be very good. Of those who specialized in editing rather than in directing, R. Q. McNaughton and Stewart McAllister are names to remember. Britten and Leigh were not the only composers to be used: among others were Ernst Meyer, Maurice Jaubert (from France), J. H. Foulds, Brian Easdale, and of course Alan Rawsthorne.

There was also the office and clerical staff essential to the smooth running of a film unit. Among them should be noted: Stanley Fletcher, who as a civil servant was assigned to Walter Creighton in the early EMB days on his *One Family* fiasco; when Grierson appeared, Fletcher became the servant of them both. With the end of the EMB, Fletcher was appointed office manager at the GPO Unit, where he continued until the war. In addition, Eric Hudson, who oiled the wheels of production – making shooting contacts, customs and travel facilities, and any odd job that no one else wanted. On the money side, there was Arthur Bray, who cursed everybody but was liked by all. Then a unique member of the Unit, Phyllis Long, Grierson's secretary for many years and with a long record in documentary. Apart from his wife and Basil Wright, Miss Long was the only person in the United Kingdom who could read Grierson's handwriting.

Overall, as a kind of production manager-cum-personal factotum to Grierson, was the *éminence grise* of Mr Joe Golightly, stern but very charming and always courteous. There was once a story current, no doubt apocryphal, that Golightly told an assistant to address Grierson as 'Sir'. The assistant refused and was thrown down the stairs. But Golightly was too slight a man to throw anyone down any stairs. It was pub gossip for days.

A precarious life indeed for them all, but John Grierson should always be on record for having stimulated, and indeed kept in work, so many people dependent on film-making. Where else would they have found work in the film industry in those days? Not in the commercial studios. Above all, it is true to record that most of these workers felt that they had a special aim beyond technical skill, and it was Grierson, and to a lesser degree Cavalcanti, who gave it to them. There was always some unease in the GPO Film Unit, as would have been expected in any creative concern, but there was also an overall loyalty which was unique in the British film industry at that time.

As with the EMB Unit earlier, the GPO Film Unit and its work was not without its hostile critics. Among these was Arthur Calder-Marshall, the novelist and essayist. In an anthology of criticism of the arts, he wrote:

The GPO Film Unit (1933-37)

In sheer technique they [the GPO Film Unit] are the most progressive unit working in England. But they are paid for by the Government to publicize Government services. The scandalous working conditions in the GPO are not mentioned in their films. All we hear is of the wonderful efficiency, the huge expansion of business handled. We are told nothing of the way the staff is limited so that the GPO can make bigger and bigger profits. . . . In the films, as elsewhere, progressive tendencies are muzzled, not by complete suppression but by semi-expression. The men working for the GPO Film Unit feel that they are doing really good work, I have no doubt. Their attitude is, 'Our job is making films. The GPO pays us for it. We go as far as we can in expressing discontent, in criticizing faults in the system. But of course we're working for an official organization, and we don't have very much rope.' If completely suppressed, that desire for reform would become revolutionary. As it is, it is kept tame. The official organization sees to that. You can admit that anything was wrong six months ago, provided that you say at the end that something is being done about it now. 'In venting this discontent,' say the reformists, 'we have been making good propaganda. And in saying that we are really tackling this problem and everything will be all right.' Says the official organization, 'You have been doing that propaganda not against us but for us. Take a rise.'[1]

In another book, this time wholly his own, Calder-Marshall extended his criticism:

The GPO also has its staff of documentarians, generalled by John Grierson, who some years ago made an excellent film called *Drifters*. Mr Grierson has collected and trained a band of young men in the technique of the cinema. They have reached a very high standard of virtuosity. And they need to: because this staff of experts is being used to advertise the efficiency of the postal services. Their function is not to comment, not to show things as they are, not to inspire any emotion except that of pride and wonder at the skill of the GPO. We see the diligent workers gallantly doing their daily task; we see the six o'clock mail being collected by the collectors, sorted by the sorters, franked by the frankers, despatched by the despatchers. It is technically very correct; everybody's tricks and mannerisms have been learnt: and if it is possible a shot or two from Mr Grierson's early masterpiece *Drifters* is cut in. [This is totally untrue – the author.] But these films are as dead as Sunday-school lectures, as lantern slides of Travel

---

[1] *The Mind in Chains*, edited by C. Day Lewis, Muller, 1937.

139

in the Holy Land, because there is nothing organic in these false-to-life, true-to-life, documentaries. They are all grimly obsequious like boys toadying to masters or clerks smarming to the boss.

This sterility is not to be blamed on to Mr Grierson or his colleagues. Mr Grierson proved in the only film he has made that he could handle real-life material with emotion. It is the fault rather of the official use to which these men are being put. They are conducting propaganda of the most reactionary all's-right-with-the-world type. The truth is that when a film is financed by interests other than those of the entertainment industry, the financiers are out to get results, either in sales or states of mind. Mr Grierson is not paid to tell the truth but to make more people use the parcel post. Mr Grierson may like to talk about social education, surpliced in self-importance and social benignity. Other people may like hearing him. But even if it sounds like a sermon, a sales talk is still a sales talk.[1]

Some tough American comments from a Mr Edward H. Shustack came somewhat later, following the wide screenings of a group of British documentary films in the US.[2] He wrote:

The work of the EMB Film Unit cannot really be classed of high quality. The young directors were in a period of technical and ideological development, of experience and exploration. When the EMB Unit was done away with by the Government, the total production was about ten good films. The rest were of interest only to the Unit itself. Their scope was of necessity limited. They could not enquire too deeply into the fundamental causes of the problems they investigated. A Conservative Government such as was in power would never countenance the filming of anything very 'revolutionary', a word whose definition extended left from liberalism. . . . Far too many of the themes dealt with a 'behind-the-scenes-of' motif, from the herring can to the bottle of milk.

Later Mr Shustack added:

The EMB and GPO films sought to 'bring alive' those many social relationships to be found in Britain. The carrying of the mail, the laying of telephone cables, the draw behind a can of herring and the value of postal savings were the subjects with which the British were concerned. Of course it is inconceivable that they would attempt any advanced analysis of things like unemployment or labor problems.[3]

[1] *The Changing Scene*, Chapman and Hall, 1937.
[2] Vide: Chapter 8.
[3] *Films and Sprocket's* Society magazine, of the City College of New York, 1938.

The GPO Film Unit (1933–37)

It is noted that neither Calder-Marshall nor Shustack paid any heed to the social films of the period, such as *Housing Problems, Enough to Eat?, Today We Live* and *Eastern Valley,* although they were all there to be seen both in England and America. The points they raise will be dealt with later in this survey.[1] Oddly enough the toughest criticism of British documentary came from a collaborator, W. H. Auden. *World Film News* reported:

Auden says that British documentary directors are upper middle class and never likely to understand workers. He says that sponsorship by Government Departments and industrial companies will never permit a truthful account of their people. Their description as 'upper middle class' will surprise and even flatter not a few documentary directors. What is more important than paternities is that documentary forces its serfs to live and learn with workmen under working conditions. Auden also complains that the documentary product lacks human appeal. It is to be noted that the human element increases as the apprentices learn their job.[2]

Of the many films made by the GPO Film Unit, some were obviously less spectacular than *Night Mail* and *The Voice of Britain,* but they had their place in the output if they did not get the limelight. They were largely required for Post Office training and for public service education in Post Office methods, those very subjects which so much infuriated Mr Calder-Marshall. They went to swell the GPO Library. This non-theatrical use of films, that is to say the screening of films to audiences outside the cinemas, in clubs, schools, institutes, libraries and so on, was to become of increasing importance in Britain in a pre-television age. Following the example of the Scottish educational authorities, the taking of 16 mm sub-standard projectors into places capable of public assembly slowly increased to form the backbone of the nation-wide, non-theatrical distribution service during the war. Here people like Thomas Baird fitted into the organization of the GPO. To Grierson was attributed the dry remark that enraged the Film Trade, that in Britain there were more seats outside cinemas than in them.

. . .

[1] Vide: Chapter 11.
[2] 'Auden on Documentary', *World Film News,* Vol. 1, No. I, April, 1936.

The GPO Film Unit (1933–37)

In 1935, Sir Stephen Tallents moved from the GPO to the BBC where he was to give up his active contact with documentary films. Two years later, in June 1937, Grierson decided to resign as Head of the GPO Film Unit to explore the world of sponsorship for documentary film-making away from Government auspices. *The Times* reported:

In his four years at the Post Office, Mr Grierson has done invaluable work in bringing to the screen valuable records of the various postal services, and the Post Master General has expressed to Mr Grierson his warm appreciation of what has been done in so short a period. The Post Office attaches great importance to the use of the film as a means of taking the public behind the scenes of its many and varied services, and the present activities of the Film Unit will not be abandoned. Mr Grierson will leave the Post Office on June 30, and will subsequently devote his experience and knowledge to the making of documentary films in a wider sphere.[1]

As will be seen later, the output of the Unit and its high standards were to be continued under Cavalcanti and, later, J. B. Holmes.

In retrospect, 1933–37, the GPO Film Unit, together with those films it inherited from the EMB, produced many run-of-the-mill films and a number of outstanding successes, such as *Song of Ceylon* and *Night Mail* which won wide public and critical acclaim both in their country of origin and overseas. Such films are still being shown nearly 40 years later. At the same time, there were some errors of judgement, which was inevitable. The pretentious *Pett and Pott* and the meretricious *Fairy of the Phone* were whimsical attempts at comedy reminiscent of amateur charades. They showed Cavalcanti's influence at its most mischievous, and are best mislaid.

With the films themselves, the prestige surrounding them and the campaign that enveloped their making, the two units had not only sold the idea of the documentary film as a public service to Government but they helped to inspire industrial and other organizations to enter into production on an imaginative scale. That will be the next part of the documentary story as told here.

[1] 11 June 1937.

7. *Director into Producer (1935–37)*

Among many social growths in the 1930s in the Western world a new kind of animal was born: not a Press officer nor an advertising manager, but a highly respectable figure, the Public Relations Man. Some were on the staff of companies or organizations, others operated on an independent basis. Of the former, Jack Beddington, of the Shell-Mex and BP company, has already been singled out for his foresight and imagination. There was also Frank Pick of London Transport, Snowden Gamble of Imperial Airways, Col. Medlicott of Anglo-Iranian oil, S. C. Leslie and A. P. Ryan of the Gas industry, Tommie Tallents of the Orient Shipping Line, Niven McNicholl, of the Scottish Office and Alexander Wolcough of the Oil industry. They were all men of ideas in whom the documentary concept might be instilled. We began to instil it.

There was, however, an obvious basic problem. It was one thing to inspire these public relations men and their organizations to bear the cost of making a documentary film which was not a straight publicity film. It was another to assure them that when made such a film would reach a wide audience through the public cinemas at no extra expense to the sponsor. The non-theatrical field existed, the showing of films mainly on sub-standard projectors to audience groups outside the cinemas, but the organization of this audience was as yet small. For public cinema showing everything depended on a film's quality and on the extent of critical and editorial attention which could be achieved in the Press.

Once the prestige documentary idea was accepted, two ways lay open to an organization to proceed. The first was for a big industrial concern to set up its own film unit, such as did Shell in time, and the second was for a film to be contracted for production with an existing film company of proved reputation. The admirable example of the Shell company was summed up by Sir Stephen Tallents:

The origin of the Shell Film Unit . . . deserves to be put on the record with some precision. It marked the beginning of a transfer of initiative from the Government to a few great industrial undertakings. . . . In 1933, the Shell Group reviewed the general policy of its approach to the public and in particular the employment of films for its purposes. Here they sought Mr John Grierson's advice; and that autumn he submitted a report, proposing six lines of film production, all to be inspired not only by the interests of the Shell Group but also by a sense of public service.[1]

It has been seen that towards the end of my uneasy relationship with Bruce Woolfe and the GB-Instructional company, several approaches had been made to me to follow up the success of *Shipyard* and *The Face of Britain*. These coincided with Donald Taylor leaving the GPO Film Unit. Linking up with Ralph Keene, who will be remembered from the preliminaries of *Contact*, and C. L. Heseltine, a South African with a small amount of private capital, they decided in 1935 to set up a modest production company to undertake making sponsored films. A sleeping passenger on the Board was the author and drama critic, Alan J. Bott, chairman of the Book Society. Of the group, I liked Heseltine for his obvious honesty and anxiety to do something worthwhile although he knew nothing about films. Keene had a good pictorial sense which later was to prove itself in some remarkable films, and Taylor had some idea about documentary. Their offer to become a director of the company was refused but I accepted the role of Director of Productions. The basis of the agreement was that my various contacts for production by sponsors should be passed to the new company.

Strand Films was known by that name for a good reason. At that time, as indeed at all times, cinema exhibitors were suspicious of what they detected might be advertising films unless they were to be paid for showing them. This was a practice often

---

[1] Foreword to the Shell Film Catalogue, 1955. Sir Stephen omits to remember that the Shell Group first came into relations with John Grierson as a result of Jack Beddington sponsoring the widely-shown *Contact* in 1932, two years before the Shell Film Unit was set up.

in use and remains today. But a sponsor of a documentary film, which did not contain direct advertising, could not be expected to pay for a film's cost of production and then pay further for its exhibition. Strand Films, Donald Taylor figured, was already known in the Film Trade as an established production company of not noteworthy feature films. It was now moribund and owned by an importer of foreign films, Cecil B. Cattermoul. Taylor and Keene acquired the company without any strings. Thus early in 1935 there began the first documentary unit independent of Government sponsorship

Strand Films moved into the same premises in Oxford Street that had been rented by the GPO Film Unit. An arrangement was made by which its films would be distributed by Associated British Film Distributors. Its first advertisement carried the fine-sounding slogan: 'We bring alive the Past and the Present for the Future.'[1] To start off production, Grierson diverted to the company two films for the Ministry of Labour, one of which, directed by Edgar Anstey, *On the Road to Work*, had some direct dialogue recording on location, a pioneering act in those days.

To turn from being a director to become a producer of films means to some extent giving up the excitement of filming oneself and assuming the role of a catalyst. It is both a pleasurable and a thankless task. Pleasurable when a film emerges bright and fine; thankless when one has to take the whole blame if the film has emerged only a part success. Knowing that the full responsibility both financial and artistic rests on the producer's shoulders, he is ever tempted to interfere with his director during production. He must share his skills and experience with his director but not restrain that director's own personal style and development as a film-maker. In my nearly three years at Strand, there were only two films on which I had perforce to take over a personal part in actual production – *Today We Live* and *The Future's in the Air* – because both films were in danger of running amok. For both thematic and budgetary reasons, I had to take an active part in the shooting and editing of the former, and in the editing of the latter. But no sore heads resulted that I recall. The medium demands a lot of cooperation and collaboration, patience and persistance, above all on the

[1] *World Film News*, July, 1936.

part of a producer with a plethora of talents on which to call.[1]

Strand had plenty of talent, all employed on a film-to-film basis at an average weekly wage of £6. As producer I drew £10. Over the next year or two, Alexander Shaw (who came from the GPO Unit and had made a group of cruising films for the Orient Line), Stanley Hawes (whom I had taken on at GB-Instructional), Jack Holmes (who had made the excellent *The Mine* at GB-Instructional), John Taylor, Ruby Grierson (Grierson's younger sister), Ralph Bond, the incorruptible left-winger, and later younger people like Donald Alexander, Paul Burnford and Jack Chambers joined. George Noble, who had done such notable work at the EMB Unit, became staff camera-man. The equipment was meagre. Two hired Newman-Sinclair cameras, a silent projector and a few bits of cutting-room equipment. But we made films – somehow. And the whole group worked very long hours without complaint. For the most part, they believed in what they were doing. They knew above all that their work was not bringing in large profits to the company and that what profits there might be would go into better equipment.

All the major films that came to Strand in those years came through my contacts. The National Book Council placed two films to embrace the impact made by writers and their books on national life. *Cover to Cover* was directed by Shaw and achieved considerable success in the cinemas. It cost £1,500 but that included a version for non-theatrical use, *Chapter and Verse*, made by Stanley Hawes. Both today would be documents of some historic value in that they contained camera-interviews (in TV style) with such distinguished authors as T. S. Eliot, A. P. Herbert, Somerset Maugham, Rebecca West, John Masefield and Julian Huxley, each in their own unrehearsed words saying what they thought about literature. *Cover to Cover*, in addition to its theatre showings, was the first film other than newsreels to be shown over BBC Television in 1936. It was very much an impressionist film with Shaw developing his good pictorial sense and with some poetic narration by Winifred Holmes.[2]

[1] Vide: Producer and Director passages in *Documentary Film*, Faber, 1952, pp. 127–183.

[2] In July, 1971, enquiry to the National Book League (successor to the National

Director into Producer (*1935–37*)

The same year a further small but significant source of finance occurred. In the grim 1930s, with high unemployment figures and wastage of human wealth, there were certain charitable bodies who salved the national conscience by raising money by voluntary means to help community life in the what were called Black Areas and in the rural areas where social life was disintegrating. Two such bodies were the National Council for Social Service and the Land Settlement Association. The former stimulated the unemployed to undertake community work for the social good of all, while the latter brought miners from the depressed areas to settle them on small rural holdings run on a non-profit-making cooperative basis. Both bodies asked Strand to make films, the former with money granted for the purpose by the Carnegie United Kingdom Trust. It was hoped that their showing would bring in voluntary funds.

The most important of the two, *Today We Live*, was made half in the Rhondda Valley among the unemployed miners and half in the village of South Cerney in the Cotswolds. These two alternating locations were preceded by a prologue in one reel in *March of Time* style giving the main events leading up to the crisis years of the 1930s. Two units under two directors shot simultaneously, Ruby Grierson making the village sequences and Ralph Bond the Rhondda Valley ones. Stanley Hawes acted as associate-producer to coordinate the two units. I must confess to having been present when the expensive sequences using sound on location for direct dialogue were being shot.

In my book about documentary, I wrote a great deal about the need to humanize our films if they were to appeal to a wide audience in the cinemas.[2] *Today We Live* offered this possibility. Ruby Grierson, with her gift for handling real people, gave life and feeling to the inhabitants of her Cotswold village – the local squire, the vicar and other bigwigs and especially to the woman who played the main part of the organizer of the voluntary effort needed to build a village community centre. In the South

Book Council) brought the reply that it had no knowledge of the preservation of the negatives, no copy of *Cover to Cover*, but that it believed that a battered 16 mm copy of *Chapter and Verse* was still in use. It is strange how such a body can take the trouble to make such films and do so little to preserve them for the future.

[2] *Documentary Film* (1952 edition) p. 147 *et seq.* Vide also *Rotha on the Film*, Faber, 1958, 'Films of Fact and Fiction', p. 207 *et seq.*

147

Wales valley, Bond and his assistant, Alexander, picked a fine group of articulate, out-of-work miners and let them speak *ad lib* what was in their minds. They were told the gist of what they had to say but put it into their own words.[1] The film left its audience not only with a basic message for the need of alleviation among the community but with the characters of the kind of people involved. For all its technical immaturity seen today (and remembering its modest cost), it was a film which lived by its passionate desire to be truthful.

The one-reel prologue had a narration written by Stuart Legg, of which one passage ran:

On 24 October 1929, the breaking point came. That day saw the Wall Street crash. After a year of crisis, it spread to nearly every country. Many branches of industry stopped work. The economic crisis held Britain in its grip. The gates shut behind three million workers.

Today depression is giving way to boom. Many men who were out of work have been reinstated but the crisis has left its mark. Some of the old industrial areas in the North, Scotland and Wales, once centres of great activity and prosperity, now found themselves without a share in the revival of work.

The majority of their people were still unemployed, unless it was to break up factories where they had once worked. Streets which were once filled with people with money to spend are now empty except for those who try to kill time. Men who once hewed coal in the mines, coal to send great ships to sea, coal to fire the furnaces of industry, now snatch fragments from slag heaps to keep a fire in their own grates.

The film was also memorable for a sequence made by Donald Alexander, shot on the slag heaps where miners were searching for waste coal. These remarkable shots have been used many times since in other films.

The British Press was very favourable to the film. Under the heading HUMANITY IN DISTRESSED AREAS, *The Times* wrote:

Documentary films have reached the stage when information is no longer enough. Mr Paul Rotha's new film, *Today We Live*, is a long

[1] Of the documentary films I took to the United States the next year, *Today We Live* was one of the most popular in spite of its two dialects. I was sure that this was because it presented its subject in human and easily understandable terms.

step forward. This impression of life in the distressed areas is not propaganda; it is a film with a purpose. . . . In 35 minutes the film sums up the changes in industrial conditions since the War, shows the decline in community life among the people oppressed by unemployment, and offers them the hope, if not the work, at least of mitigating the effects of compulsory idleness. . . .

. . . the struggle between scepticism and hopefulness is all the more moving for being shown, not by actors, but by real and homely people. The beauty of some of the faces is remarkable, being the beauty of expression and experience rather than of features, and the scenes of the people at last enjoying the centres they have been encouraged either to build or to convert are lively, humorous and warm.

Pictorially this is an important development in Mr Rotha's work. The fondness for ingenious pictorial effects that has led him, in some of his earlier pictures, almost into affectation is here entirely subordinated to his interest in the subject matter. The pictures of slag heaps where men out of work glean coal, of their houses and amusements, and of the corresponding situation in the village are plainer than usual and less selfconsciously lovely. The explanation would seem to be that Mr Rotha has transferred his interest from things to persons and there discovered a wider and more stimulating field. His people are alive in the film as well as at home, and this encouragement to the men to work out even part of their salvation is immeasurably more important than, say, the agonizing pictures painted by those serious novelists who have looked on unemployment and despaired.[1]

Today We Live was one of the few British documentary films to try and present truthfully the British social scene in human terms in the mid 1930s. It was certainly the first to tackle in any depth some of the terrible results of mass unemployment. I was proud to have produced it and edited the prologue. There was a non-theatrical version made under the title of *Today and Tomorrow* which had a direct appeal for funds from the public. Both films were made for under £2,000.

The same year Stanley Hawes directed the film for the Land Settlement Association called *Here is the Land* made for non-theatrical distribution. Donald Alexander was to develop his feeling for human and social problems in a modest two-reeler called *Eastern Valley*, this time produced by Stanley Hawes. It was about a cooperative formed in South Wales for the unem-

[1] 7 July 1937. The reviewer does less than justice to the film's two directors, Ruby Grierson and Ralph Bond.

ployed. Learning from the earlier film on which he had worked as an assistant, Alexander showed again a sensitive feeling for real people which was to stand him in good stead in his later work. *Eastern Valley* was also a success in the US. Another film of the same period at Strand was *The Way to the Sea*, by Jack Holmes, about the electrification of the London–Southampton railway. With a difficult sponsor, the Southern Railway, it had good passages, especially the crowds going on holiday to the coast. Music was by Britten and verse by Auden. It had considerable theatre showings.

A contract with Imperial Airways involved three films at a total cost of £5,000: a major one of the air-route between England and Australia, *The Future's in the Air*, which to a great extent was to take over from where *Contact* had left off, and two short films, *Air Outpost*, by John Taylor, dealing with an overnight stop by the airplane in the desert on the Persian Gulf, and *Watch and Ward in the Air*, by Ralph Keene, a film about air safety. Alexander Shaw directed the main five-reel film from a script on which I collaborated, George Noble photographed it brilliantly, and Keene went as unit manager and also did some filming himself. Shaw shot some very handsome footage. Before editing, Graham Greene was asked to write a narration, and William Alwyn, at very short notice because the original composer had let us down, wrote a memorable music score, the first of his many in later years.

There were problems in the editing stage of the main film. During the summer Alexander Korda had, as was his wont, called me very late one night at my home. He had a problem which only I (in his most honeyed tones) could solve. He had half-made a kind of documentary-cum-reconstruction feature film to be called *Conquest of the Air*. A great deal of footage had been shot, including restaging Bleriot's Channel flight and Leonardo's experiments. But no one could edit it into any kind of a film. Would I personally take it over, no matter the cost? More out of curiosity than anything else, I agreed to go out to Denham Studios that week and screen all the material. I did. To be brief, there was no film there, but some lovely footage. Whoever had scripted and whoever had directed the isolated odd sequences should never have been given the assignment in the first place. To cut his losses (or those of the Prudential Assurance Company), Korda wanted a salvage-man. I called him and said he should have known that I didn't pick up half-dead things from the gutter. He laughed and said, 'I don't blame you.'

As part of my duty to Strand, however, I had mentioned the matter to Donald Taylor. He jumped at the chance, and made an immediate agreement with Korda by which he (Taylor) and Alexander Shaw would be paid a fair sum (in documentary terms) per week, and they took over the resurrection of *Conquest of the Air*. Many months later, United Artists gave it a trade-show but the film was never, to my knowledge, booked into any cinema. It was a dead loss. But it had meant that I had to take over from Shaw the editing of the main Imperial Airways film; Strand's contract stated that I was to be personally responsible for its production. John Taylor and Ralph Keene finished their two short films and the three were presented at an all-star premiere in November 1937 at the Piccadilly Theatre. All three films were given a good release in the cinemas, especially the main one, *The Future's in the Air*. Imperial Airways were vastly satisfied.

On his way back from Australia, Shaw had stopped off in Malaya to shoot a film for its Government. This he later edited into a very nice picture, *Five Faces of Malaya*. After shooting the material for *Air Outpost*, John Taylor had gone up to Iran to shoot for a short film for Anglo-Iranian Oil, to be produced by Arthur Elton. In *March of Time* style, Taylor edited it into a good two-reeler, *Dawn of Iran*, with music by Walter Leigh.

While I was at Strand, Moholy-Nagy came to see me on an introduction from Julian Huxley; he had already seen Grierson. I must have been in a mischievous mood because I asked him what he did, knowing perfectly well. He picked up a paper-clip from the desk and bent it into a shape. Without taking my eyes off his, I picked up a similar paper-clip and also bent it into a shape and placed it by his. 'So what?', I asked. He was very angry and quickly left. Later I persuaded Imperial Airways to hire him to take some photographs of their latest aircraft. None of his photographs was usable, but that could have been the fault of Imperial Airways. Someone else who came to see me, again at Huxley's suggestion, was Wolfgang Suschitzky, also a Hungarian, whose work I did not know. He was a gifted photographer, especially of animals and children, but had no experience of film work. His photographs impressed me and I was happy to have him join the Unit. He worked with young Paul Burnford, who was then shooting material for the Zoo films series. 'Su', as he came to be known, learned fast and well to use a movie-camera and soon became an admirable cameraman, later shooting feature as well as documentary films.[1]

Another visitor to me at Strand was Kay Harrison, who was in charge of the newly started Technicolor laboratory in London. He said he knew my documentary work but also knew that I had been trained as a painter. He thought, therefore, that I would be the right man to make a short sample film of his colour process and Technicolor would bear the cost. I took him to the window and pointed down into busy Oxford Street. I indicated a red bus and asked him what colour it was. I showed him Frascati's gilded façade and repeated the question. Then I picked out a girl in a blue dress among the crowd and again asked him the colour. He now thought I must be mad. But he thought me even madder when I asked him if he could turn the bus blue; the front of the restaurant red, and the girl in the blue dress yellow. He agreed his process could do it but would never try because it would not be 'natural'. 'Let me distort and change natural colours,' I said, 'and I will make the film for you.' Needless to add, the film was never made.

Sometime in the mid-1930s a young man named John Cousins came to see me seeking stock footage for a short film to be called *Action!* that he was making for Mosley's Fascist Party. Tactfully I refused but kept him at arm's length because I was curious to see the final film and know who financed it. Eventually I saw the film; it was very bad and was presumably lost in celluloid dust. About the same time, Harold Nicolson was editing Mosley's weekly paper, also called *Action!* One evening some of us concocted a phony article under a pseudonym and sent it to the journal. It was printed. A few days after publication a cheque for 30 shillings was received. It was signed by Sir

[1] He shot my first feature film in Ireland, *No Resting Place* and also the film I made of the Abbey Theatre, *Cradle of Genius*.

William Morris, later Lord Nuffield. Among the most fervent of Mosley's followers was John Calthrop, son of the actor. He and his black-shirted friends pestered me at my Hythe cottage and local pub. They had a tough reception (not physically) and soon gave up. I imagine that he and his comrades confined their activities to Mosley's so-called Brown House in Chelsea's King's Road, where castor oil and rubber truncheons were said to be in common usage, upon whom was not known. Many times I myself saw Mosley's recruits strutting in pairs along the King's Road dressed in what would today be called para-uniforms.

It was at Strand, as in later years, that I was able to indulge in two special pleasures among the many that add up to the making of a complete film. The first was control over the design, type and speed of the main and credit titles of a film. In personal collaboration with the excellent title-making department of Studio Film Laboratories, it was a source of infinite reward to determine the titling of all films with which I was associated. In those years it was not *chic* to have half-a-reel unfold before the first title appears. The lay-out and hence impact of the main title and its background could, with its music, set the mood and perhaps even the style of the subsequent film.

The second pleasure was an indulgence which many documentary directors must have had. After hours of preliminary discussion, the time arrives for the music score of a film to be recorded. You can sit and just listen to music being played and recorded which has been specially created for your work. It has been my good fortune to have collaborated with some very talented and cooperative composers – among them William Alwyn, Walter Leigh, Britten, Clifton Parker, Elisabeth Lutyens and Siegfried Franz. Whenever possible they have entered the film at an early stage. Alwyn would often take part during the scripting. I have never been disappointed by the music written for any of my films, largely because of collaboration and flexibility. I remember that when I showed my first feature film, *No Resting Place*, without music but with speech and sound effects only, to a well-known British producer, he made what to me was a classic remark, 'Slap some music on it, old boy, and you'll have a picture!'

153

Composers like Leigh and Britten also contributed to the sound effects of a film in addition to their musical creation, three major examples being *Song of Ceylon, Coal Face* and *Night Mail.* And in many cases it must not be overlooked that we had the benefit of having available the creative appreciation as well as the technical expertise of Ken Cameron, recordist for so many years at first at the GPO and later at the Crown Film Unit, but on occasions ready to record music for an outside film especially if he knew its maker.

The overheads and salary bill of such films as above by Strand were not high. The contracts showed a small profit. Any returns, however, from cinema rentals via a distribution contract were neglible because of the scandalous rentals paid for short films by exhibitors. If there should be a profit, the distributor retained it under the dubious items 'cost of copies' or 'advertising'. The only exception at that time was *The Future's in the Air*, booked as a second feature. This showed a fair return on production cost, which Imperial Airways generously allowed Strand to retain.

But, as has been seen, the important thing was that films were being made and people were being trained who took an immense pride in their work, and above all, the documentary idea was being spread.

The possibility of seeking industrial and other forms of sponsorship for documentary production was not of course confined to Strand Films. It is important to retell here something of the background to the non-Governmental economics of the movement in the 1930s, especially so far as films dealing with social problems were concerned.

It was S. C. Leslie who as public relations officer for the Gas industry was one of the first to link the documentary approach with contemporary social problems. His predecessor, A. P. Ryan, like Leslie an Australian, disclaimed any real responsibility for this but added:

My first interest [in documentary] was excited by John Grierson's thesis on the American Cinema when he sent it to Sir Stephen Tallents, under whom I was working at the Empire Marketing Board in 1927.

Director into Producer (1935–37)

It was a masterly study. When he was making *Drifters*, it enlivened the Board. It was, for me, a quite novel development in serious public relations, but I contributed nothing to it beyond dogsbody chores – administration and publicity. Going round the London docks with Grierson and his cameraman was a most stimulating experience. It was an eye-opener for a journalist to see this new expertise in action – like talking to a painter and getting his reactions to what can and can't be recorded on to canvas. But . . . I contributed little except appreciation. The same applied to my spell later at the Gas industry.[1]

S. C. Leslie's reminiscences are more revealing. At that time, in the early 1930s, Leslie was working with the London Press Exchange, the advertising agency which handled the Gas industry's account. He came to hear of Grierson's work and the documentary idea around 1934–35, when he was a director of Publicity Films, a subsidiary of the London Press Exchange, which produced straight publicity films. He tried without success to get that concern interested in the documentary form. When he succeeded Ryan at Gas in early 1936, he decided to develop the documentary idea in Gas industry films through its associate, the British Commercial Gas Association. To quote Leslie:

In my own mind were three ideas. One was to modernize the gas 'image' by associating it with ideas of public service and contemporary problems. Another, closely related, was to combat the prevalent identification of Electricity with the millennium as accepted in the London Labour Party then running County Hall [the London County Council] and so Gas's major customer.ª [The Gas industry was busily fighting the disposition of 'Socialist' boroughs in the East End of London to build all-electric houses and shut out Gas. Sir David Milne Watson as Governor, though a Conservative, was also quite enough of a businessman to see the point.] The third idea was a merely personal bonus. It was very welcome to be able to do something positive to lift us out of the mass of poverty in which so many were floundering, at least to the extent of making the facts better known. I wanted nothing better than to get in on the documentary act and learn from you boys. The relation between the documentary idea and Gas was obvious.

[1] In a letter to the author, 17 December 1970.

155

There was of course a risk of seeming to get involved in party politics by boosting ideas with which Labour was identified. David Milne Watson accepted that risk, and not only for films but with a Moholy-Nagy poster – 'Helping to Build the New London' – which was helpful not only to Gas but, inevitably, to the ruling party at County Hall.[1]

In some ways, the above supplies as good an answer as any to those many persons who over the years have asked, 'Why did the Gas people sponsor films about slum clearance, smoke pollution, bad school buildings and nation-wide malnutrition?' It should be noted that the Electricity industry during the same period relied on straight-selling advertising pictures which, after cost of production, they had to pay to have shown in public cinemas. No better illustration can be found to demonstrate the basic difference between the documentary approach and the advertisement method in the public relations media.

Before looking at the first Gas film to create attention, it should be noted that in 1935 Arthur Elton, still at the GPO Film Unit, had on behalf of the Ministry of Labour made a short one-reel film in an Employment Exchange called *Workers and Jobs*. Up till then, documentary had little or no experience of direct sound recording on location; it was both too expensive and results often left much to be desired in the quality of the sound. But now Elton took a camera and microphone crew into an actual place and recorded with sound and picture real people using unrehearsed speech with no script. Today this technique is ubiquitous using lighter and more economic equipment and with much improved film stock; in 1935 it was pioneer stuff. Elton's film did not use any of the techniques of editing and camera angles and impressionist sound so exciting to most documentary film-makers. It resembled more a newsreel but without a sensational news item. *Workers and Jobs* was not important as a piece of film-making but it predated television reporting methods by many years.

For the first of the significant Gas films, *Housing Problems*, in 1935 a similar operation was used but improved. First, Ruby

---

[1] In a letter to the author, 21 November 1970.

Grierson, who had a natural gift for handling people, and John
Taylor sought out the slum-dwellers who were to tell their
'stories' and broke down their inhibitions against the intrusion
of a camera and microphone into their homes. Then Elton and
Anstey would appear and supervise the actual shooting of what
were really interviews, and later the editing. Nobody pretended
that this was good film-making; it was factual film reporting of
a kind not before done. The film created attention because of its
subject matter and the spontaneity of the people chosen by Ruby
Grierson. Its whole approach was as different from that of *Song
of Ceylon* or *Shipyard* as can be imagined.[1]

The only adverse comment was to come from Joris Ivens,
himself a documentary film-maker of strong social impulse. In
hindsight, he wrote:

There have been cases in the history of documentary when photographers became so fascinated by dirt that the result was the dirt
looked interesting and strange, not something repellent to the
audience.[2]

In a footnote, he added:

In my opinion certain of the early British documentary films, for
example, *Housing Problems*, fell into this error of exotic dirt. You
could not smell these London slums.

Later, Ivens had this to say about the problems of sponsorship:

Maybe here we should point to the English school [of documentary];
it became somewhat stale in avoiding the real drama before the war.
Yes, a bit on the soft side, I should say, if you compare a film like
Borinage or *Maisons de la Misère* with the English *Housing Problems*.
Without wishing to generalize, I think that the English trend was away
from realism. If the British films could have been sponsored directly
by social organizations fighting the bad housing conditions instead of
by a Gas company, they would have closed in on such dramatic
reality as rent strikes and protest movements.

Mr Ivens overlooked the one significant fact that *Housing
Problems* would probably not have been made at all if the Gas
industry at S. C. Leslie's instigation had not sponsored it.

[1] Cf. Chapter 11.   [2] *The Camera and I*, Seven Seas, Berlin, 1969, p. 216.

The slum clearance reporting film was followed the next year by Anstey's film about nutrition, *Enough to Eat?* Based on Sir John Boyd Orr's famous report *Homes, Food and Income*, it told the stark facts about Britain's health in relation to food and wages with the aid of diagrams and camera-interviews. Again, it was outspoken and explosive. The Press was much impressed.

It is the first film to show the effects of poverty on the diet and growth of the nation and it is to be hoped that it will prove the starting point for a series of similar productions on problems which should be the concern of every member of the community.[1]

In March 1937, Basil Wright left the GPO Film Unit to set up his own production company, Realist Film Unit, following in the steps of Strand Films. Proudly it announced in *World Film News* that its consultants would be Robert J. Flaherty and Alberto Cavalcanti and that its films would be produced and directed by Wright himself, Cavalcanti and John Taylor. Stuart Legg was also to join the Unit from time to time. Of its early films, the two most notable, both sponsored by the Gas industry, were *Children at School* and *The Smoke Menace*. Wright directed the first, while Grierson produced the second, with John Taylor directing. *Children at School* exposed the appalling conditions of so many hundreds of Britain's schools and was made in almost a journalistic style far removed from the lyrical poetic quality that had distinguished Wright's *Song of Ceylon*. *The Smoke Menace* dealt with the pollution of city atmosphere through smoke and the resultant danger to health. It followed closely the now familiar *March of Time* technique, telling its story more by narration than by visual images. It had camera-interviews with the distinguished scientist, Professor J. B. S. Haldane. In the same year, Stuart Legg made for Realist a reportage film in Geneva called *The League at Work*, a film of some historic value depicting the machinery behind this international organization. It should have been preserved, and for that reason probably has not. All Realist's work was noteworthy.

We have noted more than once that the hard-hitting *March of Time* series of film journalism, started by Louis de Rochemont

---

[1] *Manchester Guardian*, December 1936.

in the US in 1935 with the backing of *Time* magazine, had made its impact on British documentary. Not only did its style influence several British films, such as *Dawn of Iran* and *The Smoke Menace*, but Edgar Anstey spent a few months in 1938 in New York at the reel's headquarters, to become its English link in London. It also employed several British directors such as Harry Watt and John Monck to shoot material to be sent back to New York for editing and editorializing. Its outspoken issue dealing with Britain's Black Areas caused much comment.[1]

After the major air film by Alexander Shaw, *The Future's in the Air*, Strand Films did not come up with anything of real importance. It made two series: four modest shorts for MGM release, and six excellent films for the Zoological Society in collaboration with Professor Julian Huxley. MGM wanted the four short films to meet its quota requirements under the Cinematograph Films Act of that time, which laid down that in order to secure quota, 'interest' films should contain a minimum of human beings.[2] Donald Taylor was delighted by this deal; it meant the sum of £250 for each film, of which the Company would take £50. For the producer, it set the problem of finding subjects with very few human beings which could be made for as little as £200 apiece. Ruby Grierson, Paul Burnford and Ralph Keene faced the problem cheerfully and thought up subjects best exemplified by their titles – *Statue Parade, Rooftops of London, Parks and Palaces* and *London Wakes Up*. They were innocuous little films but provided good training experience in economy. The Zoo series produced by Stuart Legg was far more ambitious. The first six were: *Monkey into Man* (Stanley Hawes), *Zoo Babies* (Evelyn Spice), *Size and Weight* (Donald Alexander), *Whipsnade Freedom* (Paul Burnford), *Animal Legends* (Alexander Shaw) and *Animals Looking at You* (Ruby Grierson). The total cost of the series was £2,000, most of which Prof. Huxley obtained from the Carnegie Trust. They were admirable examples of popular education filled with information and very

[1] There are various descriptions of the birth and rise of *March of Time* but perhaps the fullest is in *Documentary In American Television*, A. William Bluem, Hastings House, New York, 1965.
[2] This qualification for a film by the Board of Trade has always remained a classic example of that kind of official mind's approach to the cinema. Vide *Documentary Film*, Faber, 1936, p. 20.

159

nicely made. They were distributed by Technique Films to cinemas but there is no record of their fate.

Apart from the mainstream of the documentary movement, there is little to add about non-fictional film-making in those years. Mention should be made, however, of the Progressive Film Institute, which operated as a left-wing producer and distributor largely in the non-theatrical field. Among its prime supporters were Ivor Montagu, Dorothy Woodman, D. N. Pritt and Geoffrey Vevers (of the Zoo). It distributed a number of Soviet films, among them the very fine *Professor Mamlock*. Money for actual film-making was scarce but a unit was sent to work with the Government during the Spanish Civil War. Several films were the result – *Defence of Madrid*, produced and directed by Ivor Montagu; and *England Expects*, also directed by Ivor Montagu, with Alan Lawson at the camera, on the bombing of Potato Jones's cargo boat off the Basque coast. Franco's advance hindered completion of some of the projects but the crew emerged with *Spanish ABC* (1938), by Thorold Dickinson, *Behind the Spanish Lines* by Sidney Cole, and *Testament of Non-Intervention*, by Ivor Montagu, which included footage of prisoner interrogation.[1] In 1937, Basil Wright and Ian Dalrymple made on a voluntary basis a short film dealing with Basque children in England, called *Modern Orphans of the Storm*.

The year 1936 was important for British documentary in other ways than by film production. It will be remembered that early in 1934 Grierson had suggested the setting up of a kind of guild of documentary film-makers.[2] Associated Realist Film Producers was formed in 1935. An advertisement in *World Film News* in 1936 stated that the group was an independent body of directors who had established themselves among the leading makers of documentary films. The combined experience of its members and its consultants placed ARFP in a position to guide the making of any type of documentary or publicity film. Its twelve members were listed as: Edgar Anstey, William Coldstream, Arthur Elton, Marion Grierson, J. B. Holmes,

[1] In a letter to the author, 12 February 1970.   [2] Vide: p. 111.

Director into Producer (1935–37)

Stuart Legg, Paul Rotha, Alexander Shaw, Evelyn Spice, Donald Taylor, Harry Watt and Basil Wright. Its consultants were: Andrew Buchanan, Alberto Cavalcanti, John Grierson, Prof. J. B. S. Haldane, Prof. Lancelot Hogben, Prof. Julian Huxley, E. McKnight Kauffer, Walter Leigh and Basil Ward. Its office was at No. 33 Soho Square. Its members paid a weekly due of £1 of their salary and were entitled to place the letters ARFP after their screen credit on films.

Thus there was a formal attempt to build the documentary movement into a kind of unified guild. A Benevolent Fund was at once established, which if it had been continued would have become wealthy. It was, however, discontinued in 1938.[1] The formation of the group attracted considerable Press coverage from papers as disparate as *The Times* and the *Evening Standard*. The minute books of the Association were scrupulously kept but were subsequently lost.[2] It will be noted that the term 'documentary' was not used in the Association's title but 'realist' substituted. Around this time, the term 'documentary' had become commercially a dirty word and aroused derision in Wardour Street. Not all of the association's members agreed with this change; documentary was our label and some hundreds of lectures and articles had made it so. Today, of course, it is ubiquitous and not only for films. It is used widely and often mistakenly in television, literature, theatre, radio and journalism.

In the same year Grierson launched *World Film News*, a monthly journal that took over the goodwill of *Cinema Quarterly* which was considered too parochial, published and edited as it was in Edinburgh. At first the paper was edited by H. N. Feld, a refugee from Nazi aggression, but he was soon replaced by Marion Grierson. Later Reg Groves acted as editor. It was, under Grierson's mercurial executive editorship, quick to attack and expose. It carried devastating revelations about the British Board of Film Censors, it pulled the gauze off the crooked financial dealings within the British feature film industry, and it kept up a barbed and much-needed attack on the behaviour of the British Film Institute, of which the following was an example:

[1] Vide: pp. 199, 200.
[2] For many years they were in my safe-keeping but at the end of the war they were deposited elsewhere and now, alas, cannot be located.

Past association [of the Institute] with the International Institute at Rome, and German expeditions on the invitation of Hitler, have been compromising. The international Institute is not as international as it sounds, and is too closely associated with Mussolini and Fascism. Shaking hands with Hitler is not the most lucid of cultural gestures. Beware, too, in this connection, of foreign exhibitions. In common belief they are a hotbed of log-rolling and ballyhoo. An educational and cultural organization must cultivate detachment in such matters.[1]

In its three years of existence, *World Film News* was a dynamic paper, certainly the best of its kind in the film world. That it was to run into debt was partly due to lack of professional experience of production and printing costs.

Visitors continued to call at No. 21 Soho Square to see films or just to talk with whoever might be around. All visits were not serious. One Sunday afternoon I had a call to my flat from a Mr Paul Strand, a distinguished American still-photographer. He was just in from Moscow and would like to meet Grierson and some of the boys, and also show them some of his photographs. It was arranged for him to come to the Unit the next evening. We assembled in the projection theatre. Mr Strand had requested an easel and a spotlight, which were supplied. He opened his large portfolio and placed the first of his photographs on the easel, dusted it with a white silk handkerchief and switched the spotlight on to it. It was an excellent picture of the white wall of an adobe house in New Mexico. He left the photograph there for several minutes and then replaced it with a second. This was also of an adobe wall, very similar to the first, but taken from a slightly different angle. We looked at that for several more minutes. The experience was repeated until we came to the fifth adobe house from still another angle. Then Grierson growled, 'You know, Mr Strand, we're not much interested in art photography here.' Strand was deeply hurt and departed a very angry man.

Thus in 1937, the British documentary movement, now four production units – GPO, Strand, Realist and Shell – was making different styles of film to meet different purposes. The ARFP

[1] June 1936.

group helped to maintain its unity. The attacking voice of *World Film News*, with its dynamic Griersonian editorials, made documentary opinion felt in Government, Film Trade, Film Society and industrial Public Relations circles. It was felt overseas too. It was a tragedy that it had to fold but I am afraid that it was Grierson's own fault.

8. *The Peace Film (1936)*

One afternoon in March 1936, two or three of us at Strand Films were looking down from the third-floor windows at the newspaper placards outside Frascati's Restaurant in Oxford Street. They shouted BRITAIN TO REARM. One of us said (I do not remember who), 'Why the hell are we making films if we don't do something about urging people to demand peace by collective security?' It had an electrifying result. Within a few minutes we agreed to make a very short film (so that it could be slotted into any cinema schedule without due interference) to be shown free as widely as possible asking the audience to appeal to their MP to support the policy of collective security at the League of Nations. All work on the film would be voluntary; money would only be needed for film stock, cost of laboratory processing, sound recording and copies of the finished film.

It could not be called a documentary film in the meaning of the term; it was more in the form of the old EMB Poster films. But the events which surrounded the making and eventual showing of the little film were all a part of the documentary attitude of the time.

A rapid meeting took place with our friend, Ritchie-Calder, as a result of which a kind of script mainly of drawings and titles was drawn up. The script stressed the futility of the world's armaments race, the urgent need to maintain peace by international discussion through the League, and ended with a plea for people to write to their MP about it. We then saw Mr J. J. Taylor, political secretary of the Transport and General Workers' Union, to get his support and to see if he had any suggestions as to how the money could be raised to produce the film. Mr Taylor thought an approach to private sources would be best and he arranged that the three of us should see Sir Stafford Cripps that night in his flat in Abingdon Street. Our

John Grierson

Sir Stephen Tallents

Jack Beddington

Flaherty on Aran

Cavalcanti

Grierson making *Drifters*, 1929

Basil Wright

Edgar Anstey (enlargement from film)

Rotha making *Contact*, 1932

Stuart Legg

Elton making *Voice of the World*, 1932

ACES: 21 Soho Square: the GPO Film Unit's offices on first floor,
later used by Paul Rotha Productions and DATA

Right: 37 Oxford Street: the
EMB and GPO Film Unit's
offices on third and fourth floors,
later used by the Strand Film Co.

Below: Dansey Yard, off Lower
Wardour Street: the first EMB
Film Unit cutting-room

Drifters, by Grierson (1929)

EMB Poster Film (1931) by Rotha, for Australian Wine

Contact, by Rotha (1932-33)

Contact, by Rotha (1932-33)

Aero-engine, by Elton (1932–33)

Aero-engine, by Elton (1932–33)

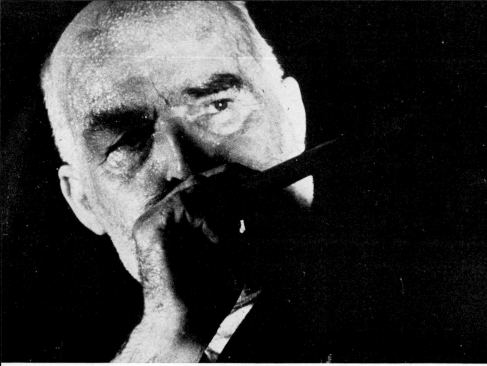

Industrial Britain, by Flaherty & Grierson (1931–32)

Song of Ceylon, by Wright (1934–35)

Granton Trawler, by Grierson & Anstey (1934)

Windmill in Barbados, by Wright (1933)

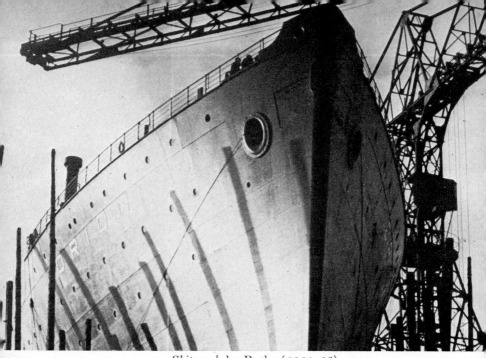

Shipyard, by Rotha (1934–35)

Shipyard, by Rotha (1934–35)

The Face of Britain, by Rotha (1934–35)

The Face of Britain, by Rotha (1934–35)

Night Mail, by Watt & Wright (1936)

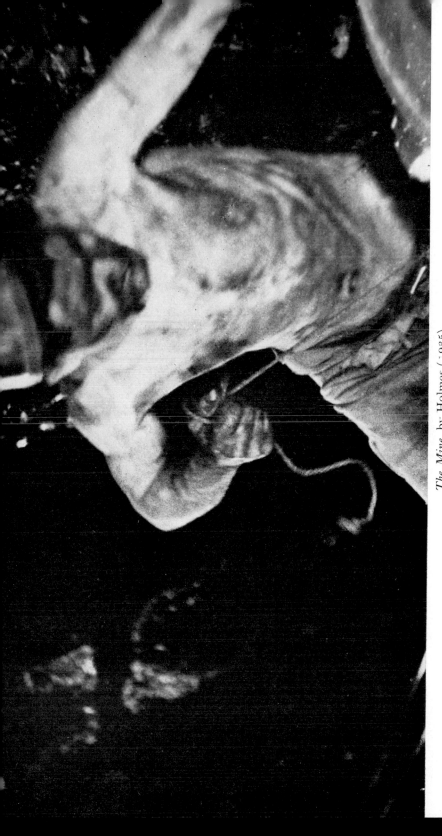

The Mine, by Holmes (1935)

Coal Face, by Cavalcanti (1936)

Weather Forecast, by Spice (1934)

Today We Live, by Rotha, Ruby Grierson & Bond (1936 37)

Cable Ship, Legg (1933)

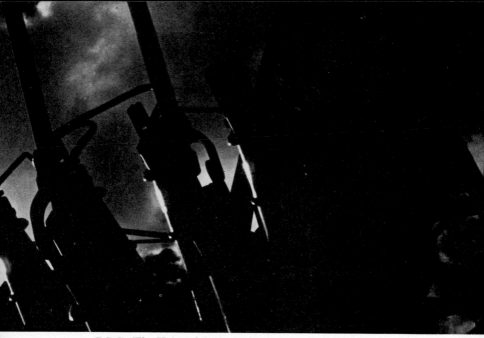

BBC: The Voice of Britain, by Legg & others (1934–35)

Cover to Cover, by Shaw (1936)

The Future's in the Air, by Shaw & Rotha (1937)

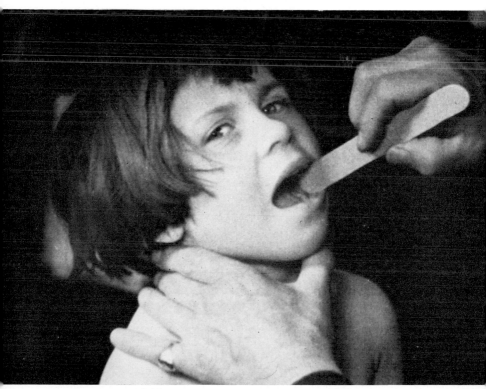

Children at School, by Wright (1937)

The Face of Scotland, by Wright (1938)

Housing Problems, by Elton & Anstey (1935)

Enough to Eat? by Anstey (1936)

Enough to Eat? by Anstey (1936)

March of Time, Inside China (American, Ca 1937)

March of Time, The Black Areas (American, Ca 1938) shot in England

The River, by Lorentz (American, 1937)

The Plow that Broke the Plains, by Lorentz (American, 1936)

Dawn of Iran, by Taylor (1938)

We Live in Two Worlds, by Cavalcanti (1937)

The Children's Story, by Shaw (1938)

Wealth of a Nation, by Alexander (1938)

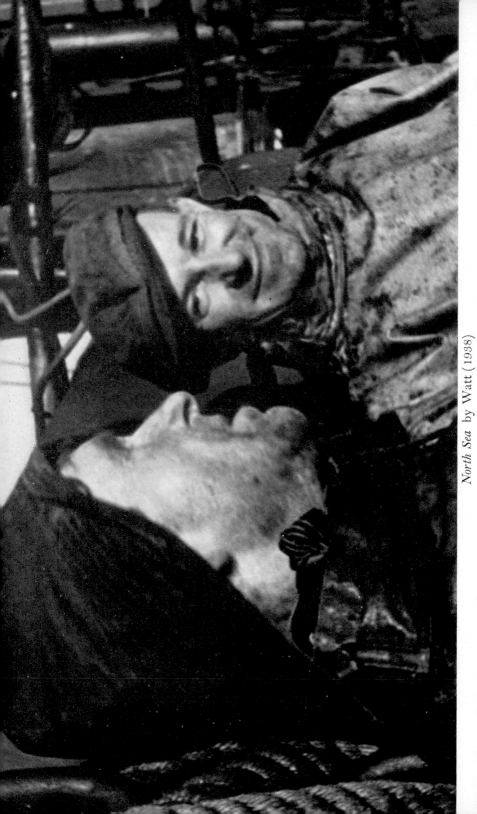

North Sea by Watt (1938)

The Saving of Bill Blewitt, by Watt (1937)

Roads Across Britain, Rotha & Cole (1938)

The Smoke Menace, by Taylor (1937)

Spare Time, by Jennings (1939)

New Worlds for Old, by Rotha (1938) The Controversial Dancing Girls

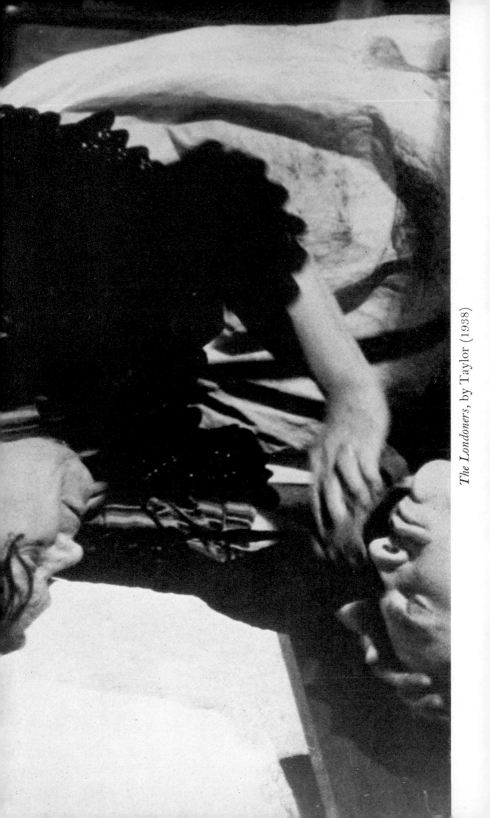

The Londoners, by Taylor (1938)

The Fourth Estate, by Rotha (1939–40)

The Fourth Estate, by Rotha (1939–40)

The Author and Quinn, July, 1972

estimate was about £250. Within minutes Cripps took out his cheque book and wrote out a cheque for £100. He further undertook to find a similar amount or more the next day. He did. Money came from Mr D. N. Pritt, Lady Parmoor, Mr George Cadbury and Sir William Jowitt.[1]

Those of us who worked on the little film worked fast. They shall mostly remain anonymous except for Ruby Grierson who was to play a major part in the subsequent troubles. The film was ready by 23 March. It had music by Benjamin Britten (without payment) which was provocative and stirring, perhaps the best thing in the film. It was obvious that it had to be made under some commercial film trade name. It was not possible to use Strand. An introduction was obtained to Freenat Films Ltd, a small company formed some years earlier by two members of the League of Nations Union to produce two propaganda films – *Thunder in the Air* and *The World War and After*. The negatives of these two films were put at our disposal. We used one shot of a tank, for which Freenat held a receipt from Universal News, New York, on which it stated that it was an American tank filmed in Texas. The League of Nations Union also had printed 5,000 leaflets about our film, urging their members to ask local cinema managers to book what had now become known as the Peace Film. Details about the film were also sent to all TUC branches. When complete, the film was viewed by Cripps, and Mr Surrey Dane, advertising manager of Odhams Press Ltd, who offered free advertising space in the film trade journal *Kinematograph Weekly*. Cripps, Freenat Films and the League of Nations Union all accepted the film. Freenat agreed that it should be submitted to the British Board of Film Censors for a certificate; this was necessary for all films except newsreels.

A copy of the film with the usual signed trade agreement which the Board required was left at the Censor's office on 27 March. In those days it normally took two days for a film to be seen by the Board, who then notified by telephone the producer that his certificate could be collected. If there was a problem with the film, the producer was sent a red form which told him of the objections and requested an interview.

---

[1] At the time these names were kept confidential but in later years their owners agreed to them being made public.

Seven days passed without there being word from the Board. On 3 April, Freenat Films were notified in writing by the Board that exception had been taken by the Examiners to the film but that, should they (Freenat) desire to discuss the matter with the Secretary of the Board, he would be pleased to make an appointment for that purpose.

At the suggestion of the producer, Freenat Films gave a letter of authority to Miss R. I. Grierson, empowering her to act as their representative. An interview was fixed for the next day. There were present Lord Tyrrell (President of the Board), Mr Brooke Wilkinson (Secretary), and two unidentified men, one in a major's uniform.

On behalf of the Board, the Secretary stated:

(a) Objection was taken to the film on the grounds that it was controversial propaganda.

(b) It was suggested that certain war scenes in the film might be the property of the War Office, who would have to be consulted.

The Secretary added that the whole matter might take some time and meanwhile a certificate could not be granted to the film. Miss Grierson rightly made no comment at this stage, although she knew of course that the shot of the tank (the only war scene in the film) was of American origin and a receipt for it lay in Freenat's file.

The next day and the next day but two, the producer sought legal advice as well as trade advice on:

(a) The authority of the British Board of Film Censors to consult a Government department about a film.

(b) The possibility of exhibiting the film without a certificate by obtaining LCC permission.

(c) The possibility of holding a private show to the Press and Members of Parliament.

On 6 April, Miss Grierson saw the Board's Secretary again. This time he was alone. She was informed that no decision had been reached about the film, that it was being submitted to the War Office, and that, if the War Office gave permission for its material to be used, or, if the War Office could say that the scenes in question were not its property, then the film would be further considered on the grounds of controversial propaganda. Mr Brooke Wilkinson mentioned the Home Office.

Miss Grierson then informed the Secretary that the scene of the tank to which he referred was American and that she had with her a receipt from the Company (Universal News) from which the shot had been bought, and further that the scene in question had already been passed by the Board some years earlier when it had been included in a film called *Thunder in the Air*. Mr Brooke Wilkinson then asked Miss Grierson if she knew where the money came from to make the film? Miss Grierson replied that she was not aware that the Secretary of the Board had the authority to ask such a question. The interview ended in an impasse.

After discussion with Freenat Films and their approval had been given, it was agreed to make the facts known to the Press. It was to be made clear, however, that it should specifically not be stated that the film had been banned by the Censor but that, as was the case, a certificate for public exhibition had been indefinitely withheld, and that in the opinion of the Board's Secretary the matter would probably take some weeks to resolve.

The following Press release was issued the same day.

FILM CENSOR WITHHOLDS CERTIFICATE FROM PEACE FILM
A short three-minute film has been made appealing to the people of Britain to insist that their MPs should support collective security. Ordinary people are interviewed in the film and give their personal reactions to the present world situation.

Many cinema managers have already applied to show this film. The League of Nations Union has circulated its members in each of its 3,000 branches with leaflets informing them about the film.

The film was submitted in the usual way to the British Board of Film Censors. The producers have been notified that 'exception has been taken by the Examiners to the film'. In discussion, it transpires that the Censor regards the film as being 'controversial' but declares his intention of submitting it to the War Office.

This film is intended as an expression of the universal desire for peace and it is felt that the Press should be informed of the fact that a certificate is being withheld by the Censor Board.

At 4.30 pm on the same day, 7 April, the Press was invited to a private screening of the film. A large number came. Mr H. G.

Wells was present and made a statement: 'This is outragrous. We cannot allow our affairs to be ruled by a gang of mystery men.' During the evening, after a second screening of the film, Sir Archibald Sinclair, the Liberal leader, said: 'I deplore any attempt to hold up a film of this nature. It is a grave mistake. The moment is particularly appropriate for showing a film which illustrates the horrors and actualities of modern warfare and there should be no delay in letting the public see the Peace Film.' Mr George Lansbury also told the Press: 'This film should be shown as quickly as possible. It is vitally important that people – and particularly young people who know nothing of the last war – should be shown what war is really like.' In its News Bulletin the same night, the BBC announced that a 'Peace Film had been held up by the Censor'. That evening invitations were issued to as many MPs as possible to see the film at a private screening in the morning.

The next day saw almost every national daily newspaper give front-page coverage to the Censor and the Peace Film. In some cases, as in the *News Chronicle*, it was the banner headline followed up by a two-column story and an editorial inside. The *Daily Herald* did the same. It is doubtful if any film up to that date had ever received so much simultaneous publicity. The stories in the nationals were repeated in all the main provincial newspapers. During the presentation of the film to a large audience of MPs at 12 noon, I was informed by a journalist from the *Manchester Guardian* that he had just spoken to the Secretary of the Censor Board on the telephone, who had said that a certificate for the film had been granted 'several days earlier' and was awaiting collection by the producers. It was not, however, until 4.30 pm the same afternoon that a telephone message was left at the registered office of Freenat Films Ltd to the effect that a 'U' certificate for the Peace Film was waiting in the Censor's outer office.

In an interview with a member of the Press, the Board's Secretary stated that the film had been granted a certificate several days earlier, indeed before Miss Grierson had her second interview, but no explanation was offered for the fact that the producers of the film had not been notified at that time. The following communiqué was then issued by the Board:

The Peace Film (1936)

This short film measuring 300 ft was submitted for censorship by Freenat Films Ltd on 31 March, and a note was sent to the publishers to the effect that as the film was controversial it was desirable for us to discuss the subject with them before action was taken.

The publishers were interviewed on 3 April when it was made quite clear to our representatives that the Board was quite ready to pass the film if they could give an assurance that the military portions of the film were not Crown property, or if they were, they had permission to use them in what was a controversial film. Provided this authority had been granted, there was no reason that the film should not be certified.

The film was viewed at our request by the proper authorities [sic] who came to the conclusion that the military sections were not Crown property.

The publishers knew that the certificate would be granted immediately such confirmation had been received from the authorities concerned, and is now awaiting them.

The discrepancies (even in dates) in the above statement made by the Board are clear when the previous facts are recalled.

At midnight on 8 April, the Peace Film was booked to three London cinemas, one being the big London Pavilion in Piccadilly Circus. At the same time, a copy was sent by post to the Manager of the Victoria Cinema, Inverurie, in Scotland, who had telegraphed for the film immediately after hearing the BBC News Bulletin on 7 April.

As a result of the nation-wide publicity given in the Press, applications were received all over the Easter weekend for copies of the film. In anticipation of this demand, 100 copies had been ordered on non-inflammable stock, with wood containers for same. Over Easter, 30 copies of the film were showing in London alone. Copies were sent by post to all those many cinema managers who had applied for it as a result of the advertisement in the *Kinematograph Weekly*.

It was the first time in British cinema history that a film received such a simultaneous release. Copies were sent on request to the League of Nations in Geneva, the Rotarian Convention in Atlantic City, and to Sweden, Belgium and Russia.

The Peace Film (1936)

Total expenditure on the whole operation, production as well as distribution, was less that £500.

The story of the Peace Film (taken from a day-to-day memorandum kept at the time) has been given in full here for the first time. It marked, I suggest, the defeat of a would-be political censorship, for which the British Board of Film Censors at that time had no authority, by simple democratic action by a few individuals. The film itself was not important as a piece of film-making; the motives behind it and the subsequent actions were; hence its full record here.

When war broke out in 1939, the original negative of the notorious Peace Film was sent to the Museum of Modern Art Film Library in New York for safe keeping, where presumably it still is; later a new print was placed on loan at the National Film Archive, London.

How many people in the United Kingdom, as a result of seeing the little film at their cinema, actually acted on its suggestion to write to their MP will always remain unknown. But as Ritchie-Calder and J. J. Taylor agreed in later years, it was an eventful and exciting few weeks with something achieved at the end.

Not long before the war in 1939, someone had the brilliant idea of holding a Soho Fair in the square. Restaurateurs and shops opened small stands and there was a funfair with a shooting-gallery, where to Mr Golightly's annoyance I beat him nine shots out of ten. As part of the celebrations, the British Board of Film Censors opened its beautiful building, Carlisle House, to the public. I went at an off-peak moment and had the pleasure of being shown round by Mr Brooke Wilkinson himself. He had no idea who I was. In his own room, I took down a copy of *The Film Till Now* from a glass-fronted bookcase. 'This looks like an important work,' I said. 'Yes, indeed,' he replied, 'We use it a great deal.' When I came to sign the visitors' book I put after my name, 'In memory of the Peace Film and the Can-Can girls.'[1] I shall always remember the expression on his face. It was the only time I met him.

[1] Vide: p. 228.

9. New York (1937–38)

In the spring of 1937, Iris Barry, film critic of the *Daily Mail* in London in the mid-1920s, a founder of the London Film Society in 1925 and author of *Let's Go to the Pictures*, and her American stockbroker husband, John Abbott, came to Europe to find films for their newly established Film Library at the Museum of Modern Art, New York. Abbott was the Library's Director, Miss Barry its Curator.

Over lunch at Scott's, Iris asked me if I would like to go to the US and be attached for, say, six months to the Film Library. If in principle I agreed, she would try on her return to get me a Rockefeller Foundation Fellowship in the autumn. The Foundation through its General Education Board partly subsidized the Film Library. She said that *The Film Till Now* was quite well known over there and that, as well as giving advice to the Library in a general way, lectures could be arranged at universities, educational organizations, government departments and perhaps some useful contacts might be made with the American motion picture industry. It was a stimulating offer but clearly needed some discussion with the people at Strand Films, where I was obliged to see through the Imperial Airways film programme.

In a week or two, a still more stimulating motive for such a visit arose. Miss Barry had seen some of our documentary films – among them *Night Mail* and *Today We Live* – and she had at once grasped that the idea which underlay our work had no counterpart in the US, except perhaps for the isolated *The Plow that Broke the Plains* in 1936 by the movie critic Pare Lorentz, which Miss Barry said had been inspired by *The Face of Britain* when it was shown at the White House. She saw now that my proposed visit might be given an added purpose, that of introducing the whole documentary idea of public service using social purpose for progress, to sections of the American public, especially those who might be concerned to promote a documentary movement among American film-makers and imaginative educationists. At the same time, I saw in this an opportunity to foster Anglo-American relations on a solid democratic basis, something about which Eric Knight and I had written a great deal to each other since 1932. In a way, the path had been blazed by Thomas Baird, a specialist in the non-theatrical and educational use of films attached to Film Centre, who had made a short visit at the invitation of the Rockefeller Foundation a little earlier and had met with an encouraging reception.

In addition, John Abbott had just heard that the Film Library had been promised the sum of 50,000 dollars to script and produce a film on the History and Technique of the Motion Picture, with material drawn from its own vaults. It was Abbott's idea that, added to my other activities, I should work on this new project.

Iris Barry had arranged with Grierson that copies of the following films should be deposited at the Film Library: *Night Mail*, *Granton Trawler*, *We Live in Two Worlds*, *Roadways*, *Weather Forecast*, *The Smoke Menace*, *Children at School*, *Today We Live*, *Eastern Valley*, *Housing Problems* and *Enough to Eat?* A copy of *Song of Ceylon* was already in an agent's hands in New York and an American book association had a print of *Cover to Cover*. It was from this collection that I should draw to back up my lectures and to give private screenings. After that, the Film Library would distribute the films non-theatrically to approved enquirers.

Before leaving, the Abbotts said that during the summer a Dr David A. Stevens, the director of the General Education Board who looked after its film interests, would be in London and would contact me officially. Dr Stevens duly arrived, took me to lunch at Leoni's Quo Vadis? restaurant and formally offered me a Fellowship valued at 4,500 dollars to include all expenses. After an uneasy discussion tinged with envy at Strand, it was agreed that my contract be suspended for the time I should be abroad and that I was free to leave London when my work on the Imperial Airway films was done. This was

New York (1937-38)

not made easier, as has been seen, by Donald Taylor abruptly taking Alex Shaw away to salvage Mr Korda's air epic. Actually Taylor had no right to do this as I was in charge of all production personnel at Strand, but I had no wish to aggravate an already tense situation and preferred to take over and finish the air films myself. I resented, however, the fact that Strand later refused to send a copy of the main film, *The Future's in the Air*, to New York, mollifying Imperial Airways by telling them that a commercial distribution had already been fixed in the US, which was untrue. American exhibitors would hardly be likely to book a film extolling the efficiencies of British air routes!

The English Speaking Union in London, a highly respectable body much occupied in improving Anglo-American friendship, heard of my proposed visit through the Press. They asked if they could give a showing of three of the films I should be taking with me to some 800 members of its society at the Phoenix Theatre in the presence of the US Ambassador. Mr J. B. Priestley, who had had much to do with one of the films – *We Live in Two Worlds* – introduced the occasion, which he was to repeat later in New York with much success and publicity.

A few evenings before departure, Grierson gave a small party at his house, during which he presented me with an inscribed silver hip-flask, which was to have a curious story.[1] I took the opportunity of saying that I was not going to the US to further my personal prospects but rather to promote the interests of British documentary as a whole.

The only tourist passage that could be found at short notice was in the German liner *Europa* on 22 September. The trip was without event except for the ship standing on its stern when it met the tail-end of a hurricane. I recall that the *Europa* was em-

[1] In 1942, when Eric Knight was in London working with me on the script of *World of Plenty*, he suddenly decided to return to the US as a result of Pearl Harbour bringing America into the war. (The script was completed by cable and air-letter.) I loaned him the silver flask. In January, 1943, he lost his life in a US transport plane that crashed into the marshes on the Dutch Guiana coast. He was then a major in the US army and posted for information work in Cairo. After the war, the US navy salvaged the aircraft, found among other things the flask, sent it to Knight's widow, Jere, who, in turn returned it to me. It has been often used since its four years' hibernation in Guianan mud.

173

blazoned at every available place by portraits of the Führer. Sleep was impossible because of the vibration; it was the time when Britain, France and Germany were rivals for the Atlantic blue riband. Passenger comfort came second to knocking half-a-day off the crossing. I remember sharing a small cabin with a Captain Jones. We drank whisky most of the day and night while I listened to his sea-faring reminiscences.

On this trip the *Europa* was about two hours late, which did not worry me. I was not to know that the Film Library had arranged a Press party at David O. Selznick's luxurious projection theatre and that the party had been kept waiting two hours. Thus I was idly scanning the sights of Manhattan Island from the Hudson River when I heard my name being called over the loud-speaker system, asking me at once – repeat, at once – to go to the first-class passenger lounge. There was John Abbott in a hopping frenzy. He had boarded from the pilot ship. I was to leave my baggage and follow him. 'Collins,' he explained breathlessly, 'will see all your things ashore.' (Later I found that Collins was the general dogsbody around the Library.) We made the quay – or a quay – in a fast motor-launch and were whisked into a waiting automobile. If there wasn't a fleet of outriders with sirens as we sped across town, then it was not John Abbott's fault.

The theatre was packed to its 200 capacity. Everyone was drinking. Iris Barry had sensibly shown them Len Lye's *Colour Box* (of which she had stolen a copy in London) three times with much success. As I was some two hours late, Abbott had told me in the car (as if it was my fault), the company would be several dry martinis and Scotches ahead of me. This, I thought, was a good thing. However, they were shown *Night Mail* with great effect. I muttered some words of the expected kind, and after a few interviews with persons whose names were inaudible, the guests departed leaving Miss Barry and Abbott beaming with delight and me rather winded and very thirsty. 'Now for some dinner,' said Abbott excitedly, 'We'll take him to Pierre's, wonderful French cooking.'[1] When I came to find my hat, coat and scarf (all new for the trip), they had gone.

[1] Not the hotel on Fifth Avenue facing Central Park but a small so-called 'exclusive' place somewhere in the East mid-50s.

'Tut, tut!' said Abbott, 'there must be some mistake. We'll rectify it in the morning.' It was never rectified.

Dinner was as expected but very expensive. 'You'd like some wine?' asked Mr Abbott, clicking his fingers. The wine waiter came with his *carte*. Abbott waved it aside. 'Just some red, waiter!' he snapped. I stuck on Scotch without the rocks. At midnight, Abbott confided, 'We've not booked you into a hotel, Paul. We thought you would prefer somewhere more English.'

The St Nicholas Club was very nice; it had everything except the Beefeaters. In my bedroom, Collins stood regarding my baggage, looking at the same time a little hangdog and a little pleased, as I was to find only Collins could do. 'It was a little difficult, Sir. I forgot to ask you for the keys. But,' with a smile, 'the Customs Officer was an Irishman, you see, Sir. There was no problem.'

Next morning I reported to the Film Library, which had offices just round the corner on the 12th or maybe the 15th floor (I don't remember) in the CBS building at 485 Madison Avenue. A nice girl at reception (she was paid 20 dollars a week, I found out later) said that Mr Abbott would see me at once. He had a big but not sumptuous office and was sitting back in a chair, draped in a white sheet. A barber was trimming his scanty hair while Abbott was on the telephone to his broker. He waved me to take a chair.

I must confess now that from then on during the next six months, my opinion of John Abbott as the Director of a Film Library declined, while my respect for Iris Barry as a Curator, with a genuine passion for the cinema, grew all the time. Later that morning I met the staff, few enough of them, and admired the well-stocked shelves of the book library where Miss Barry had her desk and typewriter. Allocated for my use was a small office with a window through which Madison Avenue could be seen I don't know how many feet below. I don't like heights. There was a fine view of Grand Central Station which, on a visit to my office some time later, Graham Greene mistook for New York's Roman Catholic Cathedral.

To Abbott I said that I should report to Dr Stevens as soon as appropriate. It was already fixed. I would not be seeing

175

Stevens (who was on a vacation), but Mr John Marshall, who was Stevens's assistant (and later his successor), would like to see me.

John Marshall I liked at once. He was quiet in manner, soft spoken and obviously well informed on most aspects of the educational and documentary film field. He spoke warmly of Tom Baird's recent visit and what a good impression he had left. Such contacts would be helpful to me. He asked me to keep in close touch during my visit but if any film matters were to be discussed, then Abbott must be there too. 'I hope,' he said, 'that some of your documentary knowledge and experience will brush off on some of our people here. They have a lot to learn.'

When I had been at the Film Library a couple of days, Iris Barry came into my office one evening and said, 'You'll need an assistant. Have you anybody in mind?' I hadn't. She said casually, 'There's been a tall, gangling young man hanging around reception for a day or two. Says he knows you. His name's Griffith and he's come up from Virginia.'

Within a few minutes I was buying Richard Griffith his Scotch at a bar along the street. In the morning, he began work as my assistant. His first letter to me as a result of *The Film Till Now* appearing in America was dated June 1931, when he was still at college; the last, October 1969, only a few days before an automobile killed him. (Like me, he did not himself drive.) He collaborated with me in the updated edition of *Till Now* in 1949 and again with the North American sections in *Documentary Film* in 1952. He was to become an author in his own right in 1953 with his *The World of Robert Flaherty* and a close friend of that fine film-maker. In collaboration with Arthur Mayer he produced the massive *The Movies* in 1957, followed by *The Movie Stars*, published posthumously in 1970. During the war, he was researching into stock footage for the Capra Unit which made the *Why We Fight* series. Later he held the post of Executive Director at the National Board of Review of Motion Pictures. He was then assistant to Iris Barry at the Film Library and, on her retirement, took her place as Curator. Our correspondence over nearly 40 years ran into some five million words and ranged far and wide, not confined only to films. He was one of the few Americans who at that time grasped the purpose of the documentary idea. He was a loyal, talented and most trusted friend, worthy to rank with Eric Knight, Carl Mayer and Richard Winnington.

The Film Library in those days had no projection theatre of its own but had the use of that of David O. Selznick in Grand Central Building when it was vacant, which was most often. Selznick saw in the Film Library, I suspected, a small but culturally useful side to his public relations. I was to find that if the Film Library organized an exhibition of, say, set-designs, the examples shown would without question be from a new Selznick production. John Hay Whitney, part owner of Technicolor, a Trustee of the Museum of Modern Art and Chairman of the Film Library, also held stock in Selznick's company. Abbott later revealed that the script I was supposed to write on The Technique of the Motion Picture was to be financed either by Whitney or Selznick, or both. Anyway, it was made clear that if I wanted any clips from Mr Selznick's films, past or present, no problems would arise. They didn't.

In the first week my tentative schedule was discussed and agreed with Abbott. There was the course of 28 three-hour lectures to give in collaboration with Columbia University, for which some 35 students had been enrolled at a high fee. The lectures were to be given in the Selznick theatre so that film clips could be shown. I was slated to give 13 of them. Now Abbot had one sensible idea. Movie people from the West Coast were often in New York for a few days and Abbott suggested that suitable ones be contacted and persuaded to talk to the students informally. King Vidor gave a good evening on film direction with clips from *The Big Parade*, *The Crowd* and *Hallelujah!*, while James Cagney was first class on spontaneous acting, with clips from *The Public Enemy* and *Lady-Killer*. (Much later that night, Cagney took me drinking to some bars he knew in the docks where everyone knew him as Jimmie and there was no red carpet stuff.) Arthur Knight, then one of the students, recalls:

For me, it's where it all began. Among the people I remember in the class are Rudy Bretz, now one of the leading American authorities on TV installations; Irving Reis, then a CBS radio producer but who became a good movie director in Hollywood before his untimely death; Felicia Lamport, who became a novelist and critic; Janet Graves, who still does film criticism for *Photoplay* and was a fan of Eric Knight's; Robert Giroux, now a director of a leading publisher; Mgr. Little, who later headed the Legion of Decency for a number of years; Ezra Goodman, of course,[1] and Griffith. We all met on a Tuesday night and after the sessions we would leave the cavernous Grand Central Building and slip across Lexington Avenue to a friendly bar, usually with the guest, and talk would go on until they threw us out. Then some of us would head for an all-night movie on 42nd Street.

Hitchcock, making his first trip to the US, gave us a marvellous evening, as did the writer Talbot Jennings (who, I think, had worked on the first *Mutiny of the Bounty*). Alistair Cooke was in for several sessions; he was still wrapped up in philology and etymology . . . I recall Gilbert Seldes talking to us about television while it was still a twinkle in CBS's corporate eye, and Eric Knight came to talk to us about his work both as a critic in Philadelphia and as a story editor in the film factory at Fox in Hollywood. Among the documentary boys were Joris Ivens, John Ferno and yourself.[2]

As Arthur Knight says, some of the students went on to make some kind of a career in or around the movies. Thereby hangs a favourite story of mine, which happened sometime later.

One day in New York around 1952 (on my way to Mexico), some twelve years after the course at the Film Library, I went out with Dick Griffith for a drink. He had called two other old friends to join us. All three had been students at the lectures. 'You know,' I said, looking at them, 'I ought to be a proud man, you are all now successful. Dick Griffith, Curator of the Film Library; Ezra Goodman, movie critic of *Time* magazine; Arthur Knight, much-sought-after lecturer and film critic. And I'm told there's some guy named Jules Something-or-other, who was also a student, he's pulling down a fat wage in Hollywood. But now, fellows, tell me what ever happened to that terrific strawberry blonde who sat in the second row?' They looked at

[1] Critic and columnist for several movie journals but especially for *Time* magazine. His book *The Fifty-Year Decline and Fall of Hollywood* (Simon and Schuster, New York, 1961) is good if light reading.

[2] In a letter to the author, 29 April 1972. Arthur Knight is now a professor in the Cinema Department at the University of Southern California and was the author of *The Liveliest Art* (Macmillan, New York, 1957). He adopted Knight's name in respect and admiration of Eric.

each other, and one of them said, 'Why, didn't you know, she became the most sought after call-girl in New York.'

Eric Knight had written me from Croton-on-Hudson, where he lived some fifty miles from New York City, to say he wouldn't come to the city to meet me and spoil Abbott's proprietorship, but that his wife, Jere, who was story editor at Selznick International Picture's East Coast Office, would call me during the week, fix to meet and she'd take me out to Croton for the weekend. His letter also contained the following cryptic remarks, 'I am convinced you must have some swell friends in England – the kind that always scrape their initials off the stiletto handle before plunging it in your back. I do not know for sure, but I feel very much that someone tried some last-minute knifing of you, and almost succeeded.' When I took Knight up on this, he shrugged, 'It was just something that Abbott dropped when he asked me to lunch last week. Forget it. You're here now and that's all that matters.' I did forget; but was to remember his warning some months later.

Thus on a very dark evening Knight came to greet me at Harmon rail road station; he was red-headed, in a white sweater and jeans, with a smile you could never forget. So two people who had exchanged hundreds of thousands of words across the Atlantic about their respective lives met for the first time.[1]

The Knights rented a converted stable wing on an estate called Finney Farm, accessible only by a rocky dirt road. Built by Horace Greeley, of *Go West, Young Man* fame, the main barn was said to be the first concrete structure of its size built on a stone foundation in the US. The original mansion had burnt down and the great barn was gutted, but its roofless shell still stood. The various outbuildings were converted into houses, the two stable wings adjoining the barn being called Cherry House and Peach House. It was all surrounded by beautiful woodland. The Knights lived in Cherry House, where Mabel Dodge Luhan (of D. H. Lawrence connotation) had lived. It was also said that Robert Flaherty had rented it but I could never

[1] A selection of Knight's letters between 1932 and 1942 were collected by me in *Portrait of a Flying Yorkshireman*, Chapman & Hall London, 1952.

find any confirmation of this; Mrs Frances Flaherty certainly did not remember. The long low living-room with its huge log fire in winter; the inner room where Knight was supposed to work but which he invariably deserted with his portable type-writer for the outdoors; the surrounding grass lawns and creeper-covered walls – these all created a memorable atmo-sphere. I was to spend many long weekends at Cherry House, grateful for the Knights' stimulating talk and for the relief its calm gave me from the febrile atmosphere of New York.

The first private show of three of our documentary films was given in the Selznick theatre, the films being *Today We Live*, *Night Mail* and one other I forget. Knight came down from Croton and then wrote,

4 November 1937

I can't tell you how terrifically exciting I found the films. While the excitement came partly from the subjects, it came (I can analyse my-self) even more from the remarkable and unbeatably stirring cutting. Visually they were astounding, showing me things I had never seen before. You know me well enough not to know that I need not write this if I do not feel it. I swear we have never had in America before any films which, even for a second, showed the remarkable brilliance of cutting that the films revealed throughout their entirety. It was to me a revelation, a sort of coming true of things that had always been to me the theoretical. Especially was this visual perfection, a hitherto un-revealed flow and contrast and contradiction and rhythm through the cutting, staggering in the first film.

The one great drawback to the films, and a problem you must tell them immediately in England if they are to be removed from all criticism here, is the sound quality. There are faults in both the technical and in the creative use. The first fault, the technical, is one of which you must be aware. In America we are so used to lacquer-finish perfection in sound recording that we are always upset by British pictures. While you explain to me that the reason for the use of inferior sound equipment is cost, I say that this *must* be rectified. The films are so remarkable that you must in future make your spon-sors underwrite the finest sound recording. It is heartrending to see such creative genius destroyed by inferior technical methods. It is not the dialect of your voices that will be difficult for American aud-iences, it is the poor sound.

The sceond fault I have, creative, is forgivable. From your showing,

I am utterly convinced that poetry – and most especially rhythm poetry – has no place in the spoken field in films. I do not know why yet; I can only guess at the reasons and tell you. The poetry of a film lies in its visuals. When it is also placed in the aural, we get an over-effect that goes beyond its goal and reaches over into the comic. It was a laudable try with Auden yet not a success. But it is fine that such experiments should be made.[1]

We must talk of all this, but I thought I'd get this off to you while I am still burning with enthusiasm for what I saw. The films are a revelation to us; we have had nothing quite like them before in America.

By now I was meeting with some of the film-makers in New York who were each in their own way using documentary techniques. I was glad first to meet Pare Lorentz, who was just finishing his second film for the Government's Farm Security Administration, *The River*. He showed me his cutting-copy on which I complimented him. He said that he had some money left in his budget and asked how he could best use it. His film, I felt, was beautiful and emotional, but lacking in human qualities. In all honesty, since he had asked my opinion, I suggested that he should take a sound crew and go and record some of the real people to find how they reacted to the problems of soil erosion and lack of flood control. Some time later, I heard that he had taken my ideas in bad grace. It seemed that Lorentz did not like frank suggestions from a fellow film-maker even when he asked for them. Needless to add, he did not utilize my ideas but finished his 'poem' in his own way. But it must be clear that both his films were a big success in the public cinemas in the US, even if exhibitors got them free.

Among others whom I met and found most anxious to discuss common ideas and problems were Ralph Steiner and Willard van Dyke, both very good cameramen who had worked on the Lorentz pictures. All through my visit, I was to have many friendly talks with these two. They were trying to operate pro-duction on an independent basis, which was not easy.

Backed by the General Education Board and with the some-what reluctant cooperation of the Hays Office, the Progressive Education Association under the highly intelligent guidance of

---

[1] I have heard similar criticism of the verse in *Night Mail* elsewhere.

Dr Alice V. Kelliher had gained access to some Hollywood feature films for re-editing purposes. A sequence was taken and recut to be used as a basis for future classroom discussion of Human Relations. She had first Joris Ivens working with her, and then Joseph Losey. She hoped one day to get enough money to go into actual production. Another meeting was with Bob Kissack who was attached as a trainee to *March of Time*. His aim was to build up a documentary and educational film school at Minneapolis. He hoped to obtain extensive GEB support to equip a production unit, as well as to make four films a year on aspects of local administration.

I paid a visit to Frontier Films, reportedly a far-Left unit under the supervision of Paul Strand. Maybe I was tactless in asking him how his adobe house was getting along. The unit had several interesting films to its credit, mainly edited from footage shot by others on foreign battle fronts. Such were *Heart of Spain* and *China Strikes Back*. The shooting in the former had been supervised by Herbert Kline, who was the militant editor of the journal *New Theater and Film*. Also at Frontier was 'Robert Stebbins', who wrote for *New Theater*, but worked too as a skilled editor. Jay Leyda, who had a job at the Film Library, also did part-time chores at Frontier. Their films were destined mainly for showing to trade unions and Labour groups, but had occasional theatre bookings.

Early in 1937 Contemporary Historians Inc. had been formed by a group of writers including John Dos Passos, Ernest Hemingway, Archibald MacLeish and Lillian Hellman. Finance was found to send Joris Ivens and Hemingway to cover the Spanish Civil War. They brought back excellent footage which was shaped by that brilliant editor, Helen van Dongen (who had cut most of Ivens's earlier films) into *The Spanish Earth*, with a commentary written and spoken by Hemingway. It was running to good audiences in New York while I was there. I also talked with Julien Bryan who, since 1930, had been a world cameraman traveller. He had brought back footage from many countries, some of which was edited into what could be loosely called educational films, and some of which was sold as stock material for use by others. All this activity so far as I could see was unrelated. There were also people on the fringe of film-making, such as the young poetess Muriel Rukeyser, who had written commentaries and through whom I met the German composer, Hanns Eisler, whom I liked and whose film music was very good indeed.

Alistair Cooke one day introduced me to Irving Reis, who was making some highly experimental radio programmes on Sundays for CBS Workshop, using sound and voice effects in exciting new ways. He was unwise to go later to Hollywood and bash his good brain against an unresponsive wall.

During my first weeks, a courtesy call had to be made to the British Library of Information, the Government department for British public relations in the US in the days before there were British Information Services overseas. I was asked to tea by Sir Angus Somerville Fletcher, K.C.M.G., C.B.E. After the usual pleasantries, I asked him what his office was doing about presenting the British people and their way of life to the Americans. He beckoned me into his office and pointed to a roll-up map on the wall. It was of the British Isles. The map had small circles dotted about it and in each circle was a little thatched cottage; this was as true of the industrial North as of sunny Cornwall. The only exception was the capital, which boasted a Tower of London. A decorative border of interwoven leaves surrounded the map, broken here and there by portraits of Lord Roberts, Lord Kitchener, Field Marshall Haig, Earl Jellicoe, Lord French and other distinguished warlike figures. 'Thousands of those maps,' said Sir Angus, teacup in hand, 'have gone out free of charge to American high schools'. Later, when he was asked to come and see some of the British documentary films I had brought, he winced. They were not the kind of England he was paid, or indeed chose, to present to Americans. Mr J. E. M. Carvell, the Trade Commissioner at the British Consulate, who was reporting to the Foreign Office in London on American reaction to British feature films, tried to understand but hedged when I told him that one of my aims in the US was to tell audiences something about how democracy worked in the United Kingdom. 'Do you think that's wise, old boy?' he asked. I was a private citizen representing nobody except myself in the US, and anyway I was the guest of the Rockefeller Foundation. This attitude to presenting ourselves to peoples overseas was very general then, and still prevails in some places now.

One major thing came as a surprise to me in the New York film scene in which I was most interested, and that was how isolated one American film-maker was from another. Unlike in London where all of us in documentary knew pretty well what the other was doing, in New York each seemed to be operating in a vacuum. A guy living and working in one street had no idea that another guy with similar aims and projects lived two blocks away round the corner. Maybe they had distantly heard about one another but it never occurred to them to meet and discuss their common interests. In fact, I found that on more than one occasion I was introducing two would-be American documentary film-makers to each other for the first time, yet they had lived and worked within the same city for years. It is possible that this shell-like existence was due to the fear of competition. Joris Ivens corroborated this strange lack of cameraderie; he put it down to personal jealousy and vanity. Pare Lorentz, who had made the two best American documentary films, never trained anyone with his unit. He operated as a loner. Such an idea would never have occurred to us in England; that is why our movement spread in the 1930s. If John Grierson's attitude after he made *Drifters* in 1929 had been that of a Pare Lorentz, there would have been no British documentary film movement.

People now write about the American *documentary* novel, American *documentary* photography, American *documentary* radio and American *documentary* theatre and of the socially aware 1930s, but it is worth noting that the term *documentary* was not used in America until the mid-1930s. Until the introduction of our films in 1937–38, the influence of Grierson's writings circulating in the US, and perhaps the reaction to my own *Documentary Film* book, the use of the documentary label was unknown there. In the last half of the decade leading up to the war, the Americans seized on the word documentary as if they had dreamed it up and applied it to anything that remotely touched on reality. The same happened in British television after the war, when a reporter talking to workers coming out of a factory was said to be making a 'documentary'.

New York (1937–38)

In America the search for an expression of social realism in the depression years in the early 1930s was pioneered by the fine work of such camera-writer teams as Agee and Walker Evans, Dorothea Lange and Taylor, and Bourke-White and Caldwell. Alfred Kazin put this very well:

Here was America, all of it undoubtedly America – but America in a gallery of photographs, an echo of the people's talk, a storehouse of vivid single impressions.

Here was America – the cars on the unending white ribbon of road; the workers in the mills; the faces of the farmers' wives and their children in the roadside camps; a thousand miles from nowhere; the tenant farmer's wife with her child sitting on the steps of an old plantation mansion, where the columns were gray and crumbling with age. Here was the child in the grimy bed, the Okies crossing the desert in their jalopy, the pallor of August in the Dust Bowl, the Baptist service in the old Negro church. Here was the greatest creative irony the reportorial mind of the 1930s could establish – a picture of Negro farmers wandering on the road, eating their bread under a billboard poster furnished by the National Association of Manufacturers – 'America Enjoys the Highest Standard of Living in the World.' Here was the migrant family sleeping on sacks in the roadside grass, above them the railroad legend 'Travel While You Sleep.' Here was the Negro sitting in the fields near Memphis (more men than jobs at Bridgehead labor market), saying: 'They come off the plantations 'cause they ain't got nothin' to do. . . . They come to town and they *still* got nothin' to do.' Here was the treeless landscape in southwestern Oklahoma, a country strewn with deserted and crumbling houses, the farmers driven off by the tractors, a picture of land where the tractors now kneaded the earth right 'to the very door of the houses of those whom they replace.'

Here, indeed was an America that could only be quoted and photographed and described in pictures or in words that sought to be pictures.[1]

Walker Evans and Dorothea Lange had caught attention with this dual use of the media in their books *South Street* (1932) and *Main Street* (1933).

For RRA, (the Rural Resettlement Administration) [William Bluem wrote] Evans went to the American south to photograph the squalid life of the sharecroppers. Dorothea Lange, working with Paul Taylor,

[1] *On Native Grounds*, Cape, 1943, pp. 496, 497.

185

an economics professor, had been hired earlier by the State of California to document the ugly story of the Okies, California's migratory workers, and here gained the insight and experience which resulted in such photographs as in *In a Camp of Migratory Pea-Pickers* (1936). Her portraits of the lives of the migrants inspired two later motion pictures – Lorentz's documentary film *The Plow that Broke the Plains* and a fiction film based on John Steinbeck's novel, *The Grapes of Wrath*.[1]

And there were other books out in the field: *An American Exodus: A Record of Human Erosion*, also by Lange and Paul Taylor; James Agee and Walker Evans's *Let Us Now Praise Famous Men*; and Margaret Bourke-White and Erskine Caldwell's *You Have Seen Their Faces*. All these were superb examples of photographs interwoven with text.

It was a visit to Washington that first called my attention to this awakening of social consciousness on America's own back doorstep. I met that remarkable man, Roy E. Stryker. Under the New Deal's National Recovery Administration, various Government bodies had been set up to aid fighting the economic and human depression. Among them was the Rural Resettlement Administration, later called the Farming Security Administration. One of its activities was to record by photographs (and later the Lorentz films) the social and economic conditions that were the scourge of so many millions of the American people. Stryker headed a photographic unit to engage a team of first-class photographers to go out across the US to capture pictures of the devastation that had fallen on people and land alike. He was of course following in the wake of the pioneer work already described but this was with Government backing. Stryker is quoted as saying,

Documentary is an approach, not a technique, an affirmation, not a negation. . . . The documentary attitude is not a denial of the plastic elements which must remain essential in any work. It merely gives these elements limitations and direction.[2]

[1] *Documentary in American Television*, Hastings House, New York, 1965. To the two films mentioned, there should of course be added Robert Flaherty's extraordinary *The Land* (1939–40) about which vide *The Innocent Eye*, A. Calder-Marshall, W. H. Allen, 1963. The outspoken narration is printed in full.

[2] *The Complete Photographer* (1942, IV) quoted in *The History of Photography*, Beaumont Newhall, (Museum of Modern Art, 1949). It should also be on the record that Stryker was the public relations officer at Standard Oil (N.J.) when Robert Flaherty was commissioned to make *Louisaina Story* in 1946.

New York (1937-38)

If in my simple way I did not quite understand what Mr Stryker had in his mind about documentary, I was at once excited when he opened his file of photographs. Some of the photographers he sent out, such as Dorothea Lange and Walker Evans, were already known, but he also commissioned Arthur Rothstein, Russell Lee, Ben Shahn, Carl Mydans and Theodor Jung. This was a superb visual survey of many aspects of the American social and economic scene. Some of the prints were used to illustrate such books as: *Land of the Free—USA* (Boriswood, London, 1938) by Archibald MacLeish, and *American Photographs*, by Walker Evans (Museum of Modern Art, 1938). Here, I find myself echoing Mr Alfred Kazin, was America!

Along with documentary photography, the other dynamic movement that I found in the US was the New York theatre, or at least a part of it. To someone who doesn't usually adapt to theatre (I am for ever searching for my scissors to cut out its static waste of time), the work of the Federal Theater came as a surprise, not all its work, some of which was conventional, but that which was called *The Living Newspaper*. Unhappily I was able to see only one production, *One Third of a Nation*, at the Adelphi Theater, but seeing that and reading most of the scripts, I fed my excitement. I also talked with Arthur Arent, who wrote some of these scripts from material provided by a team of researchers, and with Joseph Losey, who directed most of the productions.

To a young generation it should be briefly related that under the National Recovery Administration initiated by Roosevelt to help combat the great economic depression there were various projects aimed to alleviate unemployment in certain areas. It has been seen what the Rural Resettlement Administration had done for photographers. The Federal Theater Project and the Federal Writers Project were two further examples of Government aid. I at once grasped that the potentialities of *The Living Newspaper* could be extended into the film medium, not to amplify theatre technique but to develop it in film terms.[1] The

---

[1] This was attempted in *New Worlds for Old* (1938), *World of Plenty* (1942-43) and *Land of Promise* (1944-45). I must admit, however, also to being influenced by *Hellzapoppin'*!

187

following are extracts from some notes made at the time in
1937.[1]

The Federal Theater Project was set up under the general
Government work relief programme (the WPA) early in 1934.
At first, 150 actors and technicians were employed on the
scheme, which was supervised by the kind of army officials who
directed relief work in general. The plays were old favourites
and were presented in obscure theatres without proper equipment or professional advice. Most theatre people were loath to
associate themselves with the Project.

Criticism of the whole Project, backed up by letters in the
Press from serious playwrights and actors, eventually reached
responsible ears in Washington. A change in administration
was authorized. Mrs Hallie Flanagan, for many years an
organizer of independent, progressive theatrical ventures, was
given sole charge of the Federal Theater Project, while Elmer
Rice, the distinguished playwright, became Regional Director
for New York. Mr Rice was trusted to make the Project something more than a meagre labour bureau for unemployed theatre
workers. This he did, and today (1937) the Federal Govern-
ment-backed plays have an audience of half a million people a
week in many parts of the US. People in such areas as New
England and the Deep South are seeing theatre for the first
time in their lives.

The Living Newspaper is only a small section of the main
Project. According to Morris Watson, original supervisor of
the scheme, the idea was born in October 1935, and arose
directly from Elmer Rice. No one person, however, can take
credit for the productions. It had grown as a result of the
collective effort by producers, writers and actors. At the same
time, the talents of Morris Watson, Arthur Arent and Joseph
Losey were more than just inspiration. About then, the Newspaper Guild of New York was looking for some way to absorb
its unemployed journalists into the Theater Project. Its committee saw Elmer Rice, who suggested that a project be formed
to present live news on the stage. The first idea was to use
snippets of news items to precede a rather longer piece. Arent
was given the assignment to write the first longer episode on

[1] Later written up as an article, *World Film News*, Vol. III, No. 2, May, 1938.

the subject of Mussolini's invasion of Ethiopia. When his script was delivered, it was liked so much that it was decided to drop the notion of the preceding short news items and concentrate the whole production on one main piece.

There were some precedents for presenting news on the stage. In 1933–34 a smart commercial revue, *As Thousands Cheer*, used newspaper headlines as a structure for its satiric sketches. The Workers' Laboratory Theater and some vaudeville producers had attempted to dramatize news events. Of most of these precedents Morris Watson, Elmer Rice and their associates were not aware. They did, however, acknowledge a debt to both the radio and movie versions of *March of Time*.

The final script by Arent was based on research over many weeks by twenty newspapermen who brought in some 20,000 pages of reports, pamphlets and Press stories. An assessment was made of the crucial episodes of the Abyssinian 'war' and its international repercussions. Only incidents admitted to by all parties were used; claims and counterclaims of importance were given as such in the words of the officials who had presented them at the time. No claim was stated without the reply coming from the opposition. Opening scenes in Italy and Abyssinia were followed by relevant League of Nations's conferences, the outlining of the infamous Hoare-Laval plan, Hoare's defence in the British Parliament and a cross-section of scenes depicting the currents of British public opinion that forced Hoare's resignation and Premier Baldwin's admission of error. Statesmen, soldiers, politicians were all represented on stage by actors.

Ethiopia was shown privately to the Press on 24 January 1936, and was very well liked. It was recognized as being something wholly new in theatre technique. Just before its public opening in New York, however, officials from the WPA stepped in and stopped its performance. 'Almost certainly,' they said, 'a Government-sponsored play about such a subject would be construed by Italy as an unfriendly act'. Press and theatre critics protested against the ban but it was maintained and the production cancelled. Elmer Rice, stating that he had been given complete authority to produce, resigned. 'Government censorship of *The Living Newspaper*,' he said, 'would mean the end of its usefulness.'

189

Undaunted, the production team at once set out on a new venture to dramatize a home subject this time – the problem of over-production in American agriculture, the efforts of the New Deal to solve the problem by legislation and the results of the Supreme Court's invalidation of the Agricultural Administration Act. *Triple-A Plowed Under*, as it was called, was directed by Joe Losey. It received very wide Press acclaim. The story of the agricultural problem in its developing phases was narrated through swiftly shifting scenes in which type characters expressed the viewpoints of the classes which they typified. Drama critics were surprised by the liveliness of these figures which were not characterized fully because of lack of space and the desire for fast tempo. Use was made of expressionist scenery and contrapuntal dialogue. In addition, this second edition of *The Living Newspaper* gave a brief background of the post-war years of boom and slump in relation to agriculture, rather like the prologue to the film *Today We Live*. This part of the play raised a storm of protest from Conservative newspapers.

The next edition, also directed by Losey, was a survey of the events of 1935 in social terms. It was dismissed by critics as weak and diffuse but it is worth noting that each successive edition of *The Living Newspaper* proceeded further away from immediate news towards a generalization of its root causes. Next came *Injunction Granted!*, a story of American Labour in 30 scenes, again directed by Losey. It drew the conclusions that throughout their history the American workers have been always exploited by their employers with the aid of the courts, that the latter issued injunctions all too freely, interpreted the Constitution in favour of the employer and utilized the legal frame-up to send working-class leaders to gaol and even death. *Power*, the fourth edition, dealt with electricity and the Tennessee Valley Authority plan. It was most successful.

Then was to come the major work – *One-Third of a Nation*. The title was taken from Roosevelt's second inauguration speech when he found: '. . . one-third of a nation ill-housed, ill-clad and ill-nourished.' It told swiftly and vividly the story of Manhattan's slums, of the greed of its landlords, of public apathy towards the injustices and legal violations that permitted this ghastly state of human existence to occur. Against Howard

New York (1937–38)

Bay's magnificent set of a cross-sectioned tenement, four storeys high, with rotting balustrades, inadequate fire-escapes and filthy dark rooms, there was told a chronicle of real estate rackets in Manhattan Island, embracing the system of land ownership that had permitted the Astor and Rhinelander families to exploit their property for the biggest profit, a dramatic fire outbreak, a cholera plague, an episode of juvenile delinquency, a rent strike, factual evidence by means of a film of the housing conditions in New York City today, and a lantern-slide tour round New York as it was in the 1850s. The style was bitingly satirical and openly Left-wing and had no respect for persons either dead or living. No small part was played by The Voice of *The Living Newspaper* itself, questioning and explaining through a loud-speaker at the back of the auditorium. On a much bigger scale and with far greater emotional and dramatic impact, *One-Third of a Nation* was the theatrical counterpart of the British film *Housing Problems*. It was real documentary theatre.[1]

No account of the origins of the American documentary form would, I suggest, be complete without tribute being paid to the writing of John Dos Passos. His use of newsreel reportage in his monumental trilogy *USA*, begun in 1930 (which contained the novels *The 42nd Parallel*, *Nineteen Nineteen* and *The Big Money*) undoubtedly influenced later writers and photographers as well as film-makers.[2] Eric Knight used a similar technique in his first book, *Invitation to Life*.[3]

The foregoing descriptions of American documentary still-photography and writing, and American documentary theatre may perhaps seem a divergence from the film medium. They were, however, an integral part of the development of the documentary idea in the US and were, as has been seen, far in advance of the American documentary film which at that time was only really found in Pare Lorentz's two films and in Joris

---

[1] A brief summary of *The Living Newspaper* was given by Arthur Arent in *Theater Arts* (New York, November, 1938), and reprinted in *Theatre Quarterly* Vol. I, No. 4, 1971.
[2] Harcourt, Brace & Co., New York, 1937 edition.
[3] Greenberg, New York, 1934.

Ivens's film of the Spanish Civil War. The seeds were never-theless being sown, even if their flowering was to be slow.[1]

The fall in the Eastern States is something that has been talked and written about endlessly, but it must be experienced in reality to be believed. You suspect that its fantastic colours have been over-painted; that would be impossible. I have seen it more than once or twice, but the Fall that year in the woods around Cherry House on the banks of the Hudson River was something never to be forgotten.

These weekends at the Knights not only meant a welcome contrast to the turbulent weekdays spent in the city but they gave an opportunity to take stock of all that I was experiencing, to get it into some kind of perspective, and always with Knight's wise advice to draw on. Our time there was also spent in innocuous pleasures. We would pick apples by the bushel and Eric would roll off their beautiful names. We would walk for miles in the woods. There was the little local printer to visit and later in the winter there was sledging down the hill that led up to the house.

We went over to the Max Eastmans' house near by to play tennis. King Vidor, who had once made *The Big Parade* and the wonderful *Hallelujah!*, was also there. Ten and twenty years older than I was, they all played a far better game than I did. One afternoon, Max's son, Dan, who had a 16 mm movie-camera, made a Western with Knight, Eastman and me dis-guised as Indians among the reeds round the lake. Eric was a Comanche, Max an Apache, while I settled for being a mere Blackfoot. Max had not long before published his successful book, *The Enjoyment of Laughter*, and was thus in funds. We ate and drank well. At no time on these few days were such dreary things as politics discussed, something which was to be of importance later. All I recall is a rather tattered picture of Trotsky in the hall.

One Saturday morning Knight said apropos of nothing, 'Let's

[1] The fruition of the arts under the Works Progress Administration in the US is briefly described in *The Age of the Great Depression* by Dixon Wecter (Mac-millan, New York, 1948) in the chapter headed 'Reading, Writing and Revolution' The work included exciting creative activity such as County Guides and Murals in Post Offices. It was a most stimulating era.

go buy a dartboard!' 'Where?' asked his wife. 'Macy's,' replied
Eric. 'They have everything.' Jere said to call Macy's Sports
Department in New York first just to see. Sure, Macy's had a
real British dartboard specially imported from Fortnum and
Mason's. How much? Fifty dollars. 'That's a lot of money,'
said Jere. Out in the woods at the back of the house, Eric
pointed to a fallen elm. 'If we sawed a section out of that, how'd
that do?' I nodded. 'We'll buy a reel of copper-wire and some
small brass nails in Peekshill and make a board ourselves. To
hell with Macy's!' said Knight. 'What about darts?' I asked.
'Oh, sure, we'll ride into town and buy those at Macy's but the
rest we do ourselves.' On the way into New York, Eric suddenly
asked, 'Do you remember where the numbers go and how far
it is from the bull to the outer double's ring?' I did not, but had
an idea.

A suave young assistant in the Sports Department produced
a handsome hogsbristle dartboard and a set of flights. Idly I
threw a dart at the board. 'Eric,' I said in my most English
accent, 'this is not a regular board.' Eric was busy noting down
the numbers of the beds and their locations. 'The distance from
the centre of the bull to the double's ring should be $7\frac{1}{2}$ inches,' I
said soberly, 'This one is only $6\frac{1}{2}$.' The assistant called the manager of the Sports Department. Knight confided to him. 'See, my
friend here's from England. He was the runner-up in the Kent
County Darts Championship last year.' I threw another dart.
'These measurements aren't right,' I declaimed. 'I'll fetch a
rule and you can measure them, sir.' said the manager. He did.
I measured them all right. Knight wrote it all down. 'I'll send
in a complaint to London, sir.' said the manager. 'You do just
that,' said Knight, 'In the meantime, we'll take this set of
arrows.' All evening we marked off the board with nails and
wire and played our first game of darts around midnight.[1]

Oliver H. P. Garrett, experienced Hollywood screenwriter
and a good friend of Knight's (he wrote *City Streets* and *The
Street of Chance*), was a champion on the board. He threw under-
hand and explained, 'It's the Indian way.' Others who played

---

[1] Grierson also threw a straight arrow, as I found in the local pub when from
time to time he visited me in the late 1930s at the house I had in Hythe. He almost
always beat me.

were the lovely and intelligent English actress and novelist, Elissa Landi, and her friend, Nino Martini. Miss Landi had been pushed around at MGM after Irving Thalberg died; Nino Martini had failed to make the grade at 20th Century-Fox. Lissa and Nino would go off for a whole afternoon in her car. At supper late one Sunday, Eric said, 'Tell me, Lissa, whatever do you and Nino do when you disappear in the car for so long?' Lissa said, 'Oh, we just talk.' 'And then what?' asked Eric. 'Then Nino sings to me,' replied Lissa, without turning a hair. 'Times have changed since I was a boy,' said Eric.

When later the snow and ice came and the ponds froze, Jere and Eric skated in the moonlight with dazzling grace, as they did so many things together, such as horse-riding in California. Knight was a very accomplished man. He could carve well. There was an enchanting wood piece of his collie, Toots, *couchant* on the long window-sill. Toots was a prize possession of the Knights. It was she who inspired one of Knight's best-known books, *Lassie Come Home*, meant for children but read by all.[1] Made into a not very good movie by MGM, Knight unfortunately did not share in the very considerable subsidiaries of the property, residuals like dog foods, toys and so on, or from the sequels like *Son of Lassie*. I recall spending a whole week out at Croton. Jere Knight of course went into New York every day to work at Selznick International, Eric would go off in the car to Croton dam where he would work with the typewriter on his lap, and I would stay home and try and work on the Technique script.

As has been seen, the showing of our documentaries had made a profound impression on Knight, not just their technique of film-making but their subject matter. The unemployment and depressed areas sequences in *Today We Live* and *Eastern Valley* (which had only just arrived) moved him very deeply. He could hardly believe that such conditions of poverty existed in Britain. Just before Christmas, he announced that he was going to England in the New Year to see how things stood for himself. Armed with introductions from me to Sir Stafford Cripps, Ritchie-Calder, Stanley Hawes and young Donald Alexander (who had made the *Eastern Valley* film), Knight went first to

[1] Winston, New York, 1940; Cassell, London, 1942.

London and then on through South Wales, Tyneside, the Lanark Valley and his home county, Yorkshire. He wanted also to see his early childhood surroundings; he was born at Menston. So he gathered at first hand material for two long articles which were commissioned by the *Saturday Evening Post* under the title 'Britain's Black Ghosts'. They were a reportage of Britain on the dole and worthy to stand alongside Orwell. His journey also served to give him the environment for his next novel, *Now Pray We for Our Country*.[1] He was not long back at Croton when it came my turn to go back to England.

The schedule of my lectures (apart from the Film Library course) and film screenings was finalized but obviously subject to other invitations as they might arise. The lectures began at Columbia University with a repeat performance of the programme presented by the English Speaking Union in London. After dining well with Alistair Cooke and Knight, Priestley and I again spoke our pieces to a very big audience. The next day Cooke gave me some valuable advice from which I have benefited ever since. He pointed out that there are a number of words in the English language which, for one reason or another, the Americans and the English pronounce differently. Well-known examples are 'detail' and 'simultaneously'. If, was Cooke's reasonable point, the English pronunciation is used, an American audience will miss out on the next sentence or two trying to figure out the different pronunciation of a word in the previous sentence. On the spur of the moment, he listed some thirty odd words so affected and that list has been ever since invaluable to me.

In the next few months, lectures accompanied by documentary films from the collection brought with me were given at the Metropolitan Motion Picture Council, the Progressive Education Association, Smith College in Northampton, and in Washington to audiences drawn from the Department of the Interior, the Federal Housing Administration, the American Council of Education, the US Office of Education, the National Youth Administration and the Department of Agriculture. In New

---

[1] This was the English title, Cassell, 1940. In the US it was called *The Happy Land*, Harper & Bros, 1940. The English edition was a revision of the American, the last edition being retitled *This is the Land*.

York again to the National Board of Review of Motion Pictures, the Brooklyn Institute, City College and the New School for Social Research. In addition there were many private screenings to invited audiences at the Selznick theatre, including one to the Ladies Garment Workers' Union who had produced the exciting social satirical-cum-musical *Pins and Needles* which was running with much commercial success in New York at the time.

Abbott did not tell me that David O. Selznick had been in from the Coast and had asked to see some of our films. Selznick called me. 'You know,' he said, 'We've seen nothing like this over here before. Why don't you come on out to the Coast, be my guest for a month, hang around and talk with the boys.' 'Thanks a lot, Mr Selznick,' I said, 'but my place of operation is in New York.'

From all these lectures (Abbott could hardly complain he wasn't getting his money's worth) three incidents are recalled. In Washington prior to a lecture, I had been shown round the Capital and, after appropriately admiring its monumental pseudo-classical official buildings, had seen something of the appalling slum conditions, said at that time to be the worst in the country. In my programme was *Housing Problems*. In my talk I made the point that Washington D.C. also had a slum problem of devastating size and that I should like to see a film made exposing them. On my return to New York, I found a furious John Abbott. 'Where's your sense of public relations? What the hell do you mean by denouncing Washington's slums?' I told him tersely that I would denounce any slums no matter what country they were in.

A less serious occasion occurred at Smith, the big girls' college at Northampton. Inevitably the sure-fire *Night Mail* was shown, with its screen credits to Basil Wright and Harry Watt. The Chairman asked for questions. After the expected silence, a smashing young blonde rose, 'May I ask the speaker, What does Mr Basil Wright look like?' I had known Basil for nearly ten years but was unable to give a reply.

Before my talk and showing of *Song of Ceylon* at the New School for Social Research, the Ralph Steiners had given me a wonderful meal with a great deal to drink which they said I

196

would need. When the performance was over, E. E. Cummings, who claimed to have come only because he loved elephants, said, 'Rotha, you must be the only man to have uttered three Good Gods, five Christs and four bloodies from the stage of the New School.'

The weekly lecture course for the Film Library was in full swing. What hours remained were given to writing the Film Technique script, on which Richard Griffith gave much help. Articles were also written for the *New York Times, Herald-Tribune, Theater Arts Monthly, New Republic, Survey Graphic* and *Story Magazine*. The Film Technique script was finished before I left for England. When it came to the draw, neither Selznick nor Jock Whitney would find its production cost. Two years later, Abbott revived the project (without informing me), and issued a Press statement that he was going to direct the film himself in Hollywood. On his way to the Coast, he found that he had forgotten to bring a copy of the script with him. He called the Film Library in New York but they had no trace of a copy. In desperation, he cabled Richard Griffith, who had been fired from the Film Library after I left for England. Griffith had a faded carbon copy and felt (he wrote to me) like asking 10,000 dollars for it. Notwithstanding he sent it to Abbott. Needless to add, nothing more was ever heard of the project; so far as I know the only remaining copy of the script is in my possession.

In the winter months, after usually working in the evenings, I discovered, sometimes with Alistair Cooke as guide, the swing joints on and around 52nd Street – the *Famous Door*, the *Onyx Club* with its fabulous singer Maxine Sullivan, and of course *The Hickory House*. It was at the latter that Alistair introduced me to Joe Marsala, once a Chicago truck-driver, who blew a wonderful clarinet and led his Chicagoans playing in the centre of a 40 ft-long oval bar in what had once been a second-hand car salesroom. Many very early mornings were spent listening to Joe and his boys – Marty Marsala (trumpet), Adele Girard, Joe's wife (mean harp), Joe Bushkin (piano), Eddie Condon (guitar), Artie Shapiro (bass) and Danny Alvin (drums). Boy, how they played! One night Joe Marsala came across to our table to talk and I recklessly asked him to play a number for me. Back on the stand, and with a nod towards me, Joe went into an improvised number which he had recorded under the title *Hot String Beans*.[1]

Ellington was playing with a big band at the Cotton Club, outside which was a vast neon sign TEN TALL TAN TERRI-FIC GIRLS, but we preferred the smaller bands and less smart places. Joe Marsala was one of the happy success stories of those swing days. After making a picture in Hollywood of which I do not know the title, he and his dear wife (the mean-harpist, as Alistair called her), had the good sense to retire from jazz and take up beet farming somewhere in Colorado. Later he settled into the song-publishing business. He blows his clarinet only for visitors. When I returned to England in March 1938, my trunk was filled with as many jazz records as I could carry – 78s in those days; some I had later transferred on to LPs but the originals remain in safety.

My gratitude will always be to Alistair Cooke because he was such a benevolent and knowledgable guide and explorer in New York. Did he not take me to my first and last Burlesque show at Minsky's, which I found a degrading exhibition; shortly after Mayor La Guardia shut them all down? Did he not introduce me to the mixed delights and thundering din of a bowling alley, as well as taking me one weekend of that glorious Fall to the tip of Long Island, making me buy a pair of sneakers and then indulge in catching snappers with a fast incoming tide? Who knew then that he would make a world-wide reputation as a broadcaster, journalist and author with his knowledge and experience of the American scene? I am sure I felt it would happen, he had so much curiosity about everything American and an unbounded energy.

That sensitive poet E. E. Cummings, with his very beautiful wife, Marion Morehouse (who had been that enviable thing, a model for the great Steichen), took me to the memorable sea-food restaurant, Sweet's, down in Fulton Street in the fish market, a place to which I often returned. It was Marion who later put me in touch with Miguel Covarrubias, the brilliant

[1] The 78 record number was Vocalion v 4168; the LP *Swing Street*, Vol. 3. is 33SX 1511.

illustrator, who was then living in Mexico where he had a high post in the Ministry of Fine Arts. Just before my stay in New York ended, I had an invitation from Covarrubias officially asking me to make a film of my choosing in Mexico. For reasons which will become clear, I refused the temptation with difficulty. I took Cummings and Marion to see *Pins and Needles*, that enjoyable socially-conscious revue, about which Cummings was mildly sardonic but which Marion liked very much. Cummings did not react sympathetically to our documentary films and disliked Auden's work in *Night Mail*. Dos Passos, on the other hand, admired all the films, especially *Night Mail*. He and I went drinking together one evening in many small bars on the Eastside that I should never have found for myself; years later during the first London Blitz I took him in turn to some of the pubs along Commercial Road in the East End.

Others whom I met and liked were Otis Ferguson, brilliant film critic of the *New Republic* who at a party was seen listening earnestly to J. B. Priestley – he wrote to me in England later saying, 'If you see Jack Priestly around, tell him from me that we've now got the Red Indian problem well in hand' – Gilbert Seldes, author of *The Seven Lively Arts*, *An Hour with the Movies and Talkies* and *Movies for the Millions*, who had established himself early in CBS Television though doing what nobody knew; and of course the dynamic Louis de Rochemont, the driving force behind *March of Time*. A stranger in the city was the fine German actor, Fritz Kortner, whom I had known in London. He was staying at a big hotel on Park Avenue hoping to get to Hollywood, but he was scared of New York. He would for ever be calling me to go walk him round the block as he dare not go out alone and knew no one else in the city. He was not afraid of being 'mugged', as they say these days, but of the whole speed and noise of the town.

From England came a few letters from time to time. Two especially disturbed me. One referred to the ARFP group. To quote,

There is a movement afoot among our members to help out *World*

Film News, which very badly needs it, and this by way of the Benevolent Fund. The idea is that we should either give or loan a sum of £250 to guarantee the future of the paper. Naturally we are all interested in the paper but we are also interested in the Fund which now stands at about £350. We need all voices on the subject, especially yours.

My reply was that in principle I agreed to a loan if properly secured, but certainly not to an outright gift. No more was heard until, when I returned to England, I found that the whole of the Fund, which had been wound up, had been given to save *World Film News,* which of course it didn't.

News from the other letter was sparse but a trusted source sent me the following:

Strand Films steps in ermine these days. Keene and Heseltine have got out their velvet and Donald Taylor is buying himself a cutaway coat, it is said. First, a slap-up show of the Imperial Airways films with Cabinet Ministers and Air Ministers and Heaven knows what other Ministers. Then a Royal Show at the Regal of the two social service films, with the miner and his wife and little girl brought all the way from Durham to give the Duchess of Kent a bouquet of flowers and all the tiaras of Mayfair in the Royal Circle at ten pounds a seat; and then a Command Performance of Donald Alexander's *Eastern Valley* film in Buckingham Palace to the King (God bless him!), the Queen and the Little Ones. I wonder what they thought of the commentary which was pretty outspoken about the spoliation of the Rhondda. So now Strand puts 'By Royal Appointment' on its notepaper and should be all set to make films for the upper Eight Hundred. It's a good thing you're not here because they'd have said you were born in Moscow.

A few weeks earlier the following had come from C. F. Snowden Gamble, Public Relations Officer of Imperial Airways:

15 *November* 1937

The three films were shown on Friday night at the Piccadilly Theatre and they were an absolutely outstanding success. As soon as the show was over, the Managing Director asked me to convey to you personally his heartiest congratulations. His actual words were '100 per cent all through!'

New York (1937–38)

I enclose the list of distinguished guests who actually attended and I think you will agree to have landed five ambassadors was not so bad. The Press cuttings are extraordinarily good.

As a note he added:

I feel that if you were to stay in America it would have a profound effect upon their productions because those documentary films which I have seen which have been produced in America are far behind ours in every way.

All during the months spent in New York I sent regular reports on activity to John Grierson, from whom I had only three replies. My letters are worth quoting in extract because they summarize to some extent my work in the US. They range over five months.

10 *October* 1937

It's early yet to send you any considered report on the situation. There's a pretty closely woven veil over most things, chiefly drawn by John Abbott, but I am beginning to find the corners and lift them up.

Down in Washington I was able to alter the whole trend of the American Council of Education's report to the General Education Board of the Rockefeller Foundation. I got them to insert as a first recommendation the interchange of personnel between England and America with a view to making two example films, one here and one in England, with mixed production crews. Subjects to be chosen would include civics and public administration. When I arrived the report was about to recommend the setting up of small amateur units within each university here to find out for themselves how best to make films! I talked for a couple of hours and got the whole thing changed. . . .

I am finding it a little difficult to square the dead end of the Film Library (dusty films, the bones of *Caligari*) with the immediate documentary purposes. That unfortunately is the result of having written a goddamned book about the history of movies. Nevertheless I find that it brings a backing in a certain respect from the universities who are beginning from the historical (but not arty) end of things. In all talks, articles etc. I am keeping close to the sociological line and thus seldom far from the real documentary purpose.

Lorentz's new film, *The River*, of which I saw a cutting-copy, is a step forward from his *The Plow*. But it is important to note that the

201

latter is said to have had 16,000 showings in the US, about 9,000 of which were at theatres on a *free* distribution basis. The film has undoubtedly made a tremendous impact and can be likened to *Drifters* in the ground that it has broken, although to be bitchy Lorentz' *Plow* never did break any real plains that I could see. He is still in the symphonic impressionistic stage and is prickly to talk to due to his intense personal outlook. . . .

For the record, I cannot of course prove this but I have a hunch that someone in London (maybe the old gang at the Conservative Central Office?) tipped off someone here (maybe the British Library of Information?) who told Abbott that I was 'politically suspect'. Knight warned me about this. Abbott it seems got the jitters at the last moment and has to date checked my every utterance and meeting. It is a much trickier situation here, where politics are all on the surface, than it ever was in London, although God and you know there are no politics to be ground. That's what makes people like us all the more difficult to diagnose.

4 November 1937

Now after five weeks I can send you more of a report on things. Abbott is Wall Street trained and tries to run the Film Library on those lines. No art nonsense about him. He is on friendly terms with pretty well everyone in the industry, which makes sense and gets him patronizing support from the moguls. I give it to him that he sold the idea of the Film Library to the Industry and they have bought it so far. He does not intend to let it remain a place where *Caligari* is taken off the vault shelf, dusted and put back again. He's now drawing up a memorandum to show what the Library has done and could do in the future with more funds.

What has the Film Library done? Over and above collecting old films (which Iris Barry does well), it has organized an efficient distribution system. It has four copies (two 35 mm: two 16 mm) of each film (the Swedes, *Last Laugh's* and *Covered Wagon's*) and these are distributed from New York and California. It is in touch with some 1,500 colleges, universities and schools to which it sends either individual films or, preferably, programmes with notes. It's charges are considered high – 25 dollars a booking – and many bodies, I am told, who would like to book films cannot afford to do so. It is through this channel that our own documentaries will be distributed after I have finished lecturing with them. Although nothing has been said, it is my hunch that the GEB regard this distribution as the means of educational distribution in the future. . . .

Projects for films to be made are coming in, some via the Film Library, some direct to me. There have been four to date. One on the importance of television as a means of public information for CBS (whose production head is our old friend Gilbert Seldes); one on the Indian Conservations for the Indian Bureau under the Ministry of the Interior; one on how the emigrant population came to America for the Committee on Intercultural Relations to combat the growth of antipathy towards Jews, Italians, Poles *et al.* (this for school showings); and a fourth on public services and the training of public servants. There are others if one had the time to chase them, all as a result of the showing of our own films. I have stalled production on all these until at any rate next spring; there are no units here fit to take on such good projects.

The plan I am working on is to approach later, when the reports they have asked from Kelliher's unit, the Film Library and so on, are received, the GEB and ask them to finance an experimental unit for production, to equip it, and carry the expenses of staff if subsidized production should become slack. Distribution would best be undertaken by an enlarged department of the Film Library. The unit would have a separate budget and direction and staff. To it could come, by selection, trainees from the universities and other sources. At start, some executive posts would have to be filled from England (Legg would be an excellent person) as there are just not the people here. Any profit from production, and there ought to be some, would go back into the unit to lessen GEB subsidy. I am keeping quiet about this for the time being.

Abbott I know has his own ideas about production. But he wants to make money out of it. He'd like to see a commercial company set up to make documentaries but he cannot do anything about this while I am under an agreement with Rockefeller. So he too is keeping potential films warm. I tell you all this in case it may affect the memorandum Marshall is expecting any day from you now. Marshall will not finance production himself but is keen on the interchange of people idea.

24 November 1937

The production unit issue detailed in my last letter was forced to a rapid discussion a few days back. Kissack from Minnesota put in a request for over a hundred thousand dollars' worth of equipment to make four one-reel films a year! Marshall, uncertain in his mind, waited until the last moment for giving his okay and then asked for my advice. So I told him my whole idea for an experimental production unit centred in New York with interchange of personnel with England

and so on as I wrote you. He liked the idea, admitted its good sense, but was still determined to give a big grant (or rather recommend it to be given) to Minnesota. I asked for a full conference of all interested parties before the Minnesota recommendation went through. Upshot was that my general project for a central unit was approved (see enclosed memo) but Kissack to be given equipment up till the time a central unit is formed. Recommendation for this to go before the Board at the end of next March, by which time I shall be back in England. But to have got it accepted in principle is a worthwhile step.

9 December 1937

Marshall was reticent to me about the memorandum you sent him and he eventually got, because you addressed it to Dr Stevens where it was lost. However, Marshall said that he thought it was too early in the general scheme to embark on foreign commitments. He is fully sympathetic to all your proposals but, quite genuinely, wanted to get the central unit started here first and that can't be until after March next. So any idea for the interchange of personnel between England and the US must wait. He said that you had told him of the financial problems of *World Film News*, but that, much as he would like to help, the GEB could not finance a journal in another country however worthwhile.

There is a call on me for as much writing as can be done, which I do. I have finished the script for the Technique Film. Production would take about a year and I doubt if Abbott has the money to make it. In any case I have not the slightest wish to do so. I much regret the change in the original ARFP group.

26 *January* 1938

Abbott has suddenly taken an intense dislike to anything British! There is an 'American documentary for the Americans' attitude around. I have suspected trouble for some weeks and went out of my way to praise Lorentz's films. He has also I gather tried to discredit the central production unit plan. There is an opinion that America is being gyped by Britain in the trade agreement now under discussion. The upshot of this, so Marshall warns me, is that he doubts if the recommendation for the central unit will go through this year.

I had hopes when I first arrived that so much could be done in five months but I was wrong. Unfortunately your plans for inter-relations between the two countries will have to wait until the American plan goes through first. The GEB feels, I think, that it has already com-

mitted itself on films by backing for another three years the American
Council for Education, backing Kissack on his three-year plan plus
expensive equipment at Minnesota and aiding Kelliher's unit at the
PLA. All these will have to be tied together before any central plan
can be put up.

All the time the Industry, no doubt briefed by Abbott, sits back
watching. It will not make the first move. De Bra (of the Hays
Office) sits in at all GEB meetings. The Board will do nothing without
him being present. The Industry waits on the Foundation and the
Foundation acts very cautiously. If you can suggest any new line of
approach, please cable or write me. I have not heard from you since
I left four months ago.

When I came here in the autumn, you particularly advised me not
to get involved in any production. Well, I haven't. Instead I have
planned the central unit idea which is now on the shelf for a year. I
should appreciate word from you on the position. I only know that I
want to get back to making films again. I've had my bellyful of
Trade politics both here and in England. On the other hand, I want
to do best for the movement whether it means coming back to London
or staying here. But at least there is one result from my visit. We have
brought some fresh air into the Film Library with our films, which are
booking well. The ghosts of *Caligari* and the Lumiére Brothers no
longer dominate the vaults.

Three letters came through from Grierson and one cable.
Extracts are:

Film Centre, London, 28 *January* 1938

I have been most grateful for all your long letters and memoranda,
and am more than delighted at the great start you have given to
documentary discussion on the other side.

The main job before us here just now is the opening of new fields.
We have done a good deal of spadework with the big industries, and
mobilized a few more national forces, and I do not feel pessimistic
about the future. The difficulty is to get a quick maturing of actual
production. I expect the excitement will start in about two months'
time, when there will be too many films for the first-rate directors and
a considerable doubt about giving them to second-liners. I understand
you are to be back in March, and I am next week taking up the possibility of getting a film assigned to you right away.

As regards my own application to the Rockefeller Foundation, you
will know that a consideration of it was deferred. It is, of course, a

mistake on the American part. Frankly, I do not like a situation in which all the experience we have so arduously built up is being generously put at the American disposal with little or no sign of reciprocation. We have a great deal to give them in experience and wisdom and so far as I can make out that experience has been drawn on very freely in your person. It would be only gracious if they did not give the impression that they were exploiting our experience for American purposes, but, on the other hand, were looking to an integration of both efforts and a common policy for the future. If the latter we must, I think, look for their support in our various fields of experiment.

Film Centre, London 11 *February* 1938

It is a pity that they should fear the sensible planning of the work we want to do, the developing lines of which are now so obvious and agreed by those of us who know the field. As I told you in my last letter, it looks as though all our experience has been made available to the United States group in your person, with nothing immediately emerging in the interests of our own development. It savours of one-way traffic. I do not blame John Marshall. He has made his very fair contribution in establishing contacts between this side and the other, and for that we must be grateful. We have, however, on this side, taken a lead in the social use of films which is of first-rate importance from the sociological point of view, and which, by all Rockefeller standards and policies, deserves keeping in good strength.

Putting it bluntly, there in the US are all the tyros and amateurs being supported, while the old campaigners like ourselves, who have sacrificed everything of themselves in the field, are left to continue financing progress out of our own pockets. Even on an economic basis, £5,000 spent on people of our experience would save £25,000 of mistakes by novices.

As for yourself, I hope you will make up your mind to come back in March. There is a lot of work to do here. Prospects are tremendous, in fact as tremendous as we have initiating force to mobilize.

On 13 February, this cable arrived:

WILL YOU DIRECT MAJOR GAS FILM DESCRIBING PLACE GAS AND ELECTRICITY IN MODERN ECONOMY 2000 POUNDER COULD INCLUDE AMERICAN SECTION   GRIERSON

I wrote back:

New York (1937-38)

You are perfectly justified in your comments re Rockefeller and General Education Board. I do feel I have given something but firmly believe that in the long run it will have been worth while. In general I think that the many shows of our films, all the lectures and articles, have been in the best of documentary interests and must lead eventually to international cooperation without which documentary will be impossible in the US. I am certain that finance for the English side will be forthcoming from Rockefeller at a later date. I hope that my being here has followed up the excellent foundation laid by Tom Baird and do not wholly regard it as a waste of my time.

As a last step, I have been instrumental in setting up a production unit with Ralph Steiner and Willard Van Dyke in association with a group called Raymond Rich Inc. This is a non-profit-making body of educationists, university people etc. who undertake all kinds of public relations work for bodies working 'in the public interest'. I believe that they are a good bunch of people and, in the interim period before the GEB will set up the central unit, they might greatly influence the field towards some production here by Steiner and Van Dyke. They have some possible films lined up. It seemed to me unproductive to leave this country without something practicable being set up. It will now be up to them. Steiner and Van Dyke have called their unit American Documentary Films Inc. and the member of their Board from Raymond Rich Inc. is Donald Schlesinger. They asked me also to be a Board member; I agreed on a non-salary basis. I am sure that with me you wish them well. It is a start.

Prospects in England sound stimulating and it looks like being a hard-working summer. I should arrive in London about 21 March. I am greatly looking forward to getting down to making a film again.

I left New York about dawn on 11 March aboard the *US Farmer*, a cargo boat that carried about twelve passengers. Eric and Jere Knight and the Ralph Steiners' said Farewell and threw a bottle of whisky for me to catch as the boat drew away. The trip was uneventful but one for incident.

The Captain was a Swede. The first night at dinner he eulogized the greatness of Hitler, and held that Nazi Germany would win the forthcoming war and rule the world. I felt it was hardly his place as ship's Captain to inflict such views on his passengers. On the second night out, and after he had again held forth in the same way, I was taking a turn round the small deck when I met a fellow passenger, who had already made himself

known to me as Arthur Mann, English correspondent for the
Mutual Broadcasting Company based in London. 'I think that
guy ought to be reported,' he said. 'I agree', I replied. Arthur
Mann thought for a moment. Then he said, 'I could radio my
station's newsroom.' Armed with a bottle of Scotch, we saw the
radio-officer in his cabin. He had a healthy contempt for the
Captain, whom he called a bloody Fascist, and he quickly agreed
to radio any story we liked to write. Arthur Mann and I soon
worked out a story of the facts, which was transmitted. It was
used by ABC and a New York newspaper picked it up the next
morning.

Later in London Arthur Mann called me, 'D'you remember
that Swedish Captain, that Nazi guy?' 'Sure,' I said. 'I had news
today,' said Mann, 'He was fired by US Lines at the end of his
last trip.'

In the interest of political melodrama, the affair of the
stiletto-*sans*-initials must have its pay-off. Again it needs to be
told in the form of extracts from letters. The first to come was
from Muriel Rukeyser, the poetess, who had been trying to set
up a film for me about silicosis victims based on her poem *Gauley
Bridge*.

New York, 17 *April* 1938

Almost the minute you left, and God knows it should have come
before, a howling mess started about you, and hasn't let up yet. I
would have given anything all during this time to have been able to
talk with you about it, no matter how awkward results might have
been. It seems that because of the pushing of the Max Eastman film[1]
at the Film Library, and the fact that it was to be circulated with Leni
Riefenstahl's *Triumph of the Will* under a totalitarian grouping, and
further connections and reports and tangles and investigations which
I don't fully know about (except that some of the reports are said to
come from England), they've got you labelled here. I have held out and
disagreed, officially and unofficially, stating that you were not in any
way responsible for the Film Library's policy, that you did talk about

---

[1] The Film Library had acquired a copy of Max Eastman's film of library
material, *From Czar to Lenin*. I suggested that its material was of historic value and
should be preserved. It came as news to me that the intention was to circulate the
film along with work by Leni Reifenstahl *et al*. Could be this was an Abbott idea
after I left?

the Riefenstahl film technically to me, and that you thought the Eastman film should be preserved on grounds of historical value, as had a great many other people. I don't know how strongly you feel about the political split; what I felt was that in New York you were avoiding everything you possibly could and clearing the jams as they came up. But there is a jam left behind you. I hope you will write and tell me your place in the Film Library story and if it is true that you have made plans to return and work here with Max Eastman and Dos Passos? I need to get the whole matter cleared so that I can go ahead on the *Gauley Bridge* project with you. I have talked with Hanns Eisler and he defends you in all ways. This is my scare letter, I suppose, but please let me hear.

My reply went ten days later.

London, 27 April 1938

At least you have had the honesty to write. All I can say is that if your lads thought I was a Nazi agent when I was in New York, I must have been a bloody bad one! Strange as it may seem, I think the British Government thought that at the same time I was a Communist spy! Where will such stupid melodrama end? Here are answers to your questions.

(a) I hate labels. I'm no more a Trotskyite or a Stalinite or a Hitlerite or a Baldwinite than I am a Termite or a Stalactite. I'm not an insect to be labelled and stuck in a glass case. I have several fundamental beliefs, one of which is the need for the class struggle. Almost everything I do – films or books – bears witness wherever possible to my desire to ventilate the need for that struggle, that is except for my first book which has a value only as a catalogue of names and titles, and which to some extent I dispossessed in the Preface to my third book about Documentary. I do not believe that we are just saving democracy from fascism. Fascism to me is only a militant form of capitalism. It must be fought on an international front. There's no such thing for me as German, Italian or Japanese fascism. There is only world fascism against which only the working class and some intellectuals can fight. I do not believe in any firm affiliation with bourgeois democracy. That stands for the maintenance of the capitalist system under which no working class can exist in decency. I neither know nor care what this viewpoint is called. I'm not concerned with labelling things this or that. I just know that the fight has been on for a long time, and what I in my way am fighting for. I know also others who have the same belief. I can work with them. I also know that I cannot and will not work with little comrades who argue their shirts off saying, 'There, I told you he was all the time.' It's kid-stuff. If some of your sons-of-bitches comrades have got something to say to you about me, hell, let them say it. But don't let them wait until my back's turned. That is what Wall Street does.

(b) The silly stuff about the Max Eastman film. I hate giving reasons but for your honesty I argued that the film (bad as it is as a film) is worth preserving in the Film Library because it contains some interesting and valuable historical material. I do not know who got it from whom. I don't give a bugger who made it – Maxie Eastman or Eastman Kodak. The point is that it is worth preserving. If the Film Library is going to circulate it (which I did *not* know), that raises another matter about which, if consulted, which I shan't be, I should have strong feelings. Your friends' insinuations are pure mischief and Jay Leyda, who is at the Film Library as well as working at Frontier Films, should know that.

(c) Dos Passos. Of course I talked with him about a New York film. Why not? Dos knows his New York better than most people. He knows funny bits of places and people which others don't know. Listen, I'd talk to John D. Rockefeller the Fifteenth (is there one?) if I thought he's know something new or little known about New York. (I'd bet he does but he wouldn't tell me!). Do you not go to a doctor or a dentist because you think he votes Tory? Hell, you go because you think he's a good doctor or dentist. Sure, I was pursuing a crazy scheme for a New York picture to be made sometime-I-don't-know-when and Dos was a very natural person with whom to talk. I talked with him as I talked with Marc Blitzstein or Alistair Cooke or Calder-Marshall or Cummings or Eric Knight or Fiorella LaGuardia or that bum I met on Lexington Avenue one night. Jeez, must one really answer your stupid question. I do because I think you are a nice girl and an intelligent person and you are creative and worth every support.

(d) And now the *Theater Arts* piece. Since when can't the Russian cinema be criticized? Jeez, it needs it. Of course, they are facing the problem of the portrayal of human beings in their films and they're not finding the answer. Look at Pudovkin's *A Simple Case*. Read the verbatim report of the Kino Festival in Moscow in 1935 for that. Are you seriously suggesting for one moment that we should refrain from criticism of a Russian film because it is Russian? Are you imposing a control of free criticism? Of course you're not, Rukeyser, you've got more sense in your head. The point is that recent Russian films, those that we've seen, are lousy. It's my job as a critic to find out why and say so.

Finish apologia. All power to your own Silicosis film. Go to it, raise the money and have it made. Sure, I'd like to do it. But if I don't, someone else will.[1] But for Christ's sake snap out of this blinkered evaluation thing. It doesn't suit you.[2]

Then Ralph Steiner wrote:

New York, 13 *May* 1938

The Frontier Film boys have been going around town denouncing you as a Trotskyite.[3] In the *Daily Worker* there was a short piece that was nasty. It is said to have come from England. It ran like this: 'It is on very good authority from England that we hear that Paul Rotha is a thoroughgoing Trotskyite. In view of this, the infant American Documentary Films Inc, might have been more careful in its choice of directors.'

[1] Not till many years later did I learn what an impressive line-up Rukeyser had formed for the film. On 21 February 1973, she wrote:
'The film-makers I called in were a very mixed lot, politically. I don't know whether any of these names will mean anything now, but I think they might make the landscape clear to some readers: Paul Rotha, director; Herman Shumlin, distributor; Ralph Steiner, camera; Hanns Eisler, music; Paul Rotha and Muriel Rukeyser, script; cast to include Morris Carnovsky, Paul Robeson, Phoebe Brand, and possibly Franchot Tone and John (then Jules) Garfield.
Rotha was even then the great instigator and film man. It was a difficult and abrasive time in which he was in America, teaching us, scolding us, and pointing a possible way in documentary and acted-documentary film. My interpretation of the quarrel that followed was that it was based on jealousy of his work and British documentary film's place in the world, and underneath that, some resentment of his tone toward the Americans. I saw that as a teaching method, since I knew – at that time and from then on – several friends whom he treated with great generosity and kindness.'
[2] Nineteen years later, when I passed through New York on my way to Mexico, I had a drink with Muriel Rukeyser and Richard Griffith at the Berkshire bar. Muriel told me that before the letter quoted above had reached her, she had refused the party card offered her and also refused to go ahead on the film without me. On impulse I told her about Puck Fair, that amazing semi-pagan gathering and ceremony that takes place in August each year in the small town of Killorglin, Co. Kerry, Eire, about which I had heard much while making *No Resting Place* in Co. Wicklow in 1950. It was a film I much wanted to make one day, if I could find a real story arising from the Fair. Muriel Rukeyser was fired with the idea and some years later went herself to the Fair. From her experiences there arose her book *Orgy* (Coward McCann, New York, 1965). The film has yet to be made but only by someone who has taken the trouble to try and understand the Irish people.
[3] In hindsight, I don't think Paul Strand ever forgave me over that adobe house.

211

Now came letters from Knight:

Croton, 16 *May* 1938

Donald Schlesinger of ADFI called me with the anguished plaint that assertions were made in print in the *Daily Blather* saying that you are a Trotskyite. I am utterly tired of this kind of witch-hunt by which both Left wings dispel their much-needed energy, so what could I say to the Schlesinger guy except to damn him roundly and declare that you were no more of a Troskyist spy than my hat and I don't wear one. I don't give a damn whether you sleep nightly with Trotsky. Where is friendship if the minute a man's back is turned people doubt and froth at the mouthings of envious enemies? Max is suing the *Daily Worker* for 250,000 dollars because it said that he was a British agent, and here I'm ready to admit that calling anyone a British agent these days is the maximum ordinate in insults.

24 *May* 1938

Last night I had a long talk with this Schlesinger guy. He is so ridden by fear of 'The Party' that it leaves him a miserable worm. But Jere and I think we've worked out the sequence of events. Jere recalls that you once came out here for the weekend and said that in New York you had argued well into a night with a young man whose name you did not remember but you met with Muriel Rukeyser. It was about the Communist line in Soviet films, you said, with which you didn't agree on humanistic grounds. He spread the news that you were not a true adherent to the Party line. If you criticized a Soviet film, you must be unclean. I hereby invite you to join the party of one-men, to which Cummings and I belong, It is dedicated to Truth; that when all men are one-men then we shall be able to run the world without any problems except think and be true to yourself.

It did not take me long to figure out the persons involved in this sordid business, both in New York and London. Knight was wrong about the young man with whom I had a midnight argument. As the persons in question are still around the place, I won't give them the satisfaction of naming names. And, 'That,' as the riveter said in *Shipyard*, 'is that!'

10. *Back to Soho Square (1938–40)*

Although my contract had some ten months to run, Strand Films asked for my resignation (without compensation) as its producer-in-charge while I was still in the US. In the circumstances, especially after what I had heard about the way the company was heading, I complied. Stuart Legg was without doubt doing a good job as stand-in producer, particularly on the Zoological series, but was due to leave. I had no confidence in the way the business side of the company had been, or was likely to be, run. Already, in March 1937, it was advertising that its equipment was available for hire to outside bodies. This did not suggest that business would be brisk. People as loyal to the documentary idea as Stanley Hawes, Donald Alexander, John Taylor and Ruby Grierson were anxious to go elsewhere, which shortly they did.

Once back in England, there was one thing about which my mind was made up. I had no wish to revert to being a producer. I had an urge to be making films again myself. I needed to have strips of film in my fingers once more, and it was not long before I had. But I was not to be relieved of some involvement in documentary politics.

One valid thing that my absence from the British documentary movement had given me was a perspective on its situation. When he had resigned from the GPO Film Unit in the summer of 1937, Grierson had set up, with Arthur Elton, Stuart Legg and J. P. R. Golightly as secretary, Film Centre Ltd at No. 34 Soho Square. It was a promotional and consultative body not intended itself to produce films. Rather it would prepare reports and scripts, search out and inspire new sponsors and advise old ones on the use of documentary films both in production and distribution, especial emphasis being on development of the non-theatrical field of exhibition in which Grierson so firmly believed. If one of Film Centre's projects should result in a film to be made, its making would be allocated to one of the existing production units, viz: Realist, Strand and possibly GB-Instructional Ltd.

It could be said that the aims of this new body really duplicated many of those for which Associated Realist Film Producers had been set up two years earlier, a body that Grierson himself had suggested. Elton, in fact, took to Film Centre the valuable contacts with some interests in the Oil industry which had come about by ARFP publicity. The Gas industry, which had used ARFP, was also now to avail itself of the new body. So far as I heard in distant New York, no member of the ARFP group objected to this usurpation of its stated functions. I do not think that its list of distinguished consultants were asked their views. It was a highly respectable operation.

Within a few weeks of my return, I found myself writing to Griffith in New York:

27 April 1938

I hinted in my earlier letter that I was not quite happy about the general state of documentary here as I find it now. It is possible that Grierson's leaving the GPO Units began a disintegration in the movement. At Film Centre, Grierson is working as always like a giant, getting films to be made, sitting on committees, coordinating everybody and everyone in his inimitable way, and being rather Empire about it all. The Government is at least conscious of Britain's vanishing prestige overseas and is anxious to rectify foreign opinion by every means of propaganda available. But the propaganda has got to be of a special kind – Imperialism, everything's-all-right-at-home kind. It has realized that in radio it is about three years too late. The Germans, the Italians and the Japs got there first in the Mediterranean, Central and South America. So it is apparently turning to films and maybe to Grierson (always remembering his disreputable background). So far the only practical move has been made to set up a Coordinating Committee for Propaganda under Sir Robert Vansittart but I am not clear who or what it intends to coordinate.[2] Important moves may

---

[1] At that time Vansittart was Chief Diplomatic Adviser to the Foreign Secretary. He was to contribute 'lyrics' to Korda's *Thief of Bagdad* (1940). Speculation was about even as to whether Vansittart gained Korda his knighthood, or whether it was because Churchill, when in the political wilderness in the mid-1930s, was

come from this direction but one speculates on who will want to make such films? Possibly Bruce Woolfe and Mary Field? Korda most dissatisfied with the make-do-and-mend job that Strand did on *Conquest of the Air*. But *Future's in the Air* is showing widely in the cinemas having had a 16-week run in the West End. There's plenty of film work around but it's the general feeling that I distrust, people knocking one another in a way that is new to documentary. I have seen Harry Watt's *North Sea* which I like very much; I will write you about it in detail when I have seen it again. But it's the best I've seen for a long time.

To Knight I wrote:

28 *April* 1938

The bombers fly overhead with monotonous regularity. Sometimes I wish they'd drop something – a bag of flour – just so that I could be sure they are really there. This goes on every night. Earlier in the evening, lighthearted and laughing, a bunch of lads from a local bank were trying on their gasmasks in the pub across the road. Tuesday saw a real wartime budget. There is no longer any question as to '. . . if there is a war'. Every paper and every person says, 'When the war starts . . .' So Simon puts sixpence on the income tax bringing it up to 5s. 6d. in the £, only 6d. less than it was during the last war. Twopence on tea (always hitting the housewife); twopence on oil and petrol. And a £90 million loan for armaments. We are now buying fighters from the US and Canada. The newspapers welcome the budget with 'It's a hard but just demand and the nation knows that it can pay.' Hore-Belisha (war minister) visits Mussolini and it is said that Goering is coming here soon. It's one hell of a Europe. But the parks are green in London and presently the lime trees will be out in the square up the street and smelling sweet. One bomb could fell the lot.

I am still sweating on the Gas film script; I have heard that no one else wanted to make it and that's why Grierson kept it for me! The other night I ran into Bob Flaherty, wonderful old man. He was raving against the Jews, against Korda and Balcon and the Ostrer Brothers. He says he is suing Korda for his (Bob's) share of the *Elelphant Boy* receipts. He'll never see a penny, of course. But he is

commissioned by Korda to write a 'script' on the subject of Gold, which was never made. Churchill's favourite film was *Lady Hamilton*, made by Korda in Hollywood in 1941. If these rumours were false, then the honour must have been due to the many international films made at the Denham studios on which the Prudential Assurance Company was alleged to have lost some £8½ millions.

just as lovable as ever, talking endlessly without listening, still drinking Scotch, bless him. I wonder if he will ever make another film?[1]

The first important production programme initiated and supervised by Film Centre was a series of seven films for the Films of Scotland Committee at a cost of some £10,000. They were planned for first showing at the Empire Exhibition in Glasgow, after which they had quite a wide release through MGM. The Scottish Development Council set up the films committee, which was financed by the Government, industry and other bodies with the aim, 'to tell in motion pictures the story of their country – its national character and traditions, its economic planning for industrial development, its agriculture, fisheries, education and sport'. Film Centre, in the person of Grierson, ensured that, although the films themselves were produced by different companies, a consistent policy and standard were maintained. The project was, and still is, unique in film history and was successful in every way. Stuart Legg and Donald Alexander's journalistic *Wealth of a Nation* (Strand), Basil Wright's emotional and poetic *The Face of Scotland* (Realist) and Alexander Shaw's *The Children's Story* (Strand) were the best of the series, of which the others were *They Made the Land* by Mary Field (GB-Instructional), *Sea Food* (Pathé), *Scotland for Fitness* and *Sport in Scotland* (made by indigenous units). None of the films was notable; but the project itself was. A useful assessment by Ritchie-Calder appeared in *World Film News*.[2]

Perhaps the most far-reaching international report to be drawn up by Film Centre (with Grierson and Basil Wright responsible) was that commissioned by the ILO (International Labour Organization) in Geneva, set up under the League of Nations. It was first broached in 1936.[3] Grierson wrote of it,

We said in effect to the ILO, 'Why do you not create a great international interflow of living documents, by which specialized groups

[1] He did indeed; two of his best works – *The Land* (1939–42) and *Louisiana Story* (1946–48). For the record of how Flaherty left London to return to the US, vide: *The Innocent Eye* by A. Calder-Marshall (W. H. Allen, 1963).

[2] Vol. III, No. 7, November 1938.

[3] So far as is known, no copy of this historic report exists today.

will speak to their brethren in the fifty countries that come within your system? You are anxious to raise the common standards of industrial welfare. Why do you not use the film to do it? If France has the best system of safety in mines, let other countries have the benefit of this example. If New Zealand is a great pioneer of ante-natal care, let other countries see the record of its achievement.'[1]

The report was delivered in 1937. If the project had been acted upon, which it was not because the war was reckoned as being too near for such an ambitious scheme, Film Centre would of course have carried it out. It may be added that the report's recommendations are as valid today as when submitted 35 years ago.

Film Centre also acted as film adviser to the Imperial Relations Trust, of which Lady Stella Reading and Sir Stephen Tallents were active members. The Trust was to send Grierson to Canada in 1938, where he was to become Films Commissioner to the Government and to draw up the Act which brought into being the National Film Board, and later on to Australia and New Zealand. Film Centre also acted for the International Wool Secretariat, the Times Publishing Company and the Shell Company. It was also under its aegis that *World Film News* was published under its respective editors, Marion Grierson, Reg. Groves and Ronald Horton, until it stopped publication through lack of finance in November 1938.

A great deal of energy was also given to the development of the non-theatrical field of distribution and exhibition, which had already been explored with promising results by the GPO Film Library and several industrial film libraries. William Farr, sometime assistant director at the British Film Institute, took over the newly-formed Petroleum Films Bureau, while Thomas Baird looked after distribution for the British Commercial Gas Association. In this way, each of them gained considerable knowledge and success which were to be of both national and international value to the Ministry of Information during the war to come.

. . .

[1] *Searchlight on Democracy*, *Adult Education*, December 1939, reprinted in *Grierson on Documentary*, edited by H. Forsyth Hardy, (Faber, 1966).

Not long after my return, we were honoured by two visitors from the US, Pare Lorentz (with a copy of *The River* under his arm), and John Abbott (minus Miss Iris Barry). I reported to Griffith:

27 April 1938

We are all going to be very kind to Lorentz. We shall try and show him how documentary hosts should behave when foreign documentary boys go visiting. I've asked him out to dinner and then on to the show of new films that luckily the GPO is giving. I have also arranged for our old friends the English Speaking Union to put on a show of his film, and he will of course present it to all the documentary group one evening and come to a party given for him. (I doubt if the British Film Institute, who should do these things, knows he's even coming.) Next we shall have Abbott here. (I wonder why Iris is not with him?). I do not think he will enjoy Paris too much this time, where he goes first, because Cavalcanti, who knows all things, tells me that the people at the Cinémathèque Française are of the opinion that the Film Library, New York, is run to provide its Director with expensive trips to Europe every other year. He always says that the Film Library has no money with which to buy old archive films but it is noted that somehow the money is always there for luxury hotels, restaurants and first-class travel. In addition, none of the American films promised on the last visit have as yet materialized.

To Ralph Steiner, a few days later:

May 1938

Lorentz was here with his film, all smiles and charm, so we bought him a good dinner with many drinks and ran *The River* to the assembled documentary boys. As we suggested, he said a few words first, paid suitable homage to British documentary to which he added American documentary owed so much. Then he vanished like a snipe before his film was run. Some of the youngsters were caught by its lyrical appeal, they naturally responded to the novelty of great river names, the wide horizons and giant forests, but their reaction was rather like seeing Buffalo Bill and covered wagons for the first time. Most of the older boys sensed the superficiality of it all and remarked that that kind of film-making was rather old hat. But Lorentz cut a smart figure in his bow tie and dinner jacket among the shabby tweed-coated documentary boys. The English Speaking Union also gave him a joint show with GB-Instructional. Philip Guedalla, Chairman of the British

Council Film Committee, said what a wonderful film *The River* was because it had passed the main test of a documentary film in that it was beating box-office records in the States and people were lining up paying to see it as entertainment. I refrained from saying that if indeed it was beating box-office records, it was because it was given away for free to exhibitors. That old fox Bruce Woolfe was standing by me; he bent his six-feet-something down to me and whispered, 'It's very reminiscent of *Face of Britain*, isn't it?' To which I said, 'Nonsense, it must have been some other guy.' Anyway all has gone well for Lorentz and his film, which is good, and interchange between our two countries will be like the hopping of fleas from now on.

At the GPO Film Unit after Grierson's bow-out, production continued under Cavalcanti, later augmented by J. B. Holmes, who had left Strand. The situation across the Square showed signs of a little tenseness. Those at the Unit – among them Harry Watt, Humphrey Jennings, Pat Jackson and Ralph Elton – were understandably loyal and proud of its reputation. The exact reason for Grierson's leaving was clouded. When some new films by the Unit were presented on 28 April 1938, among them *North Sea*, there were a few snide remarks from across the way.[1] But the extraordinary overall critical and public reception given to *North Sea* should have dispelled such comment.

Work on the script, which was based on a cable that Elton says he had found in the files at the Central Telegraph Office, or rather the general overall line of the film, took shape while Grierson was still in charge.[2]

To Griffith I wrote:

31 May 1938

The guts of *North Sea* are simple enough. The crew of a trawler at home in Aberdeen in the early morning, their home backgrounds and human ties, their dates for what they'll do when they return home on Saturday. Out to sea. A storm, just the biggest ever, all unfaked, the real thing. The drama of radio contact with the coast station. Then the aerial snaps. The pumps jam. The trawler ships water. The coal

---

[1] The review in *World Film News*, Vol. III, No. 4, August, 1938, did not help to smooth matters.

[2] In an interview, 30 August 1967.

shifts in the bunkers. For 48 hours they hang on like grim death. They get the radio working again. They shift the coal. Contact is re-established with shore. The pumps get going. A salvage tug is not needed. So they make a cup of tea. And back to Aberdeen. No commentary. Just plain speech and a wonderful sound-track by Cavalcanti. Fine music by Ernst Meyer. As for acting, the men are magnificent. The crew was picked from unemployed. The trawler was, of course, specially chartered. They went to sea for a week. Then they shot the below-decks stuff in a studio mock-up very well done by Edward Carrick.

They showed the film to Erich Pommer and Charles Laughton, who are about to make *Jamaica Inn*, which has a storm in it. Laughton said, 'Huh, I couldn't have acted that skipper better myself.' They asked Harry Watt to go down to Elstree to do the storm scene for them. He found himself expected to make a storm in the studio-tank.

North Sea is really brilliantly cut, not by Watt but by an editor, R. Q. McNaughton, who did so well on *Night Mail*. It is superbly photographed by a couple of lads aged about 22, who used to be messenger boys at the Post Office – Jonah Jones and Chick Fowle. How they were not swept overboard I don't know. But it is the sound track by Cavalcanti that puts the drama of the film across and the quiet natural quality of the people. Everything and everyone belongs. The distant singing of the sea hymn over dawn shots of sleeping Aberdeen on the Sunday morning when the trawler is 24-hours overdue and no word has been heard from it since the radio stopped working. Sleeping, did I say? Aye, save for the men and women who keep watch, who cannot go to bed, the shore radio-operators searching the ether for the sound of a word. I don't give a damn about the cavilling; it is a bloody fine film.

Other films from the GPO Unit were not so outstanding, as could be expected, but *Men in Danger* and *Health of a Nation* were workmanlike jobs although not breaking new ground. Photographically they were of a high standard. They were muddled, however, from any social point of view. No film told its story clearly. They each started with some universal conception and then led nowhere. It was due, perhaps, to Cavalcanti's insistence on good technique at all costs. As a result the Ministry of Health film, *Health of a Nation*, left one with the impression that there was nothing the Ministry wouldn't do to improve the lot of the working man. It did not suggest that better working conditions come about in spite of the Ministry and not because of it. It showed where the pursuit of technique for its own sake can lead if a social conscience is absent. Harry Watt's *Men in Danger* said some terrifying things about industrial safety, but again it suggested that industrialists are improving the working conditions of their employees for the sake of the employees and not because it could result in higher output. Len Lye's first straight, non-abstract film, *N or NW*, supervised by Cavalcanti, was a much underestimated little film. Also to be noted were Humphrey Jennings's first real film, *Spare Time.* and a film about training a messenger boy, Evelyn Spice's *Job in a Million* which was nicely human in observation. *Spare Time* dealt with how what are called working-class people use their leisure hours. Taking three regions in the country, it showed workers from three major industries – coal, steel and textiles. Warmly observed, it gave us the pigeon breeder, the whippet trainer and choral singing, shot with a nice simplicity. The Kazoo band sequence, of the textile workers, came in for criticism at the time as being tinged with contempt, but I doubt if this could have been Jennings's intention. Rather it was a scene of pathetic display behind which lay a background of misery, a brave attempt to cover over the cracks of an industrial working-class community. The film contained many clues to Jennings's remarkable work to come in future years.

In 1936, Arthur Elton had been made film adviser to the Shell Company and taken over the productions of its Unit, ably managed by Alexander Wolcough. The Unit began to build its world reputation for films of much technical skill for explanation and information of complex mechanical and scientific subjects. Of the earlier work of this unique group, Geoffrey Bell's *Transfer of Power*, a study of the history of the toothed wheel, was a lucid filmic demonstration made with superb craftsmanship. With *Power Unit*, it was to be a forerunner of the Shell Film Library which would deservedly gain an international reputation. A point to be made is that none of these films carried any direct advertising for the Shell Company, its name only being credited among a film's titles. It can be said that this side of the Unit's work did not really fall within the category of documentary purpose, rather they were very well-made films of instruction and explanation. There is a case for this viewpoint but it can be left for argument. To disregard the Unit's output in this present survey would be irresponsible.

Basil Wright and I were asked by Grierson to join Film Centre during the summer of 1938, not to become directors of the Company but to be on its staff. He guaranteed an annual salary of £500, plus a bonus which one was tactfully told was expected to be donated to keep *World Film News* alive. We both accepted, but I did a good deal of thinking first. Letters kept coming from New York, asking me to go back. But Ralph Steiner and Willard Van Dyke were struggling to get their Unit into production and could not carry me as well. There was always somewhere to hang my hat in Cherry House. But I could see nowhere to earn my keep. Knight wrote:

6 April 1938

I cannot tell you how truly I feel you must come back here. You belong here for you are, inside you, one of the most American of persons who was ever born in Britain. There is a life here to fight, just as many burdens to carry and dragons to slay as elsewhere.

On coming back to London, maybe I missed something of the exhilaration of New York. I can't say of the US because I saw so little of it, only the tip and everyone knows that you cannot judge the 50 states by Manhattan. What, apart from friends already known through exchange of letters and from some new ones, and from the pleasures of Cherry House, did I remember worth while? Not New York's brash rudeness or its febrile way of living, but a certain indefinable character among its unsmart neighbourhoods, something not experienced since on return visits after the war. Maybe as in post-war London, the war killed whatever it was I found in New York in 1937. Walking up Fourth Avenue to the Film Library on Madison, I used to feel an aliveness. Maybe it was just a hangover but I think not.

I was reminded amusingly of New York one day in Film Centre. A man, obviously American by his face and clothes and stance, came into the office with what looked like four bodyguards. Tight-lipped, he said to one of them, 'Tell Mr Grierson that Mr Gottlieb wants to see him.' This man turned to another man and said, 'Tell Mr Grierson that Mr Gottlieb wants to see him.' The third man approached Mr Golightly, who was standing there polishing his glasses. The man said, 'Mr Gottlieb wants to see Mr Grierson.' Mr Golightly adjusted his glasses and said, 'Tell Mr Gottlieb that Mr Grierson doesn't see anyone without an appointment.' All five men left the office and so far as I know were never heard of again. Later Grierson explained that Mr Gottlieb was trying to sell him some stock footage he had come by illegally in New York. It was good *Little Caesar* stuff.

In spite of the documentary problems looming in Soho Square, nevertheless I felt in England that there was the calm in which to think and work. This I did not find in New York but did, of course, at Cherry House with its sanity and balanced way of living. In spite of my constant awareness of social injustice and my abhorrence of the class structure still so strong, it was as well to be back in England. There is much in the English character that I despise, especially its hypocrisy, but there is also much that is admirable. My more than 40 years as a film-maker have taken me to over 70 countries but there are only three to which I should really like to return – Mexico, Eire and Italy – and they will inevitably have changed now.

In its role as consultant, Film Centre allocated three major productions to the Realist Film Unit, where John Taylor became producer when Basil Wright left to join Film Centre. They were *The Londoners*, produced by Grierson, with Basil Wright as associate producer and John Taylor as director, for the Gas industry; my Gas film, *New Worlds for Old*, and *The Fourth Estate* for *The Times*, also produced and directed by me.

The Londoners was commissioned to mark the Jubilee celebrations of the London County Council, of which Herbert Morrison was then the leader. It combined commentary, verse (by Auden) and personal camera-interview (Mr Morrison) but, an innovation except for some GPO films, its first reel was largely reconstruction of 19th century England in a studio. The hovels, schools, poorhouses and sewers of the London of Dickens and Doré were staged and filmed in a style that brought to mind the studio work of the silent German cinema.Even in its up-to-date sequences, it had none of the speed and slipshod editing with which *March of Time* had infested some British documentary work of the time. With *North Sea*, *The Londoners* showed that if necessary the documentary film-makers could use a studio and yet avoid the artificiality so often associated with studio staging in British feature films.

On the other hand, *The Londoners*, like the local government film made for the Manchester Corporation in later years, failed to humanize local administration in terms of the ordinary citizen. This I find was well put by Richard Griffith:

29 July 1939

I appreciate all you write about the London film's concern for social facts, but the more I see it, and I've seen it now five times, the less I think it comes near them. The only one time we really see the common man – and a very moving scene it is – is when he is walking home from work. We never see him participating in the government; we never get the idea that it is London's citizens who are behind all the reforms we are shown. It's the County Council, *deux ex machina*, who does everything. But the opening Victorian sequences are wonderfully done with all the humanity that the rest of the film lacks.

And again, he wrote:

31 July 1939

We all see *The Londoners* as another assured, authoritative film from the technical standpoint. But many, among them myself, don't agree that it is an important social film. True it tries to be, true it leads to the future while *North Sea*, taking your dichotomy, only leads to repetition. But *North Sea* gets its modicum of social message over with a maximum effect because it is so well constructed. *The Londoners*, with much more social import potentially, fails to get it across because the viewpoint is confused. Considering the brilliant job John Taylor did at the beginning and end of the film, I feel he must have been hampered by the LCC in making the middle and thus is not to be blamed for the lessening of impact which occurs. But the impact *does* lessen. You say that the film shows us how Londoners govern themselves. Where was that? The beginning shows the evils resulting from inefficient city government; the end tells us those evils have been corrected. In the middle, the commentary tells us in a few sentences that some Londoners got together, formed the County Council, and set to work to clean things up. And what we see is members of the Council making speeches. Balls! I wanted to be shown the awakening

of a feeling of responsibility in the individual Londoners, how they came
to get the idea of forming the Council, how they met municipal problems once they got under way. I wanted to see municipal self-govern-
ment dramatized, but it wasn't there. In conception, *North Sea* is much
less important than *The Londoners*, but the former is a swell job of
film-making, while something happened to the latter – script, production, editing or sponsors – which cut the heart out of it. There are
grand things in it. I was more moved by the opening reel and the
ending than by anything in *North Sea*. But it isn't a totality, that's all.

To which I replied:

7 August 1939

About *The Londoners*, you are right on some of your points but don't
want you to underestimate its social importance. Some of the bad
patches were due to LCC insistence; you are correct there. But I still
think that something happened between the first cutting-copy and the
final married print. I saw the former and was deeply disappointed with
the latter. I know where it went astray but it is too delicate a matter
to write about here. There is always a state of muddle-headedness that
happens during making a film. Sometimes this happens during the
script, when it is not too serious and can be rectified during production.
But sometimes it happens during the very last stages – just about the
time of the cutting-copy – and then it can be disastrous. It happened
during *The Londoners* and I saw it bloody well happening. I couldn't
do anything because I wasn't the producer and I have more respect for
Grierson than to interfere. But I shall pass your comments on to young
John Taylor and let him think it out for himself.

In England the film had in general excellent critical reaction.

My own *New Worlds for Old* scripted on my return to London
and shot during the summer of 1938 was no more a documentary
film than was *West Side Story* or *Hellzapoppin'!* It was a cod
film and I was in no serious mood when I wrote and made it.
Research and script were paid by a flat fee of £100; production
cost was set at £1,800 which, not wanting to set up a unit
myself and duplicate other available facilities, was paid to the
Realist Film Unit in return for its services.

PEP[1] had just published an independent report on the then
fierce competition between the respective virtues of the Gas and
Electricity industries. This report I realized would be impossible

[1] Political and Economic Planning. An independent research study group.

to dramatize in human terms but it provided a mine of statistical information. Thinking over how the subject could be treated in film terms and not be deadly dull – gas is not exactly easy to 'bring alive' – I remembered *The Living Newspaper* which had much impressed me in New York. I decided to try and use some of its techniques but translate them into filmic terms. I thought up two protagonists to put the pro's and con's of gas versus electricity in the sound track (they were not seen, of course), and I was very lucky in my choice of Alistair Cooke (who happened to be in London at the time) to voice the man who explains it all somewhat glibly, and our old friend Joe Golightly (Grierson's personal aide) to speak the voice of the cautious, enquiring doubter. This was the first time I tried the idea of recording each speaker separately without their meeting, and knitting their sentences together into a continuous coherent dialogue in the cutting-room. It worked, and I was to use the method extensively in later years.[1]

The whole film was a joke and to their credit S. C. Leslie and the Gas people entered into the fun. An impressionist opening of London night-life in Victorian days under the glamour of gas lamps, a trick diagram on how gas is made, a speeded-up tour of a gasworks taking off advertising films, a travelogue about Swiss hydro-electric schemes with a breakneck commentary in French which has to be translated and the pictures reshown so that Mr Golightly can understand, a short sequence of steel-making with some of the music played backwards (Alwyn was quite charming about this, saying his music sounded much better that way), and a trio of singing scientists in horn-rim glasses and bowler hats in a laboratory.

The Victorian extravaganza made on a shoestring was amusing to shoot. Vera Cuningham painted a series of back-drops on two long 'flats' each about 80 ft, which faced each other and gave impressions of such flights of imagination as the spit-and-sawdust of the Café Royal, a Gaiety Girl's dressing-room, a brothel exterior, a narrow slum alleyway in the East End and so on, all lit by gas lamps. Against these some thirty friends of mine at the time (including Basil Ward, Amyas Connell, Nicolas

[1] *World of Plenty, Land of Promise* and *The World is Rich*. In the former, one voice was recorded in New York and the others in London.

Bentley, Victor Reinganum, Texeiro Barbosa) in appropriate costumes performed a series of *tableaux vivants* with the camera tracking past. Four dancers (we could not afford more) from the young Sadler's Wells ballet school danced a can-can in authentic dresses as the camera tracked along them. In the studio yard outside in the dark, Sherlock Holmes (Stuart Legg) searched through a magnifying glass for bloodstains on the pavement, while a Stagedoor Johnny (Edgar Anstey) escorted a lovely girl in a hansom cab. James Hill, one of my assistants, as an urchin raced down an alley pursued by Gordon Roe (Editor of *The Connoisseur*) in Victorian policeman's uniform. Wax effigies of Queen Victoria, Gladstone, Disraeli and Jack the Ripper which preceded this galaxy had already been filmed in Madame Tussauds. William Alwyn wrote a colourful music pastiche for the sound track.

A silent stage in the GB Studios at Shepherds Bush had been rented for a day and a night for all this feverish activity. While we were shooting, I became aware of a tall figure watching from the darkness off the set. It was Bruce Woolfe (whose GB-Instructional offices were in the same building) bristling with disapproval at this display of debauchery. Maybe he was just envious? He shook his head in shame and disappeared. A few minutes later, Mary Field arrived to look, obviously having been told of Rotha's obscene goings-on. She gave her characteristic cackle and went back to her *Secrets of Life* series.

When I showed them the sequence after editing, the Gas people took it all in good part and seemed delighted that a piece of entertainment had been made out of the drabness of the subject and foresaw a wide non-theatrical distribution for the film. They arranged a slap-up première for the film, supported by other gas films, at the Phoenix Theatre and some 800 invitations were issued. At the last moment, it was realized that a censor's certificate would be needed for the film. Not foreseeing any possible problem, the film was slipped into the British Board of Film Censor's office and the urgency explained. Within a matter of hours, word came that the Censor had withheld a certificate because of some scenes of Victorian dancing girls which were deemed obscene. A charming assistant of S. C. Leslie, a Miss De Mouilpied, was sent round in all her glamour to talk with Mr Brooke Wilkinson, the nicotine-stained, watery-eyed old gentleman who was still the Board's secretary. He explained that whenever one of the dancing girls lifted her skirt and revealed a leg as it kicked upwards, it was obscene. Quick as a flash, and I am sure with a dazzling smile, Miss De Mouilpied suggested, 'If the producer blacks out all moments when the girls' skirts are lifted, would that meet your objection, sir?' He agreed at once and expressed himself pleased with such ready cooperation. The result can be foretold. I whipped a copy of the film along to the laboratory and on the optical-printer we blacked out every frame of film in which a girl lifted her legs. When projected, the offending sequence was far more suggestive by implication than the original. Not content, I had a huge title made and affixed to the front of the film. It read: THE CENSOR HAS TAKEN OBJECTION TO CERTAIN SCENES OF VICTORIAN DANCING GIRLS IN THIS FILM. THE OFFENDING SCENES HAVE THEREFORE BEEN BLACKED OUT.

That night, when this title appeared, a ripple of anticipation ran through the audience. The can-can girls appeared within a few minutes of the opening. They and the whole film were a chaotic success. If *New Worlds for Old* had little to do with the documentary story proper, it gave us some light relief in those months around Munich. It also helped to refute the belief that documentary had no sense of humour.

Griffith wrote from New York, 'Jean Lenauer, who runs the Filmarte Theater, thinks *New Worlds* is just about the slickest documentary job he has ever seen and wants to book it for the Fall. Just about everyone says it's a wholly new departure, the most assured documentary to come over here from England.' (23 May 1939.) There are others, including myself, who doubt if it was a documentary film at all. I certainly never wanted it to be sent to New York except to amuse a few friends.

At this time I was working also on another script for Gas, around architecture, planning and the community. It was in part inspired by Lewis Mumford's *Culture of Cities*. 'It will tell,' I wrote Knight, 'how Everytown, 1938, England, grew up; how housing and public services have been related, or in so many cases unrelated, to the needs of the community. It could be

228

something for which *Face of Britain* was a child's note-book.'[1]

From the Realist Unit there came *Roads Across Britain*, made for one of the Oil companies, a journalistic survey of British road traffic problems and an urgent plea for the adoption of a national road plan. Its direction was by Sidney Cole but some confusion arose and I was asked to take over. William Alwyn wrote good music for it. Ruby Grierson made a small film, *Cargo for Ardrossan*, about the delivery of oil by sea to a small Scottish island, nicely made. From Strand there came *Speed the Plough* on the mechanization of British agriculture, and *African Skyways*, on the Imperial Airways route from England to South Africa, both well directed by Stanley Hawes, with Arthur Elton producer on the first, and Stuart Legg on the second. All four of the above films had a good distribution in the cinemas through ABFD. Strand announced a second series of its Zoological films but these were not made in spite of the success of the first group.

Strand as a company was having its problems. In its first years, it was inspired by the human and social democratic purpose that was the essence of the documentary movement. On the one hand, its group of film-makers were learning their craft the tough way with hardly adequate equipment; on the other, they believed that the subjects they were asked to make into films were worth while. As a commercial company, Strand obviously had to operate viably and for two or three years this was achieved without any loss of dignity. As the decade neared its end, however, Strand compromised in certain ways to secure films to make. But most, though not all, of its production staff were leaving to join other units. On the business side, Alan Bott had resigned as a director of the board, won an injunction against the Company in the courts and had his capital refunded. Heseltine, another of the original directors, secured a first call on all receipts from Strand films showing in the cinemas until his capital was repaid. Ralph Keene no longer attended the office. It

[1] 20 December 1938. This script underwent many changes partly to emerge in a film called *Goodbye Yesterday*, by John Taylor, during the war and be put on ice by the Ministry of Information, and partly to be incorporated in my housing and planning film, *Land of Promise*, in 1945.

would seem that moneys paid by Imperial Airways for two films in production, and due for delivery by 1 September, had to be paid to Kodak for film stock used, to a laboratory firm for processing bills and to a sound-recording studio to prevent legal actions. It was not long before Strand negotiated a merger with Merton Park Studios, a company mainly concerned with publicity and advertising films and not with documentary as was understood in Soho Square.

In the spring of 1939, a grotesque film called *The Warning* appeared as part of the Government's air-raid precautions campaign. It had been begun as a studio picture by a feature film company, British National, but it was completed by the GPO Unit under Cavalcanti's supervision. It was to cause some unease. In a broadcast in Canada, Grierson said: 'There was not much peace in *The Warning*. It was a picture of England preparing for death and disaster; and you saw the Old England made grotesque by war as in a distorting mirror.'[1] I wrote about it to Griffith:

All the uplifted faces at the end of the picture are the staff of the GPO Unit! The Unit's grant expires in June. Whether it will be renewed depends very much on its present behaviour. If it had refused to take over and finish *The Warning*, it is possible that the grant might not have been continued. I think therefore that Cavalcanti wanted to be in well with the Government.[2]

In May of 1939, John Abbott took it into his head to call a Conference of Documentary Producers in New York at the Film Library's expense; later it was postponed to the Fall. An invitation was sent to Basil Wright but the prospect of war made a visit inadvisable. Tom Baird, who was due in New York anyway to see about our films at the New York World's Fair, went to some of Abbott's meetings and reported them a damp squib. He added, though, that Cavalcanti (presumably sent by the GPO) took the opportunity to create further tension between himself and Grierson, and those of the British documentary group who were associates with him, notably Wright and myself. This friction which obsessed Cavalcanti was crystallized in *Film and Reality*, a compilation film which the British Film Institute commissioned Cavalcanti to make in 1939–40.

[1] Ottawa, 30 November 1940. Reprinted in *Grierson on Documentary*.
[2] 27 May 1939.

Obviously fascinating in parts, this film did less than justice to the social aims of the British documentary group, whose work as shown, when at all, was inadequate and false. In spite of protests by the Associated Realist Film Producers, especially in a strong letter to *The Times*, the film was not withdrawn although some film libraries abroad would not distribute it. It is, I am told, still in use in some places today. The film was not shown to the Press until after the war had started, when in the course of reviewing some Ministry of Information films, William Whitebait (George Stonier) wrote of the MOI work: 'They set a very high standard indeed; and the tradition that has produced them owes more to Cavalcanti than to any other man.'[1] To this my reply was printed the following week:

This is no time or place to explain the real social purpose (ignored by Cavalcanti's film) behind the 1929–39 years of British documentary films, but no war excuse can allow to stand uncorrected Whitebait's fantastic claim. . . . No greater respect than mine can Cavalcanti ask for his aesthetic and technical influence on our films; yet the fact remains, and I regret that it has so soon been mislaid, that one man, and one man only, John Grierson, was responsible for the birth and inspiration of the 300-odd British documentary films made between 1929 and 1939, including those of which Cavalcanti was himself director. Without Grierson's vision, unselfishness and unceasing work, there would be no trained documentary film experience upon which films today can draw.

Next week, Harry Watt replied:

It was Grierson's drive and initiative that obtained the formation and sponsoring of the EMB Film Unit, from which eventually so many off-shoots have sprung. But I, as a film worker with both men, would like to say that I am convinced that it was the introduction of Cavalcanti's professional skill and incredible film sense that raised the standard and reputation of British documentary to the pitch where today it has become a considerable influence on the cinema as a whole.

The controversy smouldered on for many years. For my own part, as a result of my letter quoted above, I was told that references to my work were in due course removed from *Film and Reality*[2] It is perhaps for such reasons that an American

[1] *New Statesman*, 1 June 1942.

[2] I am happy to record, however, that Cavalcanti and I have always remained the best of friends.

professor took upon himself to comment, 'It would be difficult to find the growth of a movement in the history of art to parallel that of the documentary film for its internal dissensions, its violence and its bitterness.'[1]

In an interview many years later, Cavalcanti was still complaining that his name had been suppressed by Grierson from credit titles and publicity on GPO films.[2] He was especially sensitive about *Coal Face*, a film that had received greater recognition in post-war years than it had when it was made in 1935, for which he claimed he had not been given due credit. In fact, my book *Documentary Film* (1939 and all subsequent editions) gave Cavalcanti credit for script, direction and sound supervision for the film, while the Film Society programme of 27 October 1935, when *Coal Face* had its first performance, printed a credit to him for sound recording [*sic!*]. Recent enquiry to the National Film Archive in 1972, however, revealed that its two copies of the film bore credit titles to only two names – Auden and Britten. When I had viewed a copy from the same source in 1968, the names of both Cavalcanti and Grierson, as well as of Auden and Britten, had been on the screen. There seems to be no explanation for this.

In afterthought, I think Grierson had a valid point in this one-sided argument when he recalled that Cavalcanti had asked for his name to be left off such films as *Coal Face*, *Granton Trawler* and *Night Mail* when they were made because he felt that association with such *avant-garde* work might jeopardize his chances of employment in British feature film production at that time.[3]

In the months leading up to the war in September 1939, while shooting of *The Times* film was in its last stages, Basil Wright at Film Centre had written a script for the Colonial Office about the spread of native administration in Africa. This was directed by Alexander Shaw, and later called *Men of Africa*. Wright also worked with the poet Cecil Day Lewis on a story idea by

[1] A. Nicholas Vardac, Associate Professor of Drama, Stanford University. (*Sight and Sound*, April 1951). It is possible that Professor Vardac had American and not British documentary in mind.

[2] At the 10th Leipzig Documentary Film Festival, 24 November 1967.

[3] In an interview, Devizes, 17 June 1970.

Robert Flaherty about a small boy in Newcastle who stowed away on a coastal collier and eventually arrived in the River Thames. This treatment was commissioned by the Gas industry (one of whose colliers would be used), and Technicolor was interested to find part finance if the film were made in colour. It was to be another war casualty.

On the political front, it was understood that the Government had formed a shadow committee to draw up a policy and plans for a Ministry of Information to come into being if war should break out. A good deal of mystery naturally shrouded this committee and its activities but there is reason to believe that its membership included Lord Reith (later to be the first Minister of Information), Sir Joseph Ball (Director of the Conservative Research Department and the Party's film adviser) and prob- ably Mr A. G. Highet (of the Post Office Publicity Department). As research for future use revealed, the committee appeared ignorant of the fact that there had been an efficient official machine for film-making in being without interruption since the EMB Film Unit in 1929.[1]

One month before the war there came tragic news from the US. Determined to 'put Uncle Sam out of the show business', Congress cut off all appropriations as of 30 June 1939, and the whole Federal Theater Project was closed. According to Griffith:

Since the beginning of the week, every important item in the Roose- velt legislative program for this year has met with defeat. Immediate results in fields which affect us are awful. Not only the Federal Theater destroyed and all the Arts Projects crippled, but the whole WPA idea is endangered. (July 29).

It is of significance that a Dies committee report in January of that year had stated, 'A rather large number of the employees on the Federal Theater Project are either members of the Communist Party or are sympathetic with the Communist Party.' McCarthyism had started early.

The biggest public controversy that the British documentary people ever went into and gained results arose over what kind of films about the British people should be shown during the New York World's Fair that opened on 30 April 1939.

[1] Ministry of Information files, 1939–40.

It will have been noted earlier that the strengthening of liberal, democratic bonds between the American and British peoples is an aim that has long been of importance to me and to those friends I have had (some of whom I still have) in the US. During my visit to New York, it was possible to foresee, and Baird had also sensed it, that a well-equipped cinema in the British Pavilion at the exhibition would offer a unique opportunity to present to visitors by means of our documentary films an overall picture of the British people and their chosen form of democracy at work. During the 1930s, as this survey has shown, a number of such films had been made, a selection of them being taken with me in 1937, but there were notable gaps in the national image. There were no good films about trade unionism, about scientific research in its international aspect, no really good films about steel and textile production, and only a scattered few about the work of our social services and of village and rural life. If sponsorship could be found in time, official and unofficial, to complete this cross-section, Britain would be in a unique position to present its people as they faced the world in the late 1930s.

A few of us also saw that, if war should erupt, the US would sooner or later be involved and good Anglo-American relations on a people-to-people basis would be of supreme value for the eventual victory. We knew all too keenly that the sending out free of hundreds of thousands of wall-maps of the British Isles dotted with symbolic thatched cottages would hardly evoke a constructive response among Americans towards the British people. The whole of British information sent abroad by the Foreign Office or the British Council was mid-Victorian amateurism and positively dangerous to the Britain of the 1930s.

Grierson was to put this well in his usual cogent manner:

We are talking a great deal today about the projection of Britain. I say frankly that I do not think that anyone in high quarters has seriously thought about how it should be performed in a truly democratic way, or has seen the enormous advantage in international communications which the democratic idea gives. In Whitehall there is today no philosophy of propaganda and certainly none that is recognizably democratic as distinct from authoritarian. There is the same exhausting effort to look spectacular. I am sorry to say that there is the

234

same tendency toward romanticising. Yet I believe that democratic education and democratic propaganda is an easy matter and indeed far easier than the authoritarian type, if those principles I have laid down are grasped. It will be done not by searchlight but in the quiet light of ordinary humanism. Speaking intimately and quietly about real things and real people will be more spectacular in the end than spectacle itself.[1]

In other words a Nazi film like *The Triumph of the Will* could not be countered by a film of the Trooping of the Colour.

To choose films for sending to the World's Fair, the Department of Overseas Trade had charged a Selection Committee of the British Council under the chairmanship of Philip Guedalla, eminent lawyer and historian of note, on which were represented the Post Office (A. G. Highet), the Travel Association (A. F. Primrose), the British Film Institute (Oliver Bell), the Newsreel Association (Neville Kearney) and the Foreign Office (unknown).[2] To be kind, these gentlemen were amateurs in the art and skills of national projection, placed in positions for which they had no special qualifications but, mark you, for which they were presumably paid with public money. In themselves they were not to blame for their inept statements and decisions; who should have had the scourge were the nameless and faceless civil servant(s) at the Department of Overseas Trade who made the appointments.

On my return from the US, *The Times* had carried a report on the very successful showings of the British documentary films there, and this was supplemented by complimentary letters from both American and British correspondents.[3] In a letter printed in the same newspaper, three months later, a documentary producer asked, 'those responsible for national projection oversea for a statement of policy intended for British films at the New York World's Fair, so that the Film Trade might know in good time what kind of films to prepare and what kind of audiences to expect.'[4]

[1] *Searchlight on Democracy, Adult Education*, December 1939, reprinted in *Grierson on Documentary*, edited by H. Forsyth Hardy (Faber, 1966).
[2] A Coordinating Committee for Propaganda had already been set up under the chairmanship of Sir Robert Vansittart but there is no record of what it did.
[3] 6 May 1938, and letters during June.   [4] 7 September 1938.

235

Back to Soho Square (1938–40)

No response was forthcoming, until on 26 November, Mr Philip Guedalla wrote a letter in a personal capacity. On 30 November, a reply to Mr Guedalla appeared signed by eight members of and consultants to the Associated Realist Film Producers. After referring to the letter of 7 September asking for a statement of policy, this new letter went on:

A Committee responsible for this matter exists but, as yet, no statement of its policy has been made except for the personal preference of its Chairman. Speaking of documentary films, Mr Philip Guedalla's views are quoted to be that pictures should be shown which are 'a pleasure to look at and advantageous to Britain . . . and that doesn't meant pictures of glue-factories by night, photographed wrong way up, with crude Russian music.' With reference to a famous *North Sea* herring fleet film, Mr Guedalla said: 'We don't want to leave people with the idea that Britain is inhabited only by fish.'

It is our belief that a Committee without representation from the House of Commons or from branches of the Film Trade, other than newsreels, cannot command the confidence of those who see in the New York World's Fair a unique opportunity to present a picture of British democracy at work.

British documentary films have gained their reputation on one main count: the honesty of their subject matter. It is our belief . . . that the American public would welcome documentary films because of their truthful approach to British life. On the initiative of certain public-spirited industrial and other bodies, several documentary films are now being made. These, together with existing films, can present a picture of many aspects of British life today at the Fair.

In his letter of 26 November Mr Guedalla minimizes the importance of the British Government's cinema on account of its small size. He apparently sees in it nothing more useful than a magnet to attract the casual visitor. We believe that with imaginative presentation it would be possible to use the intimacy of a small theatre to show, alongside our fiction and newsreel films, something that no other country can do – namely, selected programmes of documentary films about specific subjects to specially invited audiences. By these means we could be assured that Americans interested in social welfare, for example, could see what Britain is doing in this particular field. Such a method of presentation seems to us to be of greater value than unorganized showings for casual visitors who might seek the theatre's comfort because the roller-coasters are overcrowded. We welcome a

236

statement from the Committee as to how it will use the British Government's theatre to the best possible advantage.

We are, &c.,

Paul Rotha, Basil Wright, Arthur Elton, Robert J. Flaherty, J. B. S. Haldane, Lancelot Hogben, Julian S. Huxley, E. McKnight Kauffer.

Still no statement was forthcoming from the Committee. They were probably still on holiday. It had been a fine summer. *The Times* finalized the matter so far as it was concerned with a leader.

The choice of films for exhibition [at the British Government's cinema] is therefore a serious matter; it will influence the reputation of Great Britain, first in the mind of the people with whom we most ardently desire to remain on terms of full mutual understanding, but in some degree also of those many countries from which tourists will be attracted to New York. The importance of the selection [of films] has been recognized, as is shown by the references made in the House of Commons and by the many letters that have been received for publication in these columns.

. . . in the special circumstances of the international exhibition there is good reason to give the film of fact a larger share of the programme than it enjoys in the ordinary public cinema in either country. It is in the first place the distinctively British contribution to the art of moving pictures. English producers of fiction films can scarcely do more than show America that they have mastered a technique that was first developed in Hollywood; those who make films of fact, on the other hand, go to New York to teach. The interest in documentary films is now so great in the United States that, instead of being mere makeweights in a programme, they draw queues on their own merits; and British producers are acknowledged to hold the hegemony of the work.[1]

There was a great deal more building up the reputation of the British documentary film and levelling barbed criticism at Mr Guedalla and his Committee and behind them the British Council and the Department of Overseas Trade.

The controversy was by no means confined to *The Times*. The able and influential A. J. Cummings, political columnist of the *News Chronicle*, scathingly referred to Mr Philip Guedalla's

[1] 8 December 1938.

'undergraduate humour', while *The Spectator*, the *New Statesman* and the Londoner's Diary in the *Evening Standard* had their sarcastic comments about the Selection Committee. Oil was added to the fire when it became known that the Committee had rejected the Films of Scotland series for sending to New York. Again Grierson put the matter forcefully:

With great nations blaring their messages across space the quieter aspects of international address do not seem very urgent. Shall we worry about the pictures we shall show at next year's New York World's Fair when, who knows, it may take a flotilla of destroyers to escort them there? Yet, wandering over the States and Canada recently, I got the impression that these pictures we are building up to send overseas may be just as important as the noisy interventions from Godesberg and elsewhere. People were asking everywhere, where Britain stood in the present war of ideas, and they expected, I am afraid, a very concrete answer. . . . 'What world are we building?' is, significantly, the guiding theme of the World's Fair. Hard as it may be to doff our ambassadorial dress and show ourselves as we really are, it is expected of us. As we put the notion of democracy to the national masthead we oblige ourselves to give the world the first real and intimate sight of Britain the world has ever had. Some of us have been laying a plan by which effect can be given to this idea in New York next year.[1]

The Committee of Selection were unmoved. The outcome was that the films considered appropriate by the documentary people for showing in New York were not presented in the British Pavilion. They were shown by special invitation in the Little Theatre of the Science and Education Building. Richard Griffith was commissioned by American Film Center to make a report on both theatres screening British documentary films. Herewith are extracts from his report:

The only focal exhibit in operation throughout the whole Fair was that contained in the Little Theatre of the Science and Education Building. The British documentary movement has sent a selection of its films representing its approach to social problems as expressed in such subjects as nutrition (*Enough to Eat?*), housing (*Housing Problems*), local government (*The Londoners*) and education. Of unequal merit technically, these films indicate the magnitude of the task the

[1] *World Film News*, Vol. III, No. 6, October 1938.

British movement has tackled. The wide range of subjects reveals a disposition to present a complete picture of the modern effort to reorganize society on a scientific basis. . . . All of them have contributed to the reputation of the documentary film as an agency for bringing the ordinary citizen in touch with the forces which govern his life. The Little Theatre's programme on social problems might well pretend to represent the best achievement of the documentary film. The high standard may be attributed largely to the fact that documentary technicians themselves are deeply interested in such subjects.

Of all the official government exhibits at the Fair, the British Pavilion probably had the best opportunity to gain prestige by appealing to special groups of the film-going public. The British documentary film is world famous, and educators, publicists and technicians have long been curious in this country to see examples of its work. Instead, only a small group of documentaries is to be seen in this official Pavilion, and the selection is random. *Song of Ceylon* is there, and *Shipyard* and *The Londoners* are occasionally shown. Such historically important pictures as *Industrial Britain, Coal Face, Today We Live* and *The Saving of Bill Blewitt* are absent. . . . In place of these, the Pavilion offers a heterogeneous collection of travelogues and 'interest' films, incompetent enough and dull enough to alienate the most passionately Anglophile group, much more a lay audience accustomed to the tempo of American films.

So many of these pictures are below the lowest possible level of audience acceptance that one at first imagines them to have been selected at random by men who had never seen any of them. But repeated visits to the Pavilion gradually reveal a motive for the choice, focused on the British Newsreel which opens each programme. Last year the items in this reel were devoted almost wholly to such 'events' as the Changing of the Guard at Buckingham Palace, the visit of Their Majesties to a children's camp', or the opening of a garden party by the Duchess of Kent. Since the war, the reel has displayed the might of the military. As with the Newsreel, so with the rest of the programmes; these unimaginative and pompous films about British landscapes, monuments and sports, project the Britain of tradition and stability. They summon the past to reinforce the present, saying with J. B. Priestley in *English Journey*, 'Damn you; I'm all right!'

The documentary film in England has devoted itself over a period of ten years to dramatizing the Britain of today. . . . An excellent example of the way this job has been done under present conditions of sponsorship is seen in a new film, *Men of Africa*. . . . The film is intended by its sponsors as a defence of British colonial government. . . . It tells how Britain is trying to raise the living standard of her primitive subjects. By medical care, by education, by scientific agriculture, tropical colonies and their inhabitants are put on an equal footing with the rest of the Empire. The film thus states that Britain's right to govern colonies is determined by the extent to which she fits them to govern themselves. In articulating this idea, Basil Wright and Alexander Shaw have transformed the film from an apology for the British Empire into an inculcation of Britain's responsibility toward subject populations. Few such important films embodying this approach are at the British Pavilion; the films shown there have little relation to Britain today. They are, in fact, wholly opposed to the function for which the British documentary film has become famous throughout the world.[1]

The above viewpoint was largely borne out by other US reviews of the British films at the Fair.

The controversy in the British Press about what kind of an overall screen picture of Britain should be shown to the American public at the World's Fair may seem to have been enlarged more than the occasion required. It was, however, as must be clear by now, the ventilation of a conflict of attitudes that had been simmering all through the 1930s. It was a microcosm of the whole documentary policy for the national projection of British democracy at home and overseas. Why, it can well be asked, should we have cared? Why all this effort spent in mobilizing a campaign of opinions to expose a reactionary, amateur *status quo* policy on the part of those officially paid to select and present their obsolescent idea of a British 'Way of Life'? Why didn't we, like other film-makers, just get on with our busy work of making films to the measurements of our sponsors, official and unofficial? Why didn't we try and learn how to make good films just because they *were* good films, won awards and critical praise? Because that would have been a dead end. We learned to make films that expressed something deep in which we believed. If that belief has not come clear in this attempted survey, leading up to the outbreak of war in September 1939, then it has been wasted time on many parts.

[1] *Films*, New York, 1940, No. 1, reprinted in part in *Documentary News Letter*, London, February 1940.

11. *Making* The Times *Film* *(1939–40)*

Inevitably the idea for a documentary film about a national newspaper was born in El Vino's bar in Fleet Street. It was the spring of 1938 and I had recently come back from New York and had fixed to meet W. A. J. Lawrence, then film critic of *The Times*, to tell him about the success of our films in the US. It has been said earlier that his paper from the start had always been a firm supporter both in its reviews and its editorials of the British documentary film. I think someone on the paper (perhaps Lawrence), liked to believe that *The Times* discovered documentary in this country; we did nothing to discourage this belief. Out of the blue and a dry sherry, John Lawrence said, 'Why don't we make a film about *The Times* and its place in national life as a great newspaper?' 'Why not, indeed?' I replied. Lawrence said mysteriously that he would have a word with the 'management' at an 'appropriate moment', and we left it like that.

Lawrence was a man of his word. Some weeks later I went to Printing House Square, the home of *The Times* for so many years, to meet Mr S. Kent, the Manager. He liked the idea about which Lawrence had told him, asked what such a film as we envisaged would roughly cost and said genially that he would take the matter further, but with the proviso, and he was quite serious, that he himself should appear in the film.[1] In due course, Film Centre, of which I was then a member, was commissioned to prepare a script and submit a budget for a film based on it. Not until the end of the year was all arranged. I should begin writing the script in the New Year and production would be through Realist Film Unit under my direction. I spent several weeks almost living in *The Times* office, meeting

[1] Thus aligning himself with the Sheikh of Sharjah. I did in fact shoot a camera-interview with him but the camera had no film in it.

most of its staff, watching its daily and nightly processes of production and delving into its wealth-ridden history. In all this
research, great help was given me by Stanley Morison, an
expert in typography (which endeared him to me), who had
designed the famous Times New Roman type first used by the
paper on 3 October 1932, and used until 1972. He had also
written the official *History of The Times Newspaper* in three
volumes. It was said furtively that he had also designed the
heading for the front page of the *Daily Worker* but this was
never corroborated. His tall, crow-like figure, always clad from
head to feet in black, crowned by a very wide-brimmed black
hat, was a good sight for me. Peter Fleming, an entertaining
author-traveller of several good books, at that time writing
Fourth Leaders for the paper, had been appointed liaison officer
between the newspaper and myself. He had not the vaguest idea
of what it was all about but was always most courteous and
anxious to help. He now said that it was about time we had a
meeting, a kind of stock-taking to find out where we all stood.

The meeting turned out to be a luncheon in the dining-room
of John Walter III's house which still stood in Printing House
Square, the Walter family having been owners of the paper for
many years. The lunch was described in a letter to Eric Knight
in America thus:

20 December 1938

It was all most embarrassing, held in the holy of holies, the inner
sanctum where the fate of governments and nations had surely been
decided and where only the nobs get asked. Gilt plate and all that.
After a modest sherry by which we were introduced to our host,
Major J. J. Astor, the then proprietor of the paper, we filed into the
dining-room – Geoffrey Dawson, the then Editor, Barrington-Ward,
assistant editor, Stanley Morison, Casey, a leader writer, Peter
Fleming, John Lawrence, and from Film Centre, Arthur Elton (in a
flaming orange shirt), Basil Wright and myself (in my only good suit.)
I had assumed that we would all be expected to give little speeches
about what the film would be like, but I was wrong. Most of the meal
was spent in Major Astor discussing film censorship with Arthur
Elton, Wright keeping Barrington-Ward fully engaged with what
Wright doesn't remember, Geoffrey Dawson not talking to anybody
(I am warned that he has no interest in the film whatsoever and thinks

it all a lot of nonsense quite beneath *The Times*), while I chatted amiably with John Lawrence. Major Astor, at the end of an excellent luncheon, did make one remark for all to hear. He said that suggestions made by 'some people' that there was a connection between *The Times* newspaper and the Cabinet, No. 10 Downing Street and indeed the Prime Minister himself, were without foundation. With that historic, inaccurate and unprovoked statement, the luncheon party broke up. So far as I know, the film was not discussed at all.

I had spent the night before reading Wickham Steed's book, *The Press*, just published. Steed was Editor of *The Times* between 1919–22 and his book is a lament on the vanished freedom of the British Press. It is, of course, in spite of Major Astor's pronouncement, widely known that what happens in No. 10 Downing Street is talked about in *The Times* office an hour or two later. It is also recognized by most informed people that the paper's main leader always represents the home and foreign policy of the Cabinet. This was especially the case at the time of Munich, when *The Times* was said to be being given information by the Foreign Office hours before the rest of Fleet Street. It was even rumoured that Field Marshall Goering was in telephonic communications with the Editor at that time. The engaging part of all this, as I have found for myself over the past few weeks, is that alone and in confidence people on the staff of the paper will admit this to be true. However, that is not the kind of subject to be brought up at a lunch to launch the making of a documentary film.

Obviously I have been reading a great deal about the history of the British Press and it is very largely the history of *The Times* prior to the Great War. I have read the brilliant leaders written by Robert Lowe at Delane's orders, when Lord John Russell, as Prime Minister, told *The Times* to mind its own business as a newspaper and to refrain from any criticism of the nation's government in 1851. 'The first duty of the Press,' wrote Lowe, 'is to obtain the earliest and most correct intelligence of the events of the time, and instantly, by disclosing them, to make them the common property of the nation.' To which Wickham Steed comments, 'It would not be amiss if the Press and the statesmen of England should today reflect upon the final question which *The Times* asked so firmly some 86 years ago. Many things in Europe and the world might not have gone so sorely awry during the past decade [the 1930s] if the leading journals of the British Press had consistently observed the principles which *The Times* then laid down.'

So you can see my problem in this script is worrying. How far can I go in establishing the fact that *The Times* today is betraying many ideals and principles for which its 19th-century owners and editors fought so hard? How far can subtlety work with these people? Will they be like some of the others for whom we have made films these past ten years, so vain that they will not feel the needles we insert? We shall see how it falls out.

But for all that, it's a marvellous subject and I'm lucky to be making it. Russell's despatches from the Crimea showing up the terrible conditions of the British Army, despatches which aroused the Nightingale to go out there to administer. Lord Northcliffe's use of the paper during the last war to expose the personal vanities of the British General Staff. And, I am tempted to add, the famous day only a year or two ago when the very small lift in *The Times* building jammed between two floors with the Editor, Geoffrey Dawson, in it. They say that the foreign policy of a Cabinet meeting taking place at that moment had to be postponed until Mr Dawson could be freed.

Having done my research and seen what I could at first hand, I went down in the New Year to Hythe, near Folkestone, in Kent (where I had spent many holidays in my boyhood and where a I rented a cottage for weekend breaks while at Strand), and took a room at the *White Hart* in the High Street. My only companion was my spaniel who would make me go for walks. Two months were thus spent, with little Carl Mayer coming down for occasional talks about the general shape and continuity of the script.[1] The structure was to be like two funnels, one inverted above the other, spout to spout. A typical but non-existent day, 31 June 1939, was chosen to be the main thread of the film. Into the upper funnel was poured the world's news, expected and unexpected, being collected and sent by telephone, by telegram and by air-letter even to the office in Printing House Square. There the news, with the addition of the never-ceasing tapes from the agencies, was sorted, written up, checked and sub-edited, while staff correspondents went out and about covering this and that story. Meantime, advertisement pages were made up, blocks were made of the pictures, newsprint supplies were readied, machines oiled and so on.

Everything led up to the critical 4.15 pm Editor's Conference round a hexagonal table in a room where the shelves were heavy with old bound volumes of the paper and there hung portraits of previous owners and their editors. Here the contents

[1] This was to be the only film in England on which Carl Mayer took a credit as Script Consultant.

of tomorrow's paper, for the mythical 31 June, were discussed and agreed – the leaders, the main news stories, the arts page, what should go into the correspondence columns and so on. Interwoven with this sequence of the meeting today was a long sequence of dissolving shots devoted to the history of *The Times*, its famous editors, its news scoops and its memories. When the afternoon conference broke up, various stories would be followed up and we would meet the all-important night editor, who would prepare a dummy of the paper to be.

From now on, everything was to be a race against the clock. Home and foreign sub-editors sub-edit. Correspondents who have been out and about are back writing up their stories. In the composing-room men get ready for copy, in the furnace-room and the machine-hall all is expectancy. As the evening wears on, last-minute news comes in for which space must be made. Then the first edition for the more distant parts of the country and for abroad by airmail is made up, set in type, proof read and corrected, the formes of type are made, the plates are turned, they are locked on the machines and the presses are ready to roll.

But they do not roll, or rather they roll but we do not as yet see them. There is another edition coming later. Film-wise the presses rolling, the moment for which we have been waiting, must be kept for the last edition or else they would be an anticlimax. So there is a hushed sequence of waiting while an hour or so go by. The theatre critic leisurely writes his piece while printers have a cigarette and a cup of tea. At the very last moment, an unexpected story breaks by cable. It has to be decoded to add to the suspense. An event of world interest has happened. It just makes the last edition. Now the presses can really roll and thunder. The despatch vans scream into the yard. Trains wait at the mainline stations. And so the news of yesterday goes out to the world of today, through the bottom of the inverted funnel.

This was the rough shape of the script as written at Hythe. In a letter to Richard Griffith, I wrote:

Hythe, 16 *March* 1939

The script is almost ready in first draft but how the hell can one work on a creative job, let alone one that deals with current events, when we are sitting on a barrel of dynamite. Yet the British are strangely apathetic. I sat for an hour this morning in the public bar here. ⟦The public bar means the one used by the working people as distinct from the saloon which is used by the middle-class shopkeepers, estate agents, solicitors and the local gentry. The beer's cheaper in the public and, I swear, tastes better.⟧ Opinion was unanimous. That man Chamberlain's a bastard; he ought to be hung from a lamp post. Towards midday they drift back to their work. This evening they'll look in the paper first for the racing and football results. They may say how sorry they feel for the Czechs or the Poles or whoever, but they'll forget it quickly and have another pint.

'I've written a 103-page script for a six-reeler but have now decided it's no bloody good. So I try to get a wholly new approach. I'm going to make a picture of England as *The Times* sees her. *The Times* is the voice of opinion of the controlling class of Britain – the City, the Church, the Court, the Law, the Army, Navy and Air Force, the big landowners, the big industrialists – in other words what is called the Establishment. Can we put that on the screen? And if we did, wouldn't the boyos on the Left howl. They would be too short-sighted to see that in no other way could you make a picture of England that is gradually dying. It will take a long time to expire, but it will because it is hopelessly out of date. The history will play an important part – those great years in the last century when *The Times* told everyone including the Queen and the House of Lords to go f—— off. The leading articles in those days make a magnificent comment on our foreign policy today and no one can mistake their meaning. That could be the film. Not much about producing a newspaper in it; something of the editorial side but not to overweight the other. It will be the problem of taking the story behind each page of the paper and, using the old phrase, 'bringing it alive'. The picture that is behind the money market-prices and the shares reports and the property sales, behind this summary of a government report on health or housing, or behind this presentation at Court, so help me. But primarily it will be the story of British interests throughout the world and world events seen in relation to their British sense. As you will know, the sponsors are not the easiest with whom to deal, but I've had that problem before. They are for the most part very public school and Oxford-Cambridge and upper-upper-class, but then so can I be if need arises. So it goes. I shall blunder on maybe.

And again a month later.

Making The Times Film (1939–40)

London, 14 *April* 1939

The Times script, brand new version, is finished. They have it now for consideration. With any luck I hope to start shooting in a few weeks and go on right through the summer. I am not unreasonably unhappy. It is three months' work crystallized into a tight, fast-moving script. It is about an England of the ruling-class as seen through the pages of their national newspaper. Somewhere I've given those who put their trust in England's heritage their bellyful, a cod British Council sequence which I shall, to be honest, enjoy shooting because I too like old things in their perspective. England's pomp and ceremony, her sons at Eton and Oxford, will parade the screen. The Royal Family, the relics of England's glorious but fading past in ruins and museums and art collections and, bless me, the Tower of London thrown in. Then the England of the soil, a changing England, no longer so many vast estates but soil controlled by marketing boards and government department officials. (Trouble is they don't know much about agriculture.) Then the England of industry, not a workers' or Trade Union industry but an employers' industry. And then the England that controls these other Englands; the *mystique* ramifications of finance and banking and stock exchanges. Finally, the great main body of the film, how this national newspaper expresses all these Englands, how its foreign correspondents and its leader writers watch out for England's interests but always for the England of the minority in numbers but maximum in wealth and ownership. But I wonder if it will ever be made?

After a courteous lapse of time, Peter Fleming telephoned to say that a meeting had been called to discuss the script. A day or so before the appointment, a parcel arrived for me with the Compliments of *The Times*. It contained six copies of the script which had been set up in type! This petrified me. To a filmmaker, a script is something flexible and subject to change right up to the time a film is shot and, indeed, often after that. To have my script set up in type seemed to make it a fixture. But Fleming explained later that rather than have six copies and more typed by hand, it was quicker and more economic to have it set up in type on their own presses. That hadn't occurred to me.

It must have been the strangest script-conference ever held. It was after lunch in Barrington-Ward's room, famous for the fact that no fire had ever been lit in the open grate and that there was no other heating. Happily it was April. Barrington-Ward, a nice rather placid man, took the chair. By now the Editor had completely washed his hands of the whole matter. Lawrence, Stanley Morison, Casey (the mystery leader writer who never said a word) and Fleming were there for *The Times,* while from Film Centre came John Grierson to support me in case of need. Grierson was late to arrive and caused instant confusion (as only Grierson could on such an occasion) by asking if there was a lavatory in the building. Grierson's needs met, Barrington-Ward opened the discussion by saying with the utmost courtesy but with obvious embarrassment that he knew nothing about films and did not recall when he had last seen one. He then handed over the meeting to Peter Fleming. The latter said that although his wife was an actress he too knew little about the cinema.[1]

The script, as was usual, had been written in two columns; on the left a description of the screen visuals, on the right the draft wording of the commentary and suggested dialogue. After much business with his pipe, Fleming lost *his* embarrassment. 'You know, Rotha,' he said with diffidence, 'We hesitate to make any criticism of your script because we are not experts in this kind of thing and you are, but there is one thing here at *The Times* about which we *really* pride ourselves. We know when to use a colon, and when to use a semi-colon.' There was a pause while Grierson and I looked at each other dumbfounded. Fleming went on, 'Now in your commentary column, you frequently use a semi-colon where *we* at *The Times* would use a colon.' As gently as possible I said, 'Mr Fleming, I appreciate your very good comment but I must point out that the sentences of this commentary will be spoken, not read.' There was again a very long silence.

Then I said what I had been waiting to say, 'Gentlemen, there is one thing radically wrong with this script you have before you.' They all sat up and stared, and Grierson shifted uneasily in his chair. I went on, 'The news is collected, it is written and sub-edited and discussed and finally the paper is

---

[1] Celia Johnson who, a few years later, was to give such a moving performance in David Lean's *Brief Encounter* and has such a distinguished career both on stage and screen.

put-to-bed, as you say. But, gentlemen, actually there is nothing in the paper. There is no hard news story to seize the attention of the public the next morning when they get their paper.'

Grierson saw his opening. 'Rotha is right, we must find something big for the paper to say that night. You can't have *The Times* full of blank pages, can you, Mr Barrington-Ward?' Then in typical Griersonian style: 'Now, here's an idea out of the blue! Why not take three great nights at *The Times* and reenact what happened? Take, for example, the night when George V took so long dying that he missed the second edition. Every other paper printed the news of his death, but in the interests of historical accuracy, *The Times* didn't, although it was obvious that he would die at any minute. Then there must surely be something very interesting on the night before the Abdication? And of course the night when Hitler marched across the border into Austria and the link between *The Times* and the Foreign Office.' I saw Barrington-Ward's face go white. I am amazed to this day that the whole film wasn't cancelled then and there. Several people spoke at once. 'Such a thing would be impossible!' 'It would be far too dangerous!' Barrington-Ward abruptly but gently closed the meeting. 'We must all think about this problem,' were his final patient words, 'And, Mr Rotha, remember, we have every confidence in you, so long as you don't upset the work of the office too much!'

Outside in Queen Victoria Street, Grierson said, 'You're a lucky bastard. You've got away with murder.' And that so far as I know was the last he ever had to do with the film. He certainly never saw it because he was in Canada when it was finished.

Actually it was Peter Fleming who came up with a good idea for the important news story. From time to time, *The Times* used to sponsor climbing expeditions on Mount Everest and elsewhere, for which it took exclusive rights on any stories and photographs sent back to England. His idea was that the suspense gap between the two editions of the paper should be filled by a coded cable coming into the telegraph-room, which when deciphered should report that the climbing party had reached the summit, that Everest had at last been conquered. It was a good idea, non-controversial and non-political. It was adopted. It was planted early in the film by shots of a climbing party and later, when the Editor is about to leave for the night, he says to the night editor, 'No news of that climbing party yet, I suppose?'

Realist Film Unit and I prepared a production budget which was submitted to *The Times* by Film Centre and approved. It was for £7,500 for a six-reel film. Thus in May I set out with young Harry Rignold as cameraman on one of the happiest location trips that I can remember. We travelled in his big but shabby car and carried a Newman-Sinclair camera and a gyro-head tripod, the one used by Flaherty when he shot *Man of Aran*, and around 1,800 ft of film stock. I had chosen the easiest sequence of the film to shoot first, material for what was to be called the Heritage Sequence, that is to say the England we thought of as being the loveliest. We headed for Dorset, and the West country in general. In spite of Grierson's frequent admonitions, my delight at beautiful visuals on the screen never diminished. A letter to Knight said:

Marlborough, Wiltshire 13 *May* 1936
Blimey, this sequence should please the Merrie England upholders. The great vistas of trees, looking very shapely and green in the May sunlight, the old manor houses and castles and cathedrals, the cottages sleeping in their gardens thick with fruit blossom and chestnuts in flower, the ruins at Glastonbury Abbey, the magnificent West front of Wells Cathedral, the withdrawn red-brick houses with half-timbered fronts built for wealthy people three hundred years ago, the mellow buildings at Oxford and Eton – in other words I am wandering through Oxfordshire, Dorset and Wiltshire looking for the lovely relics which still live from the past and making them as lovely as modern celluloid will allow. Young Harry Rignold, whom I have talked about before, is the cameraman and feels this is his great break. Once I have fixed a set-up for the camera, he makes the exposure, does the focus-pulling if necessary, and I do the camera-operating, in other words control the camera's movement. It is all a picture of the English Heritage, something very real, in the early mornings before anyone is around much except for those who work on the land, and the sunlight grows warm and the chestnut candles smell sweet. It is the England we all dream about, but so few of us know because we can't afford to live there.

Making The Times *Film* (*1939–40*)

Here, in Marlborough, where we stay the night, is one of England's most famous public schools. Here, in the pub, are fathers visiting sons this weekend. The boys try to look grown up as they drink a bitter in the bar, calling their father 'sir', but 'pater' to their mothers. It is here that you feel class-consciousness at its most acute. It is amazing how this old world of privilege still clings. Here is a wide High Street – the widest in England, they say – with 17th and 18th century houses. Yet there is a Woolworth's and a super-grocer store and a movie-house round the corner. The old persists beside the new. And the chestnuts are neither new nor old. They are of all time with their white plumes and their terrific greenery which I shall make immortal in my film. We go to Cern Abbas and Sandford Orcas and God knows what other beautiful places. For the opening of the sequence we hit the ruins of Corfe Castle on a specially fine day. Even God blesses us with the weather.

So we wander for a week from place to place, and no one, repeat no one, knows where we are. We stop at a farm. I don't know their name and they don't know mine. May we take some film shots? Of course, you're welcome. They get on with their work, asking only, 'When will the snaps appear, sir?'. Occasionally we meet snooty people who don't like their houses being filmed. 'We don't like publicity. If photographs of our house appear, we get trippers asking to see over it.' A Sir Hubert Medlecott grew angry when we asked to film his very lovely 16th-century manor house. I dropped casually the sacred name of *The Times*, although I had no letter of authority with me. It worked a miracle. We ended up with glasses of sherry in his lounge.

And again:

Evesham, Worcestershire

We moved on but are now struggling with bad weather. The sun couldn't last. Overcast and wet as only England can be. How ungrateful can you get? We have had some wonderful days. I spent all day with a grand man – Bomford by name – a farmer who is just making ends meet because he has a small amount of capital and has invested it in machinery. He has invented and perfected some amazing machines, one of which plants mechanically two hundred acres of sprouts that would take ten men ten days to plant by hand. His machine does it in two days with two men. He is a specialist in tractors and other complicated forms of engine which not only plough the land but do many other things. He lives alone in a big red-brick old house surrounded by trees. His one wish now is that his experiments could be passed on to other farmers who have got the capital for expensive machinery.

How remote is this England I have been seeing from the poverty-stricken villages I saw when making *The Face of Britain* (about which I wrote you at the time) in South Wales and the misery of the Midlands and the North-East. No matter how stricken the farm worker, he has always the land on which to grow his food. That is perhaps why he does not get bitter and hostile to the injustices he suffers. In these parts the tensions of the international upheaval seem far removed. Two reminders – the radio news-bulletins at night and the newspaper in the morning. And a third which I bitterly resent. In every village, no matter how small or remote, there are these bloody recruiting posters. England needs you again! England expects you to do what you did in 1914! Every man, woman and child can play their part in the defence of the Motherland and the Empire! For what? Oddly enough, I find amazing apathy about it all. It shows how totally false is the newspaper impression of life in this country. From the Press, you would think that all England leaps to attention. In village and city, every manjack is eager to help defend England. Travelling from place to place as we have been doing, we have found very little enthusiasm about defending England.

The Heritage sequence ended by shooting the wonderful armour in the Tower of London. It was a fitting conclusion.

The sequence admits the possibility of the beauty of subject and the craft of camerawork. All through its shooting I have tried to use the camera in movement to express both content and expression of that content.

In hindsight, it can be said that there were two kinds of camera movement all through *The Times* film – panning and tilting with the tripod-head held static, and movement of the whole camera itself in a tracking shot. There were the stroking, affectionate movements of the camera which can (as we learned from Flaherty) express so much of the inner content through outer surface. (This is what I was to try and do much later in *No Resting Place* to reveal the 'character' and inner mind working of my actors.) The camera can also be used to move in anger – the whip-pan, the swift track-in. Pabst, Flaherty and Max Ophüls were the great predecessors. The Russians hardly ever moved their cameras. They were content to use movement within the picture-frame and the montage of the overlapping of action movement.

Shooting on the film continued most of the summer, both inside and outside *The Times* building. I was fortunate to have a proficient Unit manager in Pat Moyna, who juggled with an elaborate schedule. Major Astor's influential contacts were impeccable and shamelessly used. They brought entry for our Unit to many places. Some, like the Royal Enclosure at Ascot, the interior of the Stock Exchange, and the Law Courts in the Strand, had been hitherto uncharted territory to a film camera. Shots of Lloyds, strictly forbidden, were taken by my unit of three disguising ourselves as window-cleaners. The mounted band of the Royal Horse Guards was turned out for us in Hyde Park, although this cost Major Astor £250 for its benevolent fund. (It must have been the most expensive single shot in a documentary film up to that time, but it looked its £250's worth on the screen). There was the music critic making notes at a student's solo performance, the air correspondent chatting to a pilot about to take off on a flight to try and beat the altitude record, the fashion writer at a parade, the garrulous golf correspondent emerging from his 19th hole, and the racing correspondent on the Down near Newbury chatting to a trainer. Only the last brought trouble. With all our equipment (including an expensive sound-truck) ready at dawn, the racing correspondent abruptly asked, "What's in this for him?' (indicating the trainer), 'and for me?' I ignored the question. 'We want a hundred quid to split between us,' he added. 'You'd better telephone Mr Kent, the Manager, and ask him?' I said. He and the trainer, the horses and the stable boys went off to breakfast. My crew and I stayed put. Around ten they returned. The racing correspondent said grimly, 'It's settled, you can go ahead now.' We did. Whether he got his money I never found out or enquired; if he did, it was not a charge on our budget.

When the Unit went to film at the Royal Show held by the Agricultural Society in Windsor Great Park, it was a cloudy morning. We parked the car well away from the show ground on the grass verge of the tree-lined avenue that leads down from the Castle. We smoked and drank out of a thermos, waiting for the weather to clear. Then in the distance I saw a carriage approaching drawn by four grey horses. Acting on a hunch, I called to Harry Rignold to set up the camera quickly. My hunch was good. It was their Royal Majesties driving to their show. At that moment, blow me if the sun didn't come out. Harry panned his camera as the carriage passed at a slow trot. The Royal Pair obligingly waved their hands on either side of the carriage. There were only the three of us in sight. To this day, I am sure that the incident was stage-managed by Major Astor in consultation with the Duke of Norfolk. 'God looks after his own,' commented Eric Knight, when I wrote and told him. I don't know whether he referred to me or to their Majesties.

Before starting on the interiors in Printing House Square, a few days were spent in a studio at Elstree. Among scenes that had to be reconstructed was an attempt to 'bring alive' the well-known painting by B. R. Haydon called 'Waiting for *The Times*'. It portrayed an impatient gentleman (*ca* 1850) waiting for another gentleman to finish with the paper. The set was an accurate reconstruction of the painting, but through a small window at the back of the set there should have been painted a view of tiled rooftops. When we were ready to shoot at 11 am the view was still a piece of white canvas. Enquiries revealed that the scene-painter had been called away on a rush job to another studio and would not be back until after lunch. We had a tight shooting schedule and four hours could not be wasted. I called a half-hour break for tea and sent the whole Unit to the canteen. In the scene painter's shop I found brushes and paint. Within fifteen minutes the rooftops were in place. The Unit reassembled. 'My God, it's been done!' cried my assistant. 'Sure,' I said, 'the guy came back early'. It could have caused a strike if the truth had been known.

At the studio, scenes were also shot for what was called the 'One Minute' sequence. In the script I had dreamed up the idea that as the giant hand of Big Ben creeps from 29 minutes past the hour to 30, so a cross-cut series of imaginary incidents fills the 60 seconds of real time. A wicket is needed to win at Lords, the bowler runs up to the wicket, the batsman plays forward, the wicket falls. A raincoated man furtively climbs a staircase, opens a door handle, and a blonde lies dead on a bed. Two foreign *polizei* enter a house, a journalist hides a pocket radio, he is roughly arrested by the *polizei*. And other such items of fabricated 'news' added up to the exact moment when Big Ben strikes the half-hour. Later, I dropped the sequence as being too artificial and phoney; it introduced a false note and I was glad to be rid of it, although it took trouble and money to shoot and edit.

Other memorable moments occurred when the Unit, with lighting equipment, moved into *The Times* office. It was our first night's shooting. I had arranged with Charles Morgan, the well-known drama critic of the paper and distinguished author, to film him arriving back at the office to write his late piece for the last edition. It was the final performance at the Lyceum Theatre before it was turned into a dance hall. Mr Morgan insisted in being in full evening dress, with an ebony cane, a swinging cloak and a silk hat. He kindly invited me to have dinner with him at the Garrick Club before going to the office, which I did with enjoyment but had to get out my rusty dinner-jacket. At 11 pm the pair of us, well mellowed, arrived at *The Times*. My assistant had hired the oldest taxi-cab he could find in London. Mr Morgan was to arrive in this, pay off the driver and enter the building. By then, the lighting had attracted quite a crowd of spectators, who were kept back out of the picture. On my word, the taxi groaned up, Mr Morgan alighted and with a theatrical flourish of his cloak gave the driver half-a-crown, and went into the office to a burst of cheers from the off-screen crowd. He was thoroughly enjoying himself; so was I.

The next shot called for Mr Morgan to be seen leaning on his cane in the minute lift of which *The Times* boasted. The camera was set up on the second floor so that it would shoot Mr Morgan in the lift as it passed upwards to the third floor where he had his room. Without malice, we placed our lamps on the floor of the lift, lighting Mr Morgan from below. As he passed up the screen, it was worthy of *The Cabinet of Dr Caligari* at its most expressionist.

Next we moved to his office. He entered into our shot, placed his silk hat with habitual skill on to a peg, hung up his cloak and cane, and took his chair at the desk. He pulled a gold

watch from his waistcoat pocket, looked at it, checked it with a
clock on the wall, set it down on the desk in front of him, picked
up a very old pen from a tray on the desk, tested its nib on his
thumb, shot his cuffs and began to write. In the next shot, over
his shoulder, we read in block capital letters: HAMLET by
WILLIAM SHAKESPEARE.

Later that night and into the next morning, Mr Morgan got
gloriously drunk on canteen beer. It was an appropriate sequence, I felt, with which to begin serious shooting in *The
Times* building.

Our camera equipment was a Mitchell for all sound-and-
picture shooting, with the Newman-Sinclair always at hand. The
amount of lighting varied according to the size of the rooms but
a generator was required. When we came later to work in the
vast machine-hall where the paper was printed, it was a
mammoth task, the biggest undertaking at that time by a documentary unit. I asked for a track shot some hundred yards long.
past the banks of running machines. Jimmie Rogers was given a
whole day to set his lamps. Most of the time the machines were
of course running; they obviously could not be stopped for us. A
tribute is paid to the electricians; they worked long and very
hard. Detailed continuity sheets (as on a feature film) were
kept daily throughout by Yvonne Fletcher.

Two incidents during shooting are well remembered. A
scene was being taken of the Diplomatic editor at his desk
telephoning to someone in the Foreign room. It was a fake
dialogue about a report of some troop movements advancing
on a frontier unnamed, which, upon checking, revealed that a
similar number of troops were being moved away from the
frontier. In other words, as said the man in the Foreign room, a
normal seasonal changing of troops. 'Then I suppose we had
better say so,' said the Diplomatic correspondent resignedly.
The usual tape measure had been run out from the camera-lens
to the Diplomatic correspondent's nose to find the focus. He
was asked not to move his position and he sat rigid. Suddenly
there was a great explosion. With one mind all the crew ran to
the window to see if the sound-truck parked in the yard two
floors below was all right. It was. We turned back into the

room. Obeying the command, the Diplomatic correspondent had not moved an inch. He was covered with dust and debris from the ceiling. A few minutes later we were told that the IRA had exploded a bomb just up Queen Victoria Street. The 4.15 pm Editor's Conference was in progress at the time. At the sound of the explosion, I was told, the Editor had quietly remarked. 'That will be those film people, I suppose.'

Towards the end of the interior shooting, the day grew nearer to stage the farce of the Editor's Conference, a pivotal sequence in the film. With caution I had sounded out some of those who normally took part – two or three sympathetic leader writers, the night editor, the letters editor and the foreign editor. They all agreed to take part in the mock-up scene, but at the same time warned me that the Editor himself, Mr Geoffrey Dawson, would certainly have nothing to do with it. He had assiduously ignored the film unit up to that point.

Two days before the scene was due to be made, I sent a brief memorandum to Mr Dawson, in which I asked him which West End actor he would like to play his part at the staged Conference. In minutes his secretary came to me and said that Mr Dawson would like to see me urgently in his office. I took my time. When I entered his office, he said, 'What's all this tomfoolery about some West End actor? Nobody shall portray me except myself! I'll call a special Conference at 10 am next Saturday morning.' In this simple but human way, the Machiavelli behind the Abdication of Edward VIII and the Munich Pact succumbed to personal vanity, as I suspected he would.

The Editor took it all very seriously. Saturday is normally a day off for newspapermen but they all appeared on time. Mr Dawson had thought up some mythical, timeless dialogue and news items for the meeting to discuss, and submitted them to me. They seemed fine. The day's work was a great success and Dawson admitted afterwards that he had much enjoyed himself with the 'amateur dramatics'.

I wrote to Eric Knight:

London, 29 August 1939

Once again I write with maybe bombs around the corner. But this time it is strangely different. There is not the excitement there was last September, no panic, no radio-vans in the streets telling you to get your gasmask. This hot summer afternoon all is very calm. Hitler's reply is on its way, the Press placards tell us. The House is sitting and once again Mr Chamberlain refuses to tell the people what he and Hitler have been saying to one another. At night now we black things out. All work at Film Centre has stopped. All films are cancelled. The 128 tins containing the 36,000 ft of negative of *The Times* film are safely stored in the strong room at *The Times* building. With them is a copy of the final script covered all over with minute instructions as to how the film should be cut – if ever it is cut. Duplicate copies of the script are lodged away in the country, one at Grierson's farm in Kent, one at my brother's cottage in Hertfordshire. But nine months of hard work by a fine crew of technicians could be blown to bits tonight if a bomb dropped in the right place.

So far as shooting is concerned, the film is finished. I am, I must confess, pleased with it to date, judging by the rushes. *The Times* staff, being newspapermen, have done well from an acting viewpoint. If the film is ever finished, it will show how *The Times* works and what it stands for. For once, you in America will not be able to complain, as you so justifiably did, about the quality of the sound recording. It is all on violet RCA, and I am sure that being violet means it must be good.

You know, somehow I have a hunch that this war will not break. Information among the boys down at *The Times* office says that the Foreign Office have handed the whole matter over to Chamberlain, and that he and Halifax are acting wholly on their own responsibility. Except for information about troop movements and the coming and going of ministers and messengers, our Press has had no specific news since last week. That is why I smell a sell-out. If Hitler intended marching, surely he would have marched last week?

Evacuation is perplexing, except for the film referred to above. When you come to put to yourself the question, Do I really need this or that, or can I replace them? There's really little to evacuate, except yourself, when you come down to it. Maybe a few books, a few papers and letters (all yours, for example), and that's about all. Yours will go well out into the countryside and thus probably receive the first bomb to be dropped by mistake. I reckon I must be the last person left in London without a gasmask, but the very idea of it so revolts me that I would rather take the risk of being gassed than tie up my face in rubber. I'm sure they are no use anyway, except for morale purposes. I have also no bomb-proof shelter to which to go and do not know the name of my allotted air-raid warden, or even if he exists. Thus I shall probably be the only person left alive in England when the war ends. I shall then finish *The Times* film with no one to interrupt me.

In twenty-four hours we shall know . . .

A few weeks after war broke out, *The Times* decided that as all the shooting on the film had been done and the majority of the budget spent, it might as well have the film edited. With young Gerald Keene and Yvonne Fletcher as assistants, we settled down to the task in a cutting-room hired in Wardour Street. There were no bombs as yet.

Again I wrote to Knight:

8 October 1939

We've been cutting now for four weeks, working very long hours and weekends (we don't have to, but once I start cutting I can't leave the goddamned thing alone). We've got it down to twelve reels. Eventually it must come down to between five and six. That in my opinion is the maximum for a documentary, although so much of ours is in terms of story dialogue and not the orthodox commentary style. One interesting thing about the film will be its intimate use of camera and microphone. When shooting, I liked the idea that much of it in the offices must be told in terms of telephone conversations between one room and another, and thereafter the voice level must be quiet. That was not possible until we had good recording facilities which, as you know, I had this time.[1]

You write that I sound excited about the picture. Of course I am. How can you not be, when you are living three-quarters of the day for seven days a week handling the celluloid strips which bear images that you captured through a crystal lens three, four or even more months ago? I remember writing you one Sunday from Marlborough. Well, I cut that material only yesterday. That is something amazing about film. You have creative urges months back when you trained your camera at something, and then you recapture those urges when you pick up the strips of film from the rack in the cutting-room six months later. That is maybe something you don't get in any other form of expression, unless it is in music and painting. Even on-the-spot notes for a book don't come alive in such a vital way and with the same intensity.

---

[1] This was before the days of midget microphones and other such aids to recording. Unlike other technicians, the names of sound recordists are often overlooked. The patient recordist in this case was L. H. Page for all location work. He did a good job.

Music for the film, of which there was a good deal, mainly in the first half, was written by Walter Leigh who interpreted various sequences with his usual skill and sensitivity. It was played by the Sadler's Wells Theatre Orchestra, conducted by Constant Lambert. It was, I believe, Leigh's next to last work, at any rate for a film, before he was called up, only to be killed in North Africa in 1942.

In anticipation of a première for the film, which seemed to me rather optimistic in wartime, John Lawrence sent me the proof of a kind of illustrated programme, with an excellent preface about documentary films written by himself. At that stage, only six copies were printed. I made appropriate corrections but before I could mail it back, he called and said any idea of a première was off. I was not surprised.

After the first married print of the film was made at the end of January 1940, in agreement with *The Times* I decided to shorten it to five reels. There was no argument; I was the first to see the need for shortening. At the same time, they generously offered to pay for a few extra scenes I needed in the composing-room. This time, A. E. Jeakins, who has shot so many documentary films in his time, was behind the camera, and he skilfully matched his photography with that of Jimmie Rogers.

Geoffrey Dawson had been at the last showing of the film. A few days later I met him in a passage in *The Times* office. He stopped and said, 'You know, it was really very remarkable the way you got real drama into that film of yours. A most interesting medium. It was quite an exciting experience to see it, even if you are going to change it. Don't spoil it, now!' Without waiting for a reaction, he passed on to the Editorial Conference.

The first casualty of shortening was the Heritage Sequence *in toto*. It was some 600 ft long, for which Basil Wright had written what he called a Purple Passage of commentary and Walter Leigh some romantic music which would have warmed British Council hearts. It had been a cod sequence anyway, although it had some lovely visuals, and seen in perspective it could be dropped with no one the wiser. It had been a piece of self-indulgent nostalgia on my part. (For a long time, like the Industrial Sequence from *Rising Tide*, it was kept as a separate reel in the vaults but it was mislaid during the war.)

Making The Times *Film* (*1939–40*)

The shorter version was shown to a small audience of *The Times* in a private theatre in Savile Row. It was followed by dinner at Major Astor's house in Carlton House Terrace. It was a gloomy affair; the dinner was excellent. (Food rationing had not hit the Astor household as yet.) All the old familar faces of previous meetings were present. Everyone said cautiously how much they 'liked' the film. But I sensed there was no enthusiasm for it. Some of them had been receptive, it was clear, to the arrows of satire in the film, but nothing was said. They were far too well bred. I was not at all depressed as I walked home in the black-out and found a pub still open for a pint.

A few days later there was another showing to a small audience, at the Ministry of Information, which included Lord Reith (now Minister), Sir Kenneth Clark (Home Controller) and Jack Beddington (Head of Films Division). I was not invited. Before this show, however, the film had been seen by several commercial film distributors, including United Artists, Anglo-American and Associated British Film Distributors. They all liked it, and Anglo-American had the idea to present it at the Rialto in the West End supported by two other documentaries. None of them would take it, however, without it first having the Ministry of Information's approval. Oliver Bell, who had somehow managed to see the film, I suspect at the MOI, came up like a real-estate agent with an offer to house this 'valuable property of future historic importance' in the National Film Archive.

Film Centre was then informed by *The Times* that as the film was essentially one depicting a day in peacetime Britain, it was not considered suitable for wartime propaganda.[1] It had been decided, therefore, to put the film into storage in the strong-room at Printing House Square for the duration. I have often wondered if this was the real and only reason for withholding permission to show the film for so many years afterwards, even when the war had been won. Everything to do with the film, the cut negative etc., was duly sent to *The Times*. Without their

---

[1] In view of this reason, it is worth noting that quite a number of films of 'peacetime' Britain were shown in the British Pavilion at the New York World's Fair later that year.

261

knowledge, however, I had a copy printed for myself, for which I paid.

To my knowledge, only two reviews of the film appeared; it was not of course given a normal Press show. Both were in *Documentary News Letter* (June 1940). The first by, I think, S. C. Leslie, ran in part:

Here is a film about *The Times* as *The Times* sees itself. As such it is an unqualified success. It conveys perfectly the characteristic blend of starchy dignity, and rather selfconscious loyalty to an historical tradition. The film borrows the paper's practice of strict anonymity, but we are introduced to screen Presences like the editor, the chief leader writer, the dramatic critic and the night editor, all of whom play themselves with convincing poise, a fact behind which there lies no doubt a considerable achievement of manipulation on the producer's part . . . What is wrong with this film is what it leaves out. It was a pity to have employed a producer with Rotha's awareness of social relationships and perspectives and then not used him to present a study of the paper in its full setting – to let us perceive the wider relationships between it and the community it sets out to inform and guide. Institutions with more experience than *The Times* of the art of projecting themselves, long ago left behind them the notion that the way to begin was to put a picture of the works in the forefront of the announcement. *The Times*, of course, knows its own business best and has got what it evidently wanted, expertly and often brilliantly done.

The second by, I know, Aubrey Flanagan, of the film trade's *Today's Cinema*, ran:

Rotha's admirably concise and honest film is a direct and unemotional piece of reporting. It tells its story . . . which is in many respects the story of British journalism, without clichés or journalese, makes it a most fascinating and essential molehill out of a positive mountain of material. . . . Like its inspiration, Rotha's document is sober, dignified and without conscious humour. It is not without either fascination, or indeed – for the professional craftsman at least – without thrill. . . . The unsmiling and ponderous subs of *The Fourth Estate*, the weighty editorial pronouncements, the crisp Scots accent of the layout man, the pedestrian slowness, so subtly combined with infallible efficiency, to be found among the comps and in the machine-rooms, have here the flavour of reality. . . . Because Rotha has told the story simply and directly, without a selfconscious camera angle or smart-alecry with the scissors, the story has a more effective punch.

Making The Times *Film* (*1939–40*)

. . . It may not represent either the spirit or the letter of the two million net certified readers' dailies. But what it sets out to do, is to tell concisely and accurately in another medium of the purposes and the processes behind the modern newspaper. And that is a story well worth the telling.

For the historical record, among the screen credits was one made to Film Centre for its supervision. In point of fact, beyond holding a watching brief over the money side of the contract, for which it rightly took a handling charge, Film Centre had little to do with the film beyond paying me a £20 weekly salary during production and a fee of £100 for three months' work on writing the script.

For many years *The Times* kept the film, of which it owned the copyright, under covers. When it was requested for showing at the Memorial Performance held of Carl Mayer's work on 13 April 1947, permission was refused. Some time later, the Screenwriters Association wished to show it to their members. Even a personal approach by the President of the Society of Authors, Sir Osbert Sitwell, to Major Astor, brought a rebuff. I wanted to screen an extract only at the address I gave to the British Film Academy when I was given a Fellowship in the autumn of 1950. This was also refused. But fifteen years later, in 1965, the vigorous and always active Canton Film Appreciation Group in Cardiff in some way contrived to beat the curfew. They screened extracts from the film on 30 April of that year; and Richard Griffith, to whom I had screened my own private copy when he was in London, recorded the following tape which the Canton Group played before the film:

Any film long unseen is apt to develop its own legend, with consequent disappointment for those who see it for the first time years after it was made. With a film such as *The Fourth Estate* the danger was greatly increased by the fact that it was never shown anywhere. Consequently its legend, at any rate in America, reached almost the dimensions of fantasy. When I saw it for the first time in London in 1963, almost twenty-five years after it was made, I approached it with misgiving. I feared that no film could live up the expectations that had gradually been building since 1939. I was glad to have turned out to be wrong.

The material of journalistic life has long been one of the staples of movie-making. It's an easy kind of material. The noise of the City Room. The frantic City editor tearing his hair and shouting orders. The copy boys rushing everywhere at once. Wild-eyed reporters banging out their copy. The presses roaring against deadlines which are already past. Bales of papers hitting the street. All this is easy movie material for a director to dramatize, in fact it dramatizes itself. It's been done a hundred times.

What is so striking about Rotha's film is that in spite of this long movie tradition about newspapers, he took an exactly opposite approach. (As an American I may be overimpressed by this.) Perhaps the stateliness, shall I say, of newspaper procedure as exemplified in London's *The Times* is typical of British journalism? I doubt it. I rather think instead that it was a deliberate attempt on Rotha's part to give us a new kind of tension, a new kind of cinematic edge, altogether opposed to the headlong pace of the Press which movie tradition has accustomed us to. As we watch the staff of *The Times*, in all perplexity, collect, discuss, write and edit the news, they seem at first to be going about their business as calmly as book-keepers. Yet there is a sense of tension and suspense that comes out of identification with them, we are not the observer watching the wild-eyed journalist, we are as the film progresses inside them. We are waiting as they are to see if the news they have discussed at the beginning of the day is going to be affected, and their writing of it affected, and their editing of it affected by small bits of additional news which come in from time to time. This of course is their daily routine, and they treat it as routine. But I at least as a spectator, as a very involved spectator, felt their own suspense, not mine but theirs, as to just what would happen to the carefully plotted editorial plan, the carefully written lead story, the layout of the paper itself? How would these things be affected by each new phone call, by each new messenger boy's arrival?

Another element I want to stress is the beauty of this film. In many of his earlier films Rotha had achieved a camera beauty that was rare indeed in films in any country. Sometimes, as in *The Face of Britain* or *Shipyard* or *Contact*, or others I could mention, this beauty seemed somewhat irrelevant to what the film had to deliver in the way of a message or theme. It seemed tapped on, appliqued, or at any rate not really germane to, or deserving of the footage it was given as far as the central theme was concerned. What was overwhelming to me about *The Fourth Estate* was the beauty of a found beauty, its part of the life that is being drawn together into a conspectus which makes us understand what it is really like to put out a newspaper. Even in the mundane office scenes, apart from when the camera takes us round the world, a beauty of light, and texture, and surface is found, is discovered, that really builds up the theme rather than distracting from it. I call your attention particularly to that commonest, almost shrieking cliché, the rolling of the printing presses themselves. Here it is approached not for its easy drama but for the strange beauty of the machines themselves and of the extraordinary patterns that the papers themselves follow as they are fed into the machines, printed, folded and brought out at the end. I feel I must say in this connection that one of the great mistakes of documentary policy of the 1930s and later was to let Rotha be a producer rather than primarily a director, though he sometimes managed to produce and direct at the same time. It was obviously good strategy to cast him in this role in as much as he was able as producer to attract a good deal of finance to sell films, both to sponsors and to distributors, which he certainly could not have done if he had concentrated wholly on his craft as a director. Yet the sheer beauty of *The Times* film, its suspense, and what I should like to call its universality, suggest that there was something wasteful in this policy of casting Rotha as a producer even if it gave immediate beneficial results. I can only say, as I look back now, that it was a double tragedy that *The Times* film was never released when it was made, and that Rotha returned to producing soon after it.[1]

When, however, in later years Lord Thomson took over *The Times* newspapers, some relaxation occurred. The film was given its first public showing during what was called Cinema City organized jointly by the *Sunday Times* and the National Film Archive. The original negative was found to have decomposed. A duplicate negative was made from my own almost new copy in the NFA, where it had been kept under strict temperature control, and a print was made from same. When it was projected at the Round House, Sunday, 25 October 1970, its picture quality was reasonably good but the sound track had been ill reproduced. This was ironical in view of the trouble we had taken to record good sound quality after the criticism in America of our inadequate sound tracks.

It was a strange experience to introduce the film 30 years after it had been made. It was of course the first (and only) time I had seen it with an audience, some 600 persons. They reacted,

[1] Griffith forgets that a way was found during the war by which I was able to direct (*World of Plenty et al*) and produce several films at my unit at the same time.

I am glad to report, to all the small and subtle moments as planned. The suspense of the wait between editions, while Everest is climbed and Mr Morgan writes his review of *Hamlet*, and the subsequent crescendo build-up to the roaring and thundering presses had the emotional impact aimed at so many years before. I must add, in fairness to this survey, that *The Fourth Estate* was not, whatever else it may have been, a group film. *Pace*, Mr Grierson. It was a strictly personal work.

Postscript: Bits of *The Fourth Estate* were later used without my knowledge in a bastard little film called *Morning Paper*, produced by Mary Field at GB-Instructional in 1941 for the British Council. *The Times* actually used this for publicity purposes. It was shown as recently as 1970 by a speaker from the paper's staff at a meeting of a Townswomen's Guild in Wiltshire where, to my disgust, I saw it for the first and, I hope, last time.

In retrospect, *The Times* film has a macabre aspect. Of the persons appearing in it, Geoffrey Dawson, Barrington-Ward, Peter Fleming, John Maywood, Herbert Russell (the excellent night editor in the film) and others are dead. Of my unit, Patrick Moyna, Harry Rignold, Gerald Keene, Walter Leigh are no longer around. Even the old building of *The Times*, where so much was shot, was partly destroyed by fire during the war by enemy action. It thus has some historic value.

12. *Afterthought* (1972)

Discouraging as they may be, the economic facts of documentary film production and distribution have to be faced. No matter its social, aesthetic, educational or other purposes, a documentary film costs a good deal of money to make, and sometimes to show. However the cinema medium is approached, the irrevocable fact is that, even allowing for technological improvements in equipment, it is an expensive medium, even for solo amateurs. The film-maker, whatever his choice of *genre*, must depend for his materials either on his own private source of finance, or on the finance of friends or family, which is rare. The great majority have had to square up to finding private investment which requires adequate return on outlay, or alternatively involvement by a State-run industry which may carry obligations of political propaganda, or at least some kind of public education.

In the mixed economy of the United Kingdom, the documentary film has in all but exceptional cases been dependent for its production finance on (a) Government, at both national and local levels, (b) institutions or societies of some kind, and (c) industry, either private or nationally controlled. The distribution and exhibition sides of the three-tier commercial industry, as organized over many years now, do not permit the self-financed documentary film, even with quotas and funds, to make an adequate return on its production capital outlay.

A film-maker must establish a good working relationship with his sponsor. At times, a film can emerge with aesthetic qualities, and hence audience and critical appeal, beyond the expectation of the sponsor. *Song of Ceylon* and *Shipyard* are good examples; Haanstra's *Glass* and Lorentz's *The River* are others. These are the work of individuals who create a personal reputation with which a sponsor wants to be associated. In the

1930s, Strand Films secured contracts to make films with such bodies as Imperial Airways, the National Book Council and the National Council for Social Service because of the prior reputation of the producer they engaged to be in charge of production, and thus guarantee quality of product. Government departments, like the Ministries of Labour and Agriculture, went to the department of the Post Office for advice about their projected film activities not because of the Post Office *per se* but because it employed Mr Grierson, whose reputation for a quality and style of film-making had become known way outside the bounds of Post Office reference. The fact that there was an official post known as Government Film Adviser did not change this fact; it seemed he mainly swept up the dust in official film vaults.

When some British-made documentary film, as was sometimes the case, won an award at an international film festival and gained critical praise outside its country of origin, it acquired a prestige that did not pass unnoticed at home. (*Song of Ceylon* and *The Face of Britain* were examples.) The sponsor of such a film could as easily have put his requirements on the order-books of the makers of advertising and publicity films, but public relations men in the 1930s, like Beddington, Leslie and Snowden Gamble, saw in the documentary film a medium of far wider prestige and influence than the buying of space for advertising in newspapers or time on commercial radio.

At the same time, the need for sponsorship widened and the idea for documentary films had to be propagated and nurtured all through these years. Hence the reason for the formation in 1935 of the Associated Realist Film Producers group to undertake promotional and publicity work. Grierson never tired of writing that in the first place Whitehall did not *ask* to make documentary films; what few films Government ministries made were put out to tender to a handful of commercial companies that made publicity pictures. Here perhaps the experience of the Government Film Adviser was sought in comparing submitted tenders for a contract so that the lowest could be chosen. The civil servants involved were satisfied with such results and, until Mr Grierson's arrival on the scene, all jogged along smoothly. No one, least of all the Press, MPs and film critics, were aware that such films were even made. They were shrouded in peace and quiet.

Civil servants, for the most part, are not exactly renowned for their interest in creative matters, especially the Treasury when it comes to spending money, and public money at that. On the contrary, their background and training engender fear and mistrust of anything to do with 'art' or 'aesthetics'. That is why Grierson so often tried to dissociate the word 'art' from 'documentary', and substituted instead such words as 'information' and 'public service'. He analysed rightly that Whitehall would be less suspicious of 'public education' than of 'aesthetic purpose'. Tallents's (or was it really Grierson's?) happy phrase 'bringing alive' must have smoothed many a civil service qualm; it was a slogan capable of easy understanding, not the aesthetic jargon of the arts which was anathema to the bureaucrat mind. Grierson said it thus:

The story of the documentary movement is, in part, the story of how, not without a scar or two, we got by. Maybe you win more or less for keeps, as in the later case of the National Film Board of Canada. Maybe you lose, though never altogether, to the bureaucrats and the other boys behind the woodwork. . . . The fact is that there are many real sources of opposition to the idea of art (activist) in the public service; and they will only be overcome where you establish a most manifest need, secure a measure of imaginative indulgence on the part of the powers that be.[1]

Hence always the emphasis in our writing at that time for documentary 'to fill a need', but I doubt if you had asked a civil servant, 'What need?', he could have answered.

It has been seen earlier that it was Sir Stephen Tallents within the Government service (with Grierson at his elbow) who first persuaded Government officers to embark on waters outside their previous sphere of public operation. The naïve questions and some of the answers given before the Select Committee on Estimates in 1934 fully confirm this state of ignorance.[2]

Separate in identity as were the documentary units (EMB,

[1] In answer to some questions sent him by a Cambridge student (whose name is not recorded) and to which Grierson felt in a good enough mood to reply. (1967).
[2] Vide: chapter 6.

Afterthought (1972)

GPO, Shell, Strand and Realist), the unity of the groups, or movement as we liked to call ourselves, expressed itself in the main through its senior members. Only two or three of us, besides Grierson, were so involved; everyone else (including us) were at the full-time job of making films. Documentary progress was dependent on intense activity on three inter-related fronts, with a fourth to emerge later. First, in the field of finding and educating potential sponsors in the Government and industrial sectors; second, propagating the documentary idea by as widespread journalism and lecturing as possible, and here our Fleet Street contacts seldom let us down; and third, obviously in making films as good as our circumstances and abilities and finance permitted.

The fourth front, which arose as the decade wore on, and which grew to be of increasing importance, was the field of distribution for our films when they had been made. Sponsors obviously wanted good films for their money, but they also wanted those films widely seen. Welcome as was the hard-to-come-by and usually reluctant cinema release (*Drifters* via New Era, *Contact* via Wardour Films, *Cover to Cover* and *Night Mail* via ABFD) the slow but ever-widening access to the public by what came to be known as the non-theatrical market was more and more valuable and attractive to sponsors. The EMB and GPO film libraries had blazed the way. The Gas and Oil Industries were to set up their own distribution libraries, in some cases making films (like *New Worlds for Old*) exclusively for such specialist release. As will be seen, this pioneer work by the big industrialists was to be of immense value to the nation during the war, when the Ministry of Information non-theatrical distribution was to achieve nation-wide importance.

It should also be said here that we, as film-makers, had learned from Bob Flaherty that no film, however good, ever sold itself. He had gone out in the States and mobilized special audiences to go to their local movie-theatres to see his film *Moana*.[1] We in Britain used the film society movement, spreading every year, as a showcase for our films and wherever feasible made an appearance and spoke about the film. No

[1] Vide: *The Innocent Eye*, A Calder-Marshall (W. H. Allen, 1963) pp. 116, 117.

commercial distributor was interested in publicizing documentary; we were and did.

Looking back at our documentary films of the 1930s, it is important to make a point about the aesthetic of film movement. No confusion of course should be made between this use of the word and its use to describe the ideas and purposes and work output of a group of film-makers with a common aim in Britain. Of the aesthetic of film movement, something of an analysis was made in 1935 in my book at that time, but a relook can perhaps be useful here.

Several kinds of film movement are involved:

1. Movement of ideas or meaning conveyed by the contents of the film and its parts.
2. Movement of physical action being filmed in a shot or sequence.
3. Movement of camera (tracking, panning, etc.) and microphone in both visual and aural imagery; sound images can be either in harmony with the visual or in counterpoint.
4. Movement by editing, in which visual images taken by the camera and sounds recorded through the microphone are placed in juxtaposition to interpret meaning, and to make possible intellectual and emotional response in the audience. Transition can be made by placing shots one after another in continuity of meaning and also of camera movement: the relationship of one shot to the next can be made by abrupt change of viewpoint, or by a merging of one shot into the next (dissolve or mix). The same process is possible with the sound images (including speech and music).

   Movement of physical action between shots can often be made to flow by overlapping the same movement from one shot into the next, thus using the element of filmic time and filmic space as distinct from actual time and space as we know them in everyday life. The filmic reproduction of what the camera observes and the microphone records is usually made at the same rate of action as the human eye sees in everyday life; but the film camera and microphone can record faster or slower than the human eye and ear can see and hear.

These basic elements and/or principles of the film medium have not changed basically over the years. As with other art media, especially television, many kinds of tricks have been thought up to provoke new audience sensations but they are ephemeral and as soon forgotten as invented.

A good deal has been written about the symphonics of film movement and need not be restated.[1] What needs to be remembered is that visual symphonic movement, so satisfying to create and so visually exciting to the eye, can obscure the meaning inherent in what is on the screen and produce a superficial effect that masks or even ignores purpose. (The classic example of this danger is in Ruttmann's *Berlin: Symphony of a City*).[2] The film medium offers so many slick and spurious varieties of creating effects on the audience, effects which are not to be found in the other art media until television, that the film-maker needs to use the utmost discretion in his approach to the medium. The cheap, phoney technical tricks used in television have done some temporary harm to the film medium but it will not last. Contrary to all the recent hot air expended on the need to jettison the known and accepted fundamentals of filmic expression, I believe that a film-maker of any integrity must learn his craft by experience and by study of what has already been done by the great film-makers of the past, after which he may or may not, according to his talent, be equipped to express his own attitude towards the drama of life through his chosen medium. There is no quick way to learn film-making. It is a medium far more complex yet subtle, far more stimulating and evocative, in its appeal to a vast audience than any other before it. The film offers a fundamentally new creative medium of incredible powers to the author-artist, which is one reason for its magnetism today, especially to the young generation. Television has nothing in its own right comparable to offer, except prostitution.

Grierson has suggested that the aesthetic of movement disappeared from the British documentary film after about 1935 to be replaced by camera reportage, that is to say that the aesthetic qualities of *Song of Ceylon* and *Night Mail* were replaced by the journalistic reporting approach of *Workers and Jobs* and *Housing Problems*.[3] This I find an over-simplification and untrue in that it

---

[1] *Documentary Film*, (Faber, 1952) pp. 133 *et seq.*
[2] Op cit. pp. 86–88, 108, 109, 135
[3] Notes to the author, 27 December 1970.

overlooks the development of the handling of human beings in such films as *Today We Live, Bill Blewitt* and *North Sea,* all of which came later than Elton's films. Thirty years earlier Grierson had also written,

I think the greatest [documentary] advance of all came with two little films which, except among the far-seeing, went almost unnoticed. One was called *Housing Problems* and the other *Workers and Jobs.* . . . They took the documentary film into the field of social problems, and keyed it to the task of describing not only industrial and commercial spectacle but social truth as well.

These simple films went deeper than earlier films like *Drifters* and later films like *Night Mail* and *North Sea.* They showed the common man, not in the romance of his calling, but in the more complex and intimate drama of his citizenship.[1] See *Industrial Britain, Night Mail, Shipyard* and *North Sea* alongside *Housing Problems.* There is a precious difference. *Housing Problems* is not so well made nor so brilliant in technical excitements, but something speaks within it that touches the conscience. These other films 'uplift'. *Housing Problems* 'transforms' and will not let you forget.[2]

It is hard to see why Grierson overlooked the sequences dealing with unemployment in *Rising Tide* and *Shipyard,* both made prior to *Housing Problems,* and harder still to explain his ignorance of *Today We Live* and *Eastern Valley* which, three years before he was writing, went far to meet his request; they both had 'uplift' and 'transform' and certainly did not let you forget. They also had one undisputed advantage, which is why I think Grierson forgot them. They were films as well as social documents.

Basil Wright quotes from a letter he had from Grierson in 1942 which is relevant in this context. Grierson wrote:

Documentary was from the beginning – when we first separated our public purpose theories from those of Flaherty – an 'anti-aesthetic' movement. We have all, I suppose, sacrificed some personal capacity in 'art' and the pleasant vanity that goes with it. What confuses the history is that we always had the good sense to use the aesthetes. We did so because we liked them and because we needed them. It was,

[1] Neither *Workers and Jobs* nor *Housing Problems* had any remote bearing on the 'drama of citizenship'.

[2] *The Battle for Authenticity, World Film News,* November 1938, reprinted *Grierson on Documentary,* Faber, 1966.

paradoxically, with the first-rate aesthetic help of people like Flaherty and Cavalcanti – our 'fellow-travellers' so to speak – that we mastered the techniques necessary for our quite unaesthetic purpose.[1]

In this afterthought, let me try and be clear about this. Films like *Housing Problems, Workers and Jobs* and *Enough to Eat?* had little to do with film technique other than that they used celluloid, camera and microphone. Their drama lay in the (almost) spontaneous behaviour of the real people chosen to appear. Their subjects – slum clearance, the working of a Labour Exchange and the nutritional weaknesses of the British people – were of immense social significance, but their failure to use, in fact their deliberate resistance against using, the basic aesthetic qualities of the film medium caused a good deal of criticism among film-makers, film critics and general audiences. When I was showing our films in the US, it was very often said, *Night Mail* and *Song of Ceylon* are very fine films, but *Housing Problems* and *Enough to Eat?*, these are just illustrated reports of interest only because they use real human beings. I, who have always believed that an audience must be emotionally involved before it will absorb arguments, let alone facts and opinions, found myself at the time – and I still do – critical of what I consider is unnecessary suppression of the basic elements of the film medium to evoke audience response. On the other hand, it should be noted that some people became emotionally involved in *Housing Problems*. Basil Wright reminds me, for example, that when reviewing his journalistic *Children at School*, Graham Greene praised it for introducing poetry into an apparently non-poetic film.[2]

I did not share Grierson's almost blind allegiance to the journalistic style in film, denying the creative use of direction, photography and constructive editing, but I can understand its magnetism for Grierson. In one way, *March of Time* was a very bad influence before the war on a part of British documentary. Grierson, and others influenced by him, fell under its spell. Its string of images, usually thrown together with unrelated editing, its strident, staccato, one-level voice delivery, these

---

[1] In *Grierson and Film Aesthetics*, an article in the Society of Film and Television Arts journal as a memorial to John Grierson, June 1972.
[2] In a letter to the author, 3 June 1972.

made a powerful impact all right but it was an impact quickly
to become dulled. To many in the audience, the words of its
sound track penetrated one ear and left the other with nothing
behind. Its attack stunned the mind but did not make it think.
What was seen and said was all too soon forgotten. No single
issue had the long-term quality of a *North Sea* or a *Song of
Ceylon*. This technique reached its pitch for me in a NFB film
called *The War on Men's Minds*, an attempt to analyse propaganda methods during the war. I made a point of seeing it
several times, each with a different audience of moderately
intelligent persons. Not one afterwards could say what the film
was about or what it was meant to impart. It can be said that
Today We Live showed *March of Time* influence; that is true,
but only in the prologue which was less than one quarter of the
total picture.

Grierson has complained that the aesthetic of movement, the
persuasion by dialectic argument, largely disappeared from
British documentary in the mid-1930s.[1] If this is true, which I
doubt, then it was mainly due to his insistence on suppressing
aesthetic values in favour of factual reporting. His argument
that drama lay in the unvarnished facts themselves brought one
stream of documentary to a dead and rather boring end. Exactly
the same thing has happened in television, that is why all too
much of it is so dull.

Not all of the documentary group accepted this *diktat*,
however; for example, Watt, Jennings, Holmes, Shaw and I
suppose myself. And it is the films of these people that survive
today, not as a back-number department of facts and interviews
but as living works of dramatic human appeal. This experience
emerged clearly when I resaw many documentaries while
making the research for this present survey. This was to be even
more true in the oncoming war films, when pictures like *Fires
Were Started*, *Western Approaches* and *The Harvest Shall Come*
were to achieve as permanent a value as cinema can offer, whereas the journalistic output of the National Film Board of Canada,
important indeed as urgent and immediate wartime propaganda
and information, has no lasting qualities. That such a film as
Fires Were Started, made before Jennings became too 'poetic',

[1] Notes to the author, 27 December 1970.

combined an important morale message to the British people
with a full use of the cinema's technical and aesthetic assets is
for my money more valuable in the history of the cinema than
any number of the ephemeral NFB wartime films let off with
missile speed and precision under Grierson's dynamic guidance.
On the other hand, as Basil Wright has pointed out, the films
by Jennings took a long time to produce and when they appeared 'they were celebrating past rather than present heroism,'
whereas the Sten-gun output of the NFB served an immediate
short-term purpose.[1]

And yet, for all his concern with spot-recording, Grierson
still kept a nostalgia for the aesthetics of experimental sound
images that began in the 1930s, partly under Cavalcanti's
influence and supplemented by the ideas of Britten, Leigh and
Auden, and waned when the so-called factual reporting approach
loomed large. He suggested that the complex use of sound
stemmed from *Granton Trawler* and *Song of Ceylon* through
Coal Face to *Night Mail*, where it suddenly stopped. (Again
this is not historically accurate.) This use of sound images
represented noise at various levels of organization and in
various combinations of natural noises and orchestrated with
musical effects, rhetoric recitation, poetic recitation as well as
monologue and narration. Again in fairness it must be put on
record that the sound tracks of *Shipyard* and *Face of Britain*
also contained many of these sound elements including fabricated, impressionist and synthetic sound and the use of the
disembodied voice as monologue. 'But', maintained Grierson,

this experiment ended when those who contributed to it were reaching
out for direct reporting by dialogue in the search for social reality.
When documentary went missionary, the greatest single drive in
audio-visual aesthetic (*per se*) stopped and has not been resumed since.[2]

Grierson also had much to say about the self-indulgence of
the *auteur* concept in film-making and dismissed it as being
'romantic and old-fashioned'. He enunciated,

[1] In a letter to the author, 3 June 1972.
[2] Notes to the author, 27 December 1970. But again Grierson is incorrect because Elton and Anstey, the two 'missionaries' to whom he referred, had little if
anything to do with the sound-image experiments which were the work of Cavalcanti, Wright, Leigh, Britten *et al.*

Afterthought (1972)

I am not interested in single films as such, only as they contribute to the larger thesis – and individuals likewise. Film cannot of its nature be a purely personal art, except, as it were, miniature and on one's own money. A few have managed it but they are not significant. The nature of the cinema demands collaboration and collusion with others and with many variant purposes; and its significance derives from those who can operate and command purposively within these conditions.[1]

Generally speaking it is true that the

medium demands a lot of collaboration and collusion with others. It also demands cooperation and patience and persistence, one with another, not to mention as multifold and various and rich a collection of talents as the project demands and the wit of catalyst/producer dictates.[2]

But now Grierson is shifting the *auteur* status from director to producer, an argument that by no means holds true. Take *Song of Ceylon* as a good example. As its producer, Grierson contributed greatly in ideas to its final four-part shape; others, Walter Leigh, Lionel Wendt and Cavalcanti, gave much to its sound track, but it is quite impossible to deny – indeed who would wish to? – that it is a film by Basil Wright, and no other person. To anyone who has studied Wright's work, the shooting in Ceylon and the editing in London could be by no one else; they stem directly from the two short West Indian films, *Windmill in Barbados* and *Cargo from Jamaica*. The same cannot be applied to *Night Mail*. Here Harry Watt claims, and there is no reason to doubt him, that the great majority of the shooting was his. Most of the editing, on the other hand, was done by McNaughton and Wright. Grierson was the usual catalyst, Cavalcanti the alchemist of the sound track aided by Britten and Auden as his accomplices, notably to get the damned train away from Crewe and hurl it across the border into Scotland. Thus on balance it was fair that Watt and Wright should share the main credit (although I have heard Grierson decry Watt's part in it), supported by the other contributors under Grierson's parasol; but the whole is not one man's film, as was *Song of Ceylon*.

[1] Op. cit. Cambridge questionnaire. 1967.   [2] Op. cit.

Afterthought (1972)

This characteristic of the 'group' film that arose in the 1930s poses the relative merits of production by a group of creative talents, or by an individual working in close collaboration with a team of technicians. What must always be remembered, but is sometimes forgotten, is that the EMB and GPO Units needed a *flow* of overall good films and it was to meet this need that the group method was evolved. *Industrial Britain* was the first of such films and it truly grew out of necessity. As the good Bob brought back his footage, it was clear there was no film. His material, plus some additional shooting by Wright and Elton, was pulled into some kind of unity by Grierson and Anstey's editing. The series that included *Weather Forecast, Cable Ship* and *Six-Thirty Collection* were essentially the product of group working, although they were credited respectively to Evelyn Spice, Stuart Legg and Edgar Anstey. None of them had any individual characteristics of direction. Any of these three directors could have made any of the three films. Of *BBC: The Voice of Britain* Grierson said,

The whole film went wrong at one point and we had to think up (and in 24 hours) separate sequences for various people to make; people who were not originally on the film.[1]

The other development of the individually made film, apart from *Song of Ceylon*, was represented, I suppose, by *Contact, Shipyard, Voice of the World, New Worlds for Old* and *The Fourth Estate*. They were produced in the main as lone-handed works, using hired facilities. The relationship between Bruce Woolfe and myself on the first two of the films could not in any remote way be likened to Grierson's relationship to the directors working at his Unit. The personal style, or what Grierson called the 'impressionist' approach, may have risen from necessity. In no sense was it in competition with the Grierson group method; it was rather an alternative method of production using non-Governmental sponsorship.

We have seen above that Grierson did not find himself interested in individuals *per se*. He says he had no interest in Joris Ivens except as Ivens influenced the Dutch documentary

---

[1] Notes to the author, 26 December 1970.

278

movement, or in Elton beyond his teaching at the Shell Film Unit.[1] But, I almost hesitate to point out, if anyone influenced the Dutch it was Bert Haanstra, not Ivens who came earlier; nor, as Grierson also claims, did Henri Storck create a Belgian documentary group because there never was one. On the other hand, it is unlikely that the Shell Film Unit would have gained its rightful recognition without the influence of Elton, just as I am quite sure there would have been no British documentary movement as a whole without Mr Grierson, whether he would admit it or not. His argument is that the movement is bigger than its individual films, and to an extent he is right, but a movement is made up of individual films and the people who conceive and make them. The documentary movement in Britain in the 1930s can indeed be seen as a coherent relationship between peoples and policies and purposes, but these in turn cannot be analysed without regard to the individual qualities of the major films. *Night Mail* and *North Sea* cannot be divorced from the movement as a whole, nor the latter from the former, but that is what I find Grierson trying to do. He can, as he likes to do so often, talk about Mack Sennett's proletarian influence on Hollywood in the early years of comedy without naming a single film title, but the same can be said for few movements, including British documentary, in cinema history.

Critics at the time complained that the GPO films did not give, let alone comment on, the wage rates and working hours of Post Office employees in a film like *Night Mail*, or that *Future's in the Air* did not tell us the pay of aircrew or the extent of their leave periods. In view of their sponsors, how could they have done? If these films did not state these things, would it have been better that they should not have been made at all? In defence of documentary on this point, it should be remembered that the Voices of Commerce sequence in *Song of Ceylon* carried implicit but nevertheless significant comment on the low industrial status of native labour in that island. *Today We Live* was outspoken about the ravages and injustices

[1] Grierson gravely underestimates, in my opinion, the influence of Ivens on all international documentary.

279

of mass unemployment and stated bluntly that the means-test dole was no substitute for real work. But note that it was a commercial propaganda board and a charitable society that, under documentary stimulus, found the money to make these films. It was the Gas industry, admittedly with the long-term aim of selling gas where gas was most efficient, that made films about the need for slum clearance, about the need for a national nutrition policy, about the need for building new schools and the need to combat the menace of smoke pollution. These things happened in a Tory-governed country because a handful of public relations officers, prompted by a bunch of documentary film producers, had a social conscience that sought an outlet, and that outlet was not to be found in any part of the so-called Left.

If the trade unions had commissioned films in a sensible way, the request of the critics given above might have been met. But in the 1930s the unions and the cooperatives, let alone the Labour Party, had an antiquated attitude to their public image. Lack of money was a threadbare alibi that became boring by its monotony. The wealthy Cooperative movement squandered its money on having advertising pictures made by companies tainted by Conservative views. We have seen how a display of documentary films and projection apparatus arranged at the Labour Party annual conference in 1936 resulted only in funds being found to send on tour a play (not even a film!) about the Tolpuddle Martyrs. This rusty outlook was comparable with that of the British Council's use of Beefeaters at the Tower and the Changing of the Guard as symbols of modern Britain. When, after the war, *Land of Promise,* perhaps the most socially progressive film to be made in Britain about the problems of planning and housing was sponsored by the Gas industry and offered free to the new Minister of Health in 1945, the film (which incidentally carried a certificate of merit from the Royal Institute of British Architects) was rejected because it was 'thought' that an actual rent-strike march in the East End shown in the film 'had been Communist inspired'.

As Grierson so often pointed out, it was the Conservative mind that first caught on to the inspiration of the documentary idea. Labour had no ear for such an imaginative approach to public service and public education. Labour did not even have an aesthetic approach, let alone a social one. What did a Tory Minister hang on his wall at home? Maybe a fake Stubbs or a Constable copy. And a Trade Union leader? Three china ducks in flight. At one of those abortive, dreary meetings of what was called the Labour Party Films Committee which Ritchie-Calder and I attended, I once asked out of politeness my companion at the table in Transport House who the chairman was? And why he was chairman. 'Well, he plays the fiddle well at home,' was the reply. It was a hopeless struggle.

We must have been naïve to have thought that when the Labour Party actually became a more than sizeable government in 1945 it would implement an imaginative and purposeful national information service. Only one man in the Party (and I met most of them) had the instinct and wisdom to grasp that we could offer a service in the national good, but in effect it was outside his sphere of stewardship at that time. That man was Sir Stafford Cripps. Instead the need for national projection was split between the possessive vanities of Herbert Morrison and Ernest Bevin. The whole vital concept for a single National Film Board in Britain was jettisoned because of rivalry between these two politicians.[1]

In a letter to *The Times* at a later date Grierson summed the whole matter up very well. He wrote,

The Labour Movement has had from the beginning a built-in distrust of information services other than its very own, and perhaps no wonder. I was a very near and interested observer of this phenomenon in the Clydeside days and when I helped to develop certain ideas about planned and national information services in a planned society, nothing ever surprised me more than to find a welcome for them, not where I expected, but among Conservative and Liberal Ministers. When this was put to Mr Herbert Morrison he said, 'It was double-talk' but was told that 'Mr Walter Elliot would understand it immediately.' Certainly when it fell to that Labour Government to liquidate the Ministry of Information it did so all too cheerfully and without a thought for what we might be losing.[2]

[1] The memorandum on the British Film Industry, including recommendations for a National Film Board was commissioned by Cripps when he was the President of the Board of Trade. It was printed in full in *Rotha on the Film* (Faber, 1958).
[2] 19 April 1966.

This letter provoked no replies. Labour leaders failed even to defend their own effete attitude. But these are matters about which I shall expand in due course.

Even before the outbreak of war in September 1939, there were signs of unrest in the British documentary movement. The slightly uneasy relations between the GPO Unit and Film Centre could be felt across the Square, the disunity of Strand (which in 1935 had begun with such bright fervour), the decline of the Associated Realist Film Producers (set up with banners aloft in the same year), all were indications of disquiet. To me the last event was the saddest. When Film Centre took over ARFP's promotional and consultancy work (again we should remember that it was Grierson in the first place who suggested setting it up), the group changed the word 'Associated' in its title to 'Association' and opened its membership, which had been confined to only some of the senior people, to more than forty technicians and distribution officers. It was to lead to internecine dissension. The war claimed the group for an early casualty.

In this afterthought, I think that one major reason for this documentary disruption was Grierson's leaving the GPO Unit; another was that his absences abroad, in 1938 and 1939 and thereafter, left the movement without a helmsman. To those of us who knew him as well as he allowed himself to be known, Grierson had many faults – he fermented frictions and split loyalties – but he was a dominant personality who created confidence, inspiration and allegiance. He had a sense of power and a respect for it in others. If, in a dialogue, which he usually swayed, a case was well made against him, he would be known to modify his views. He did not readily accept opposition, but at the same time found a regard for it. He certainly exercised a very considerable influence on those who worked both with him and around him. His changes of mind might exasperate some of those whom he employed (not least the harassed, successive editors of *World Film News* who had to wrestle with his disregard for date-lines and printer's costs). He was ruthless in pursuit of his purpose, a purpose that was plainly declared, to accept (or reject), in his many articles and lectures. You might go along with that purpose but not always like the methods by which he sought to achieve it. He was known on occasion to double-deal but only, I swear, when he suspected that he himself was being double-dealt. 'There always has to be a bastard, as they say in Hollywood,' he once wrote, 'and there always has to be a catalyst, as we both very well know ourselves.'[1]

Grierson had an expert sense of diplomatic strategy and manoeuvre which, clear enough to himself, could baffle some of those near him. In all, his influence and guidance over the policy and development of British documentary in the decade before the war was indisputable; in fact, except for those in a political position, few would refute it. In the whole history of the cinema, it is very rare to find a man of Grierson's talents who used them without reserve to pursue ends for fundamental good purpose. This kind of man does not easily survive in the poisonous nettlebed of the film industry. It was something of a miracle built from struggle that Grierson sustained his influence so long and made it so widespread. Many today should be the more grateful for his lack of self-gain.

Although he kept in transatlantic touch by articles, correspondence and an occasional fleeting visit, Grierson's absence was, as I have said, badly felt. No one could have filled his place, although at least one tried. But I have always had the thought that if he had stayed at the head of the GPO Unit, and his relations had continued to be as reasonable as could be expected with his Post Office masters and the Treasury officers, the British documentary movement would not have disintegrated, at least not so fast. No really satisfactory reason was ever to be known for his resignation. The main purpose given at the time, as we have seen, was the need for wider promotional activity outside the limits of a government unit, but such activity could well have been undertaken, and indeed had been begun at Grierson's own suggestion, by the ARFP group. The divergence of views between Grierson and Cavalcanti could have had something to do with it. After the former's leaving of the Unit and before the coming of war, there is the record that unhappily Cavalcanti became actively opposed to the Grierson social documentary policy. But I doubt very much that a man

[1] Notes to the author, 26 December 1970.

283

of Grierson's stature would have permitted such a fractious disagreement to deflect him if he had wished to stay at the Unit. Again, there may have been political and administrative problems arising between Grierson and the civil service mandarins to whom he was ultimately responsible; that is something about which he was always reticent and about which we shall not know now.

Or did Grierson foresee that the knife-edge equation between the Government and industrial sponsorship in a capitalist system, on the one hand, and the socially progressive outlook of the majority of documentary film-makers, on the other, would inevitably come to an end? The idea of public relations and public service being interpreted in aesthetic terms by talented and honest craftsmen, like Wright and Watt, and later Holmes and Jennings, might not have lasted even without the war. The burial of *The Times* film showed that social satire, however subtle, could not be got away with under the guise of aesthetic appeal, at least not with such an intelligent and well-informed sponsor, who had to find the excuse of a 'peacetime' image being unfavourable in a 'wartime' situation to cover its confusion. And later, a great deal of pressure from high places on both sides of the Atlantic was brought to bear to stop *World of Plenty*[1] and *The World is Rich*, both Government commissions, from reaching the public screens.

Or yet again did Grierson look to Canada because he believed a liberal freedom for the documentary idea would be more capable of development by solid constitutional methods there than in a nationally-governed Britain at war? If that had been the case, as I have heard argued, it is hard to explain why Grierson later relinquished his own creation at the National Film Board (unless he felt he had done his work there) or why he flirted with failure in New York (where he ran into the repercussions of the Canadian spy-trials, became frustrated in a constipated Unesco but where he did some basic groundwork which later showed results) and finally why he returned to England, first to wage a hopeless battle in a now Treasury-controlled Central Office of Information and, second, to an ill-

[1] This title, to become world-known, was William Alwyn's idea when he wrote its music.

284

conceived, experience-lacking project attempting a wedding between 'human' story films and the documentary approach, a wedding which Grierson had earlier himself decried. These are questions not easily solved in this investigation. Let the facts speak for themselves, so far as we know them, and let them suggest the answers.

So in spite of some remarkable output during the war years which had world-wide repercussions, and which will be dealt with in depth at a future date, the British documentary film movement ceased to continue as the unity it had been in the 1930s. The existence of a Federation of Documentary Film Units set up in good faith in 1945 did not last long. But I hasten to add that the war itself was not responsible for this break-up. The war was to cause chaos and confusion in the Ministry of Information until its Films Division was restaffed under pressure, and provided with a policy for its future work by the documentary people.[1] But the Ministry itself had neither the power nor the ability nor even the wish to reunite a movement of film-makers so that its initial integrity of purpose could be rediscovered. I doubt very much if the successive Ministers – Reith, Duff Cooper and Bracken – or their aides – Sir Walter Monckton and Harold Nicolson – even knew about the potential national value for projection of the British documentary movement. When I talked with Harold Nicolson, Parliamentary Secretary at the Ministry, in the summer of 1940, he knew nothing whatsoever about documentary's existence.[2]

The purpose of the documentary idea so clearly defined in the 1930s became lost during the war among the self-centred production units dependent economically for the making of films on the Ministry's hand-outs. There was no real common policy except that their films, good though some of them were technically, were alleged to be what was called in the 'national interest.' For a time *Documentary News Letter* tried to maintain a central policy and it was a useful vehicle for printing the articles

[1] Early in 1940 we were asked to submit a memorandum for the policy of the MOI Films Division which the Head of that Division was said to have kept in his top drawer for the duration.

[2] Ministry of Information files for 1939–40 are revealing for their ignorance of what existed in Britain in films for propaganda and information purposes.

Afterthought (*1972*)

that Grierson sent from Canada, but in time it lost its nerve and became more of a house magazine than anything else. Grierson's strategic diplomacy and political know-how were absorbed in drafting a Bill out of which would come the National Film Board, and between the Bill and the Board were his visits to Australia and New Zealand for the Imperial Relations Trust. It was during that time that war broke out. Invited back to Canada to head the Board, Grierson accepted for six months only. After that he decided to stay and in senior documentary opinion in England he did the right thing. In wartime Britain he would have been both shackled in his brilliant propaganda ideas and techniques, and driven mad as were most of us, by the sheer incompetence and amateurishness of those at the top of official information and propaganda services.

As against the erosion of the movement in Britain, however, it must be remembered how in the years to come the documentary idea was, through its British exponents, to inspire growing points in many parts of the world – in Australia, India, Egypt, New Zealand and Malaysia among them. British documentary broke the boundaries of Soho Square (which it left empty), and opened up new horizons; but the first upsurge that was the ideological force behind the pioneer work of the 1930s will, I hope, be always remembered and not just in nostalgia, because it was sociologically and aesthetically unique in the cinema's scarcely eighty years of existence. In documentary, technical skill is all important but even more important and vital is social good purpose.

Selected Book List

Camera and I, The, by Joris Ivens, Seven Seas, Berlin, 1969.
Changing Scene, The, by A. Calder-Marshall. Chapman & Hall, 1937.
Cinema, by C. A. Lejeune. Maclehose, 1931.
Documentary Film, by Paul Rotha. Faber. 1936, 1939, 1952.
Documentary Film in American Television, by A. William Bluem, Hastings House, New York, 1965.
Documentary Tradition, The, compiled by Lewis Jacobs. Hopkinson & Blake. New York. 1972.
Experiment in the Film, edited by Roger Manvell. Grey Walls Press. 1949.
Factual Film, The. (An Arts Enquiry Report). Oxford Uni-University Press. 1947.
Factual Television, by Norman Swallow. Focal Press. 1966.
Film in National Life, The, Allen & Unwin. 1932.
Films Beget Films, by Jay Leyda. Allen & Unwin. 1964.
Grierson on Documentary, edited by H. Forsyth Hardy. Collins. 1946. Faber, 1966.
History of the British Film, by Rachel Low. Vol. IV. Allen & Unwin. 1971.
Ideas on Film, by Cecile Starr. Funk & Wagnall. New York. 1951.
Innocent Eye, The, by A. Calder-Marshall. W. H. Allen. 1963.
Kino, by Jay Leyda. Allen & Unwin. 1960.
Mind in Chains, The, edited by C. Day Lewis. Muller. 1937.
On Native Grounds, by Alfred Kazin. Harcourt, Brace & Jovanovich. New York. 1943.
Projection of England, The, by Sir Stephen Tallents. Faber, 1932; Film Centre 1955.
Report from a Select Committee on Estimates, H.M. Stationery Office, July, 1934.

Selected Book List

Rotha on the Film, Faber. 1958.
Split Focus, by Peter Hopkinson. Hart-Davis. 1969.
Technique of Documentary Film Production, by W. H. Baddely. Focal Press. 1966.
Thirties, The, by Malcolm Muggeridge. Hamish Hamilton. 1940.
Use of the Film, The, by Basil Wright. Bodley Head. 1948.
World of Robert Flaherty, The, by Richard Griffith. Gollancz. 1953.

Periodicals and Newspapers Consulted

Close-Up, 1927–33 (London and Switzerland)
Cinema Quarterly, 1932–35 (Edinburgh)
World Film News, 1936–38 (Film Centre, London)
Documentary News Letter, 1940 (Film Centre, London)
Sight and Sound, 1932–40 (British Film Institute, London)

With the exception of the last named, all the above journals are defunct.

and

The Times, The Observer, Manchester Guardian, News Chronicle, New Statesman, The Spectator, The Listener, Fortnightly Review, ACT Journal etc.

Index of Film Titles

Index of Film Titles

Index of Film Titles

Nana, 10
Nanook of the North, xiv, 17, 19, 25, 29, 45, 50, 53
New Babylon, 10
New Generation, The, 59
New Operator, The, 60
New Worlds for Old, 187, 223, 225, 228, 270, 278
New Year's Eve, 10
Night Mail, xii, xviii, 62, 119, 123, 125, 131–3, 135, 141, 142, 154, 171, 172, 174, 180, 181, 196, 199, 220, 232, 270, 272–4, 276, 277, 279
Nju, 10
No Resting Place, 152, 153, 211, 252
N or NW, 221
North Sea, xviii, 119, 134, 215, 219, 220, 224, 225, 236, 273, 275, 279
Nosferatu. See: Dracula

O'er Hill and Dale, 59
One Family, 22, 23, 138
On the Road to Work, 145

Parks and Palaces, 159
Passion de Jeanne d'Arc, La, 10
Pett and Pott, 142
Piccadilly, 9, 10, 12
Plow That Broke the Plains, The, 171, 186, 201, 202
Power Unit, 221
Prisoner of Zenda, The, 3
Private Life of Henry VIII, The 112
Professor Mamlock, 160
Public Enemy, The, 177

Q Ships, 16
Que Viva Mexico, 27

Rainbow Dance, 137
Rien que les Heures, 7, 10, 17, 18, 130
Rising Tide, 97, 260, 273
River, The, 181, 201, 218, 219, 267
Roads Across Britain, 229
Road to Hell, The, 110
Roadwards, 96
Roadways, 172
Robin Hood, 3
Rooftops of London, 159

San Demetrio, London, xviii

Saving of Bill Blewitt, The, 134, 239, 273
Scotland for Fitness, 216
Sea Food, 216
Secrets of Life (series), 97, 227
Secrets of Nature (series), 16, 70, 97
Shadow on the Mountain, The, 59
Shipyard, 48, 54, 61, 72, 99, 104–7, 112, 125, 134, 144, 157, 212, 239, 264, 267, 273, 276, 278
Simple Case, A, 48, 210
Six-Thirty Collection, 123, 124, 278
Size and Weight, 159
Skin Game, The, 48
Smoke Menace, The, 158, 159, 172
Song of Ceylon, xviii, 3, 51, 61, 71, 123–5, 127–9, 131, 132, 135, 142, 154, 157, 158, 172, 239, 267, 268, 272, 274–9
Son of Lassie, 194
So This is London, 60
Southern April, 23
South Street, 185
Spanish ABC, 160
Spanish Earth, The, 182
Spare Time, 221
Speed the Plough, 229
Sport in Scotland, 216
Spring Comes to England, 60
Statue Parade, 159
Storm Over Asia, 10, 25
Street of Chance, The, 193
Student of Prague, The, 9

Tabu, 50
Tall Timber Tales (series), 17
Tartuffe, 10
Telephone Workers, 60
Tell England, 48, 89
Testament of Non-Intervention, 160
They Made the Land, 216
Thief of Bagdad, The, 10
Thief of Bagdad, The (1940), 214
Three Musketeers, The, 3
Thunder in the Air, 165, 167
Today and Tomorrow, 149
Today We Live, 41, 62, 141, 145, 147–9, 171, 172, 180, 190, 194, 239, 273, 275, 280
Trader Horn, 81, 85, 86
Transfer of Power, xiv, 221
Triumph of the Will, The, 208, 235

Index of Film Titles

Index of Names

293

Index of Names

Index of Names

Flanagan, Mrs Hallie, 188
Fleming, Peter, 242, 247–9, 266
Fletcher, Sir Angus Somerville, 183
Fletcher, Stanley, 138
Fletcher, Yvonne, 256, 259
Ford, John, 9
Foreman, Carl, xvi
Foulds, J. H., 137
Fowle, Chick, 137, 220
Franz, Siegfried, 153
Freedman, Barnet, 68
Freund, Karl, 18
Furse, Sir William, 43

Galeen, Henrik, 9
Gamage, F. 137,
Garfield, John (Jules), 211
Gardner, Shayle, 39
Garrett Oliver, H. P., 193
Gauguin, 5
Gibbs, Gerald, 59, 137
Girard, Joe, 197
Giroux, Robert, 178
Glyn, Sir Ralph, 122
Goering, Hermann, 110, 215, 243
Golightly J. P. R. (Joe), 52–7, 65, 138, 170, 213, 223, 226
Goodliffe, Frank 75, 87, 100
Goodman, Ezra, 178
Graves, Janet, 178
Greeley, Horace, 179
Greene, Graham, xii, xix, 126, 150, 175, 274
Greville, Edmond, 12
Grierson, Dr Anthony, 53
Grierson, John, xiii–xv, xvii, xix–xxii, 4, 14, 17, 19, 21–50, 52–61, 63–5, 68, 72, 90, 91, 94, 97, 105, 108, 111, 114, 115, 117–19, 121–5, 127–33, 135, 136, 138–42, 144, 145, 151, 154, 155, 158, 160–2, 172, 173, 184, 193, 201, 205, 206, 213–17, 219, 222, 223, 225, 226, 230–2, 234, 238, 248–50, 258, 266, 268, 269, 272, 273, 275–86
Grierson, Margaret, 45
Grierson, Marion, 45, 49, 58, 60, 137, 160, 161, 217
Grierson, Ruby, xv, 146, 147, 149, 157, 159, 165–8, 213, 229
Griffith, Mrs Ann, xvii
Griffith, D. W., 4

Griffith, Richard, xix, xxii, 14, 15, 17, 18, 94, 176, 178, 197, 214, 218, 228, 230, 233, 238, 245, 263
Groves, Reg, 161, 217
Grundy, C. Reginald, 7
Guedalla, Philip, 218, 235, 236
Gysin, Francis, xvi

Haanstra, Bert, 267, 279
Hakim, Eric, 15
Haldane, Professor J. B. S., 158, 161, 237
Hansen, Lars, 9
Harbord, Carl, 9
Hardy, H. Forsyth, xix, 20, 45, 46, 129, 217, 235
Harrison, Kay, 152
Hawes, Stanley, xvi, xxii, 107, 146, 147, 149, 159, 194, 213, 229
Haydon, B. R., 254
Hellman, Lillian, 182
Hemingway, Ernest, 182
Henderson, Sir Vivian, 117
Herbert, A. P., 146
Herring, Robert, 22
Heseltine, C. L., 144, 200
Highet, A. G., 233, 235
Hill, James, 227
Hitchcock, Alfred, 9, 178
Hitler, Adolf, 109, 110, 162, 207, 249, 258
Hogben, Professor Lancelot, 161, 237
Holmes, J. B. (Jack), 15, 142, 146, 150, 160, 219, 275, 284
Holmes, Winifred, 146
Hore-Belisha, Leslie, 108
Horton, Ronald, 217
Howard, G. Wren, 14
Hudson, Eric, 138
Huxley, Gervase, 125
Huxley, Professor Julian, 43, 146, 151, 152, 159, 161, 237

Isherwood, Christopher, xii
Ivens, Joris, 33, 48, 157, 178, 182, 192, 278

Jackson, Pat, 219
Jacobs, Lewis, xxiii
James, Norah, C., 12, 13
Janowitz, Hans, 4
Jaubert, Maurice, 137

Index of Names

Index of Names

Index of Names

Index of Names

General Index

Abbey Theatre, (Dublin), 152
Academy Cinema (Oxford Street), 15
Action!, 152
Actor Manager, The (project), 66
Adelphi Theater (New York), 187
Age of the Great Depression, The, 192
Agricultural Administration Act, 190
American Council of Education, 195, 201, 205
American Documentary Films Inc., 207, 211
American Exodus, An: A Record of Human Erosion, 186
American Film Center, 238
American Photographs, 187
American Political Ideas, 1865–1917, 20
Anglo-American Film Corporation, 261
Anglo-Iranian Oil, 143, 151
Architectural Review, 102
Arts Council of Great Britain, xvi
Arts Enquiry Report, xvii, xviii, 116
Ascent of F6, xii
Associated British Film Distributors (ABFD), 124, 132, 145, 229, 261, 270
Associated Realist Film Producers (ARFP), xii, 111, 160–2, 199, 204, 214, 231, 236, 268, 282, 283
As Thousands Cheer, 189
Australia, Film Library, 133
Australian Government (film department), xxii

Basic Films, 123
Benjamin Britten: A Sketch of His Life and Works, 132
Big Money, The, 19
Board of Trade, 159
Book Society, 144
BBC–TV, xiii, xix, xx, 28, 146

Britannia Films Ltd, 67
British Acoustic Films, 64, 96, 115
British Board of Film Censors (BBFC), 123, 161, 165–70, 227, 228
British Commercial Gas Association, 155, 217
British Council, xviii, 219, 234, 235, 237
British Film Academy, 263
British Film Institute (BFI), xviii, xxi, 96, 115–17, 121, 122, 161, 217, 218, 230, 235
British Independent Films, 96
British Instructional Films (BIF), 70, 73, 88, 89, 92, 120
British International Pictures (BIP), 8, 9, 91, 92
British Library of Information (New York), 183
British Movietone News, 35, 122
British National Films, 230
British Paramount News, xviii
Brooklyn Institute, 196
Brussels Film Festival, 105, 125

Camera and I, The, 157
Canadian Motion Picture Bureau, 47, 49
Canton Film Appreciation Group (Cardiff), 263
Cape Town Film Society, 80
Carnegie United Kingdom Trust, 116, 147, 159
Celluloid: The Film Today, 45, 81, 108
Central Electricity Board, 103
Central Office of Information, 133, 284
Central Telegraph Office, 219
Ceylon Tea Propaganda Board, 124, 125, 128
Changing Scene, The, 140
Chesterfield Educational Authority, 59

300

General Index

301

General Index

General Index

Lyceum Theatre, 255

Manchester Corporation, 224
Manchester Guardian, 22, 158, 168
Manchester University, xvi
Marble Arch Pavilion, 3, 7,
Marine Biological Station (Plymouth), 27
Merton Park Studios, 97, 230
Metro-Goldwyn-Mayer (MGM), 81, 86, 159, 194, 216
Metropolitan Motion Picture Council, 195
Mind in Chains, The, 138
Ministry of Agriculture, 60, 268
Ministry of Health, 220
Ministry of Information, 217, 229, 231, 233, 261, 281, 285
Ministry of Labour, 60, 145, 156, 268
Miracle, The, 70
Morning Post, 110
Movies, The, 176
Movies for the Millions, 199
Movie Stars, The, 176
Museum of Modern Art Film Library (New York), xxii, 170–2, 174–8, 182, 197, 201–3, 205, 208, 210, 218, 222, 230
Mutual Broadcasting Company, 208
Mystery of the Marie Celeste, The (project), 66

National Board of Review of Motion Pictures, 176, 196
National Book Council, 113, 146, 268
National Book League, 146
National Council for Social Service, 147, 268
National Film Archive (London), xviii, 170, 232, 261, 265
National Film Board (project), xviii, 281
National Film Board of Canada, 137, 269, 275, 276, 284, 286
National Film Theatre, (London), xxi
National Recovery Administration, 186, 187
National Youth Administration, 195
Nerofilm, 67, 68
New Britain, 94
New Era Films, 17, 26, 27, 29, 59, 70, 115, 117, 122, 125, 128, 270

New Clarion, 112
New London Film Society, 58
Newcastle Chronicle, 30
New Gallery Kinema, 10
New Republic, 197, 199
New School for Social Research, 196
News Chronicle, 168, 237
News of the World, 107
Newspaper Guild of New York, 188
Newsreel Association, 235
New Statesman, 231, 238
New Theater and Film, 182
New Victoria Cinema, 91
New York Herald-Tribune, 197
New York Sun, xiii
New York Times, 197
New York World's Fair, 230, 233–40, 261
Nineteen Nineteen, 191
Now Pray We For Our Country, 195

Observer, The, 13, 33–5, 63, 108
Old and New London, 122
One Third of a Nation, 187, 190, 191
Orgy, 211
Orient Line, 72, 125, 143, 146

Palace Theatre, 22
Paramount, 130
Pathe, 216
Petroleum Films Bureau, 217
Philadelphia Public Ledger, 14
Phoenix Theatre, 173, 227
Photoplay, 178
Piccadilly Theatre, 151, 200
Picture, xxi
Pins and Needles, 196, 199
Political and Economic Planning (PEP), 225
Portrait of a Flying Yorkshireman, 179
Post Office Publicity Department, 233
Power, 190
Press, The, 243
Progressive Education Association, 181, 195
Progressive Film Institute, 160
Projection of England, The, 21, 24
Prudential Assurance Company, 151, 215
Publicity Films, 97, 155
Public Opinion, 14

303

General Index

General Index